The Face Is A Canvas

The Design and Technique of Theatrical Makeup

IRENE COREY

ANCHORAGE PRESS
Post Office Box 8067
New Orleans, Louisiana 70182

Copyright 1990
ANCHORAGE PRESS, INC.
Post Office Box 8067
New Orleans, Louisiana 70182

ISBN 0-87602-031-7

Other Books Concerned with Irene Corey's Stage Work

THE MASK OF REALITY: An Approach to Design for Theatre
by Irene Corey
Published by Anchorage Press, Inc.

AN ODYSSEY OF MASQUERS: THE EVERYMAN PLAYERS
by Orlin Corey
Published by Rivendell House, Ltd.

Both of these books are available through
Anchorage Press, Inc. P.O. Box 8067, New Orleans, Louisiana 70182

Contents

Foreword

Irene Corey has a passion for design. She loves every phase of theatrical production: sets, costumes, makeup, props, lights and sound. She sees each production as one large, creative, integrated whole. Each line, each daub of color applied in makeup is a vital contribution to the large design concept.

The Face Is A Canvas is a master work because it combines Irene's superb craftsmanship with her brilliant insight into creative design, relating all the intricate makeup elements to one artistic statement. The book has developed from thousands and thousands of hours of in-depth, hands-on study of the intricate problems of applying makeup. *The Face Is A Canvas* reflects thorough research into the social and historical background of theatrical periods.

Irene Corey understands the student's learning process and has developed each makeup problem to guide teacher and student through the makeup processes in a clear step-by-step procedure. By following the procedure, the makeup student can become a fine makeup craftsman, and if he is capable, Irene Corey's book will show him the way to become a creative artist as well.

Paul Baker

Acknowledgements

It may be that this book owes its beginning to the moment when, as a child, I traded my treasured Prang Water Colors for a tube of Blue Waltz lipstick. Since then I have learned that writing a book is not done alone, any more than "making up" is done with lipstick alone. The patience, endurance and support of my friends have helped bring the book to completion. Therefore, I extend my thanks to Bob and Candy Canzoneri for care and feeding and long walks with Bubba; to Norma Allen who was there for the highs and the lows; to Julia and Nelsyn Wade for persuading the beautiful people of San Augustine, Texas, to lend me their faces; to Joy Emery for holding the light at the end of the tunnel; to Pat Taylor and Winona Fletcher, who offered insight after proofings; to Nick Dalley, my incomparable assistant; to Susie Thennes who conquered my typewriter and my handwriting; and last—thanks to the Angels who stayed the wolf from my door so I could write this book for you.

Irene Corey

Introduction

I approach the face as if it were an artist's canvas stretched over a frame. By application of paint, the features found there can be reinforced or can be totally ignored, creating the illusion of changed form. This method opens up endless realms of variation to the makeup artist, using nature and art as well as the countenance of man as inspiration.

This book is a practical workbook, to be placed beneath the makeup mirror. The student will work from individual, full-sized face charts, showing makeup designs and character photographs. He will be guided step-by-step. Learning will be enhanced by the use of transparent overlays which illustrate how the makeup is derived. The book is arranged in a series of carefully chosen exercises which lead the student into a rapid comprehension of contouring, aging, and stylization. It can serve as a springboard for the advanced designer, while at the same time teaching the basics to the beginner. It stresses the creative potential of the student by directing him to new design departures.

The technique of makeup is presented from the viewpoint of a designer. By treating the face as a canvas, and becoming aware of the infinite sources available to him, the makeup artist can make a personal, unique contribution to the theatre.

1

Why Makeup?

In the theatre, ideas about people are expressed through the medium of people. If people are important, their faces are eminently important.

1–1   *(photographer) Marion Post Wolcott*

Every day each of us creates a little more of our own distinctive "mask". Each decision, or lack of decision, makes an eventual difference in how we look. Cosmetics provide no vanishing cream for the etchings of time and experience. Only the retouch photographer, the plastic surgeon, or the undertaker can succeed in this task.

Faces are abstracts of our lives.

In the beginning, children are unmarked, yet even these perfect faces can be quickly altered by drastic experiences such as those created by neglect and

1

1-2   (photographer) Doug Milner

abuse, poverty and war. However, given a protected childhood and adolescence, the face we inherit will stay fresh until after about age twenty. From then on, changes accumulate at a rate of speed proportionate to what goes on inside and outside our bodies.

Our faces are created by climate—

1–3   (photographer) Arthur Rothstein

Faces can reflect occupation—

ELIZABETH DAUGHTER OF Sᴿ ROBᵗ THROCKMORTON BARᵗ

1-4 Elizabeth Throckmorton.   *(artist) Nicolas de Largillière*

or lack of occupation.

1-5   *(photographer) Arthur Rothstein*

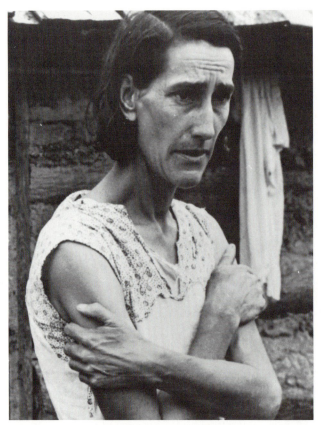

Anxiety reshapes features quickly.

Apprehensive faces are shared by the rich and the poor. Our affluent society is built on a hive of interlocked pressures, demands and competition. Facial muscles respond to the repetition of emotional expressions, and may record the tightened contractions of hatred—

1–6   *(photographer) Ben Shahn*

1–7   *(photographer) Theo Jung*

a tracery of laugh lines—

1–8   *(photographer) John Vachon*

—or the haunted gaze of suffering brought about by pain, fear, or grief.

1-9   *United Press International Photo*

Characterization is one of the playwright's most potent tools. Dialogue is shaped by the vessel from which it comes. The author molds his characters with great care so that their variations in texture, rhythm and coloration will result in compelling contradictions and resolutions. He selects from nature and heightens reality. Such meticulous observation of the human scene should lead the makeup artist to the same sources. Accomplished actors, such as Sir Alec Guinness and Lord Laurence Olivier, combine the crafts of acting and makeup to achieve great diversity. Each character they portray is given some visual facial detail which aids in the projection of that personality. They never seem to appear in the same face twice.

1–10 Sir Alec Guinness.   *Courtesy Weintraub Entertainment*

Abraham Lincoln once refused to hire a man because he did not like his face. He apparently believed that he could judge by what he saw. Today's sophisticated and educated viewpoint tends to discount and rationalize visual evidence. Although there is a danger in stuffing people into convenient pigeonholes, certain messages are present in faces, waiting to be seen.

1-12 Abraham Lincoln, 1859.   *(photographer) Samuel M. Fassett*

1-11 Abraham Lincoln, 1846.   *Daguerreotype by N. H. Shepherd*

I believe character, or lack of it, can be revealed in the face. Therefore, I present the premise that an actor should use the important medium of makeup as an aid to character interpretation, rather than presuming that God-given features work for *every* character created by *every* playwright. Makeup can be a point of reference by which an actor can steer himself.

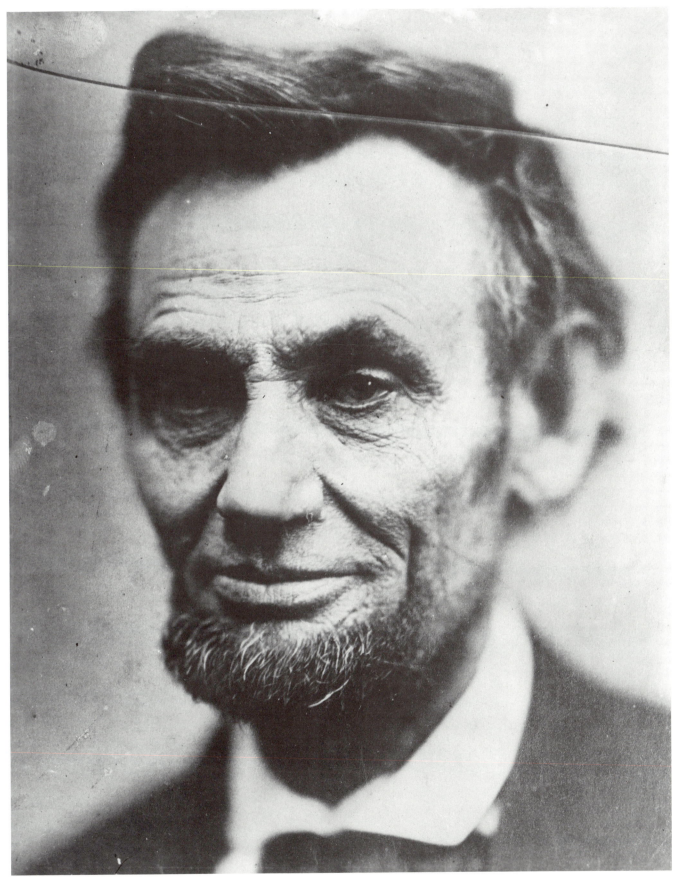

1-13 Abraham Lincoln, 1865.   (photographer) Alexander Gardner

BIBLIOGRAPHY

Liggett, John. *The Human Face*. (New York: Stein and Day, 1974). An in-depth study of the human face, its structure, its expression of emotion, its concepts of beauty.

Mellon, James, Ed. *The Face of Lincoln*. (New York: Bonanza Books. 1979).

2

Getting Ready

The makeup charts in this workbook are based on a generalized face shape with little regard for facial variation or sex. (See Basic Makeup Chart 2-3.) In order to personalize your work based on the charts in this book, it would be advantageous to have a life-sized, full-front, close-up photograph of your face. You should be looking directly into the camera, unsmiling, hair pulled back, revealing hairline, with front, flat, direct lighting. The profile view is optional, but helpful. If you are using a Polaroid camera, enlarge the photo on a copy machine until it is life-sized.

EXERCISE ONE:

Making Your Face Chart

1. Study the face outline drawn over a photograph in Illustration 2-1. Place sheer tracing paper over your photograph and trace, with a lead pencil, your face shape, ears, hairline, the eye opening, a dotted line for the top of your brow, a slight indication of the bottom of your nose and nostrils, and the line of the mouth opening—not an outline of the lips.

2. Ink these lines.

3. Type in spaces for name, role, and production title. Indicate space to list makeup colors needed.

4. Make copies of chart and use them for recording your makeup for exercises or performance roles. Always make notes while makeup is still on your face. Use colored pencils if you wish to indicate color.

5. Note your hairline, but remember it can be changed by style. The outline of the generic face chart used for all makeup charts in this book indicates the area of the face occupied by makeup.

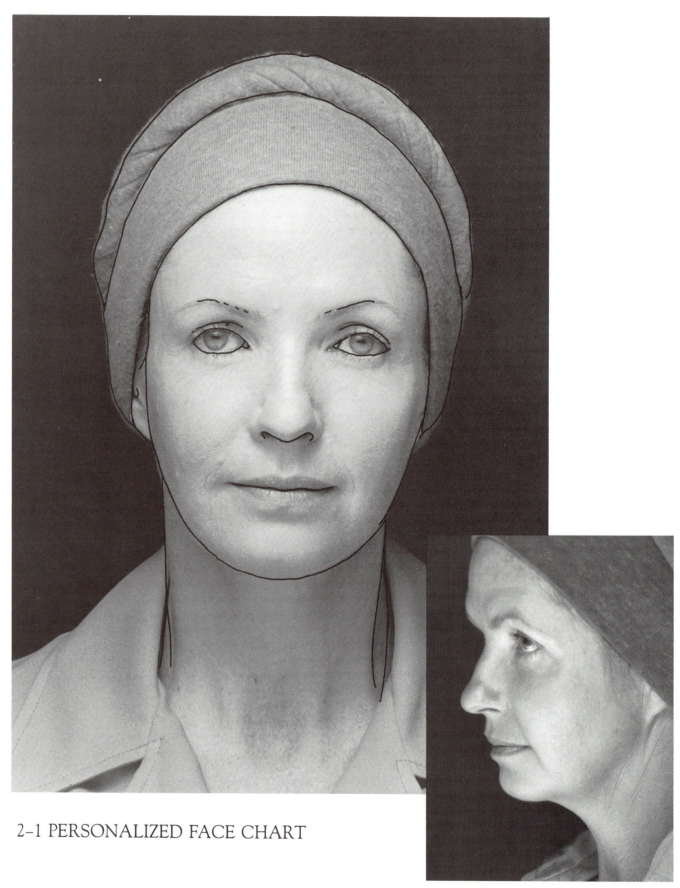

2–1 PERSONALIZED FACE CHART

2–2 *(photographer) Suzanne Dietz*

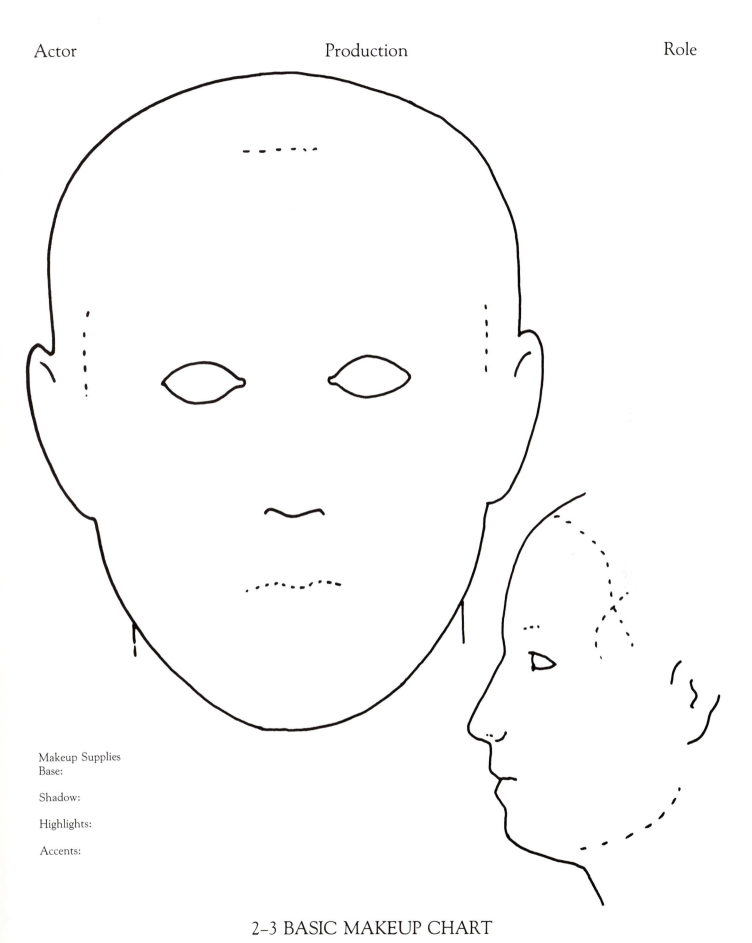

Makeup Supplies
Base:

Shadow:

Highlights:

Accents:

2–3 BASIC MAKEUP CHART

BASIC SKIN CARE

How many times has the remark been made, "Greasepaint ruins my skin"? Except in rare cases, when there is an allergic reaction to a chemical component, the "ruining" seldom comes from the greasepaint, but rather from poor skin care. When the following procedure has been followed, I have frequently heard actors remark that their skin has never been in better condition.

Before Makeup

1. Astringent and cotton balls
A mild astringent, or ordinary witch hazel (available at drug stores), is applied to the face to tighten and close the pores. Start with clean skin. If you are wearing street makeup, remove it. Saturate a cotton ball with the astringent and rub it over your skin.

2-4

2. Moisture cream
Before application of greasepaint, additional skin protection is provided by a light application of moisture cream. Many prefer the medicated variety. Or, apply a *very* sparing coat of cold cream, and wipe off the excess thoroughly.

2-5

After makeup

1. Makeup removers. Almost any kind of oil will remove greasepaint, including:

2-6

Cold cream, water soluble
There are several brands available at cosmetic counters. Apply over makeup and rub until all is emulsified. The water soluble cold cream washes away easily with soapy sponge or cloth, without excessive rubbing. This method is much easier on the skin than the abrasive removal with tissues.

Baby shampoo substituted for the soap will not burn your eyes.

Cold cream, oil emulsion
If water soluble cold cream is not available, many brands of the oil-based type can be found at drugstores. Albolene has an effective liquifying action and is inexpensive.

Baby oil
Baby oil, mineral oil, or even Crisco will remove makeup.

2. Old, soft T-shirt or cotton towel
The greatest curse to the skin is rubbing it repeatedly with paper tissues in an effort to remove makeup. Try to get a mental image of tissues as abrasive, pulverized wood pulp; imagine them "sand papering" your skin—and start saving your old T-shirts. They can be laundered for re-use.

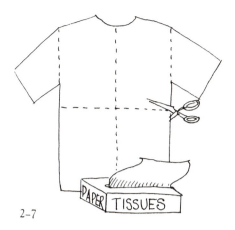

2-7

3. *Astringent and cotton balls*

Deep pore cleansing is done with cotton balls moistened with astringent or witch hazel. Wipe repeatedly until cotton comes away clean.

4. *Moisture cream*

Now that your skin has been stripped of all its natural oils, pat your face with water, patting until almost dry. While it is still damp, apply a coat of moisture cream. Now you are ready to face the elements.

2-8

A makeup mirror on a stand is useful for viewing your profile, and if the dressing table is too deep. The near-sighted may need a double mirror with a magnified side. Utilize a full-length mirror to view your makeup from ten or twelve feet away.

CHOOSING MAKEUP

Consider for a moment what makeup is made of. Basically, it is a pigment, an inert matter held together, and to your skin, by various binders. As oil is the main binder for greasepaint, the difference between types is basically in the amount of emollients used. This dictates its packaging.

2-9

1. *Stick Grease and Cream Stick*

The older form of makeup, stick grease, has less oil, and its stiff consistency allows for the softening which occurs when it contacts the skin and responds to the body heat. Cream sticks fall into this same category, except that they are slightly softer.

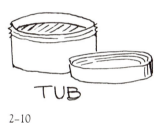

2-10

2. *Tubbed Creams*

A softer, oil-based makeup which is easier to apply, but may become slippery on the skin, making it somewhat difficult to control blending.

3. *Cake Makeup*

Popularized under the Max Factor brand name, Pancake, it is face powder compressed into a dry cake, under pressure, and is usually applied with a moistened sponge. Except when specified, the procedures in this book do not apply to the use of cake makeup. The resultant matte finish creates a mask-like effect which tends to flatten rather than enhance the features. (An excellent effect, however, for death!) It creates a resistance to subtle blending, but can be contoured with light and dark shades of pressed powders. (See *Contouring for Crowds*, Chapter Six.) Cake makeup is also useful as body makeup for covering large areas of skin quickly. However, for this purpose liquid makeup may be preferred.

2–11

4. *Semi-moist Cake Makeup**

This is a water based makeup containing glycerine. It is not totally dry, and creates a life-like sheen on the face. Contouring is achieved by using basic water color techniques of blending highlights and shadows while the surface is wet. As it does not require powdering, the result is a light weight covering. Water based makeups do not withstand heavy sweating as well as grease bases.

*Aquacolor Wet Makeup by Kryolan

*Star Blend Cake Makeup by Mehron

One of the primary premises of this book is that learning to mix your own colors will aid you in mastering the art of makeup. In order to accommodate the various types of makeup which may be in your kit, I have created generic color names which correlate with brand names. Please consult Chart, p. 19, and select the makeup which coordinates with the basic colors used in the exercises in this book. From these few colors all shades of skin pigment can be mixed. It's not that difficult.

A varied and workable array of colors and shades can be created from a limited palette of colors. It is not necessary to furnish yourself with numerous premixed colors when you can arrive at them yourself. It *is* necessary to learn to see color and to adjust it to your needs. Given the confusing list of numbers and color names provided by makeup companies, and given your need to know your skin color and to be able to adjust it to your character's needs, it is far better to learn to rely on your own eye. How can you decide via chart names whether you are Olive, Spanish, Light Negro, or just plain Suntanned? Far better to be able to mix the enormous range of tones found in the ethnic and racial groups. Be aware, also, that one cannot automatically depend on opening a certain pre-mixed color and finding the same color every time. Since color batches may not be consistent, or may be altered because of new government restrictions on certain colors, the responsibility for correct color usage is back on you.

SELECTING SUPPLIES

Brushes: Your brushes are your best friends in makeup. Don't skimp. Buy the best and take care of them. Clean brushes by dipping them in cold cream, wiping gently with tissue, and flattening the bristles between your fingers. For storage, slip a drinking straw over the end to keep bristles flat. If they should dry crooked, soap bristles with a stiff lather, shape them, and let them dry.

2–12

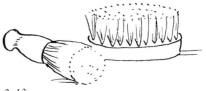

2–13

Generic Color Name	Ben Nye	Bob Kelly	Mehron	Stein/Zauder	Kryolan
White	White foundation P-1	White Creme Stick S1	White Foundation 102 White Cream Blend Stick 400	White Velvet Stick 43 Stick Grease 22	White 070
Pale Pink	Lite Warm Pink Creme Liner P-2	Pink Creme Stick S2	Shell Pink 104-9 Blushtone	Middle Age 44 Velvet Stick Pink #1, Grease Stick	Pink 03
Muted Yellow	Goldenrod Creme Liner CL-6	Golden Yellow SL 15 Liner	Mustard Yellow 107-16, Shado-liner	Mikado Yellow Velvet Stick: 40½ Ivory Yellow 5L Stick Grease	303
Primary Yellow	Yellow Creme Liner CL-5	Lemon Yellow SL-14	Yellow Foundation 102 Yellow Cream blend Stick 400 Yellow liner 107	Stick liner 16	509
Sunburn	Sunburn Stipple Creme Liner CL-9	Light Egyptian S-22	Chestnut brown Shado-Liner Light Egyptian Foundation 102-8B Light Egyptian Cream blend Stick 400	Hawaiian 37 Velvet Stick Stick Grease: Dark Sunburn #8	08
Red-brown	Dark Sunburn Creme Liner CL-10	Chestnut Brown SL 8 combined with Grey Violet SL 17	Ebony Foundation 102 Ebony Cream Blend Stick 400	Red-Brown 9, Velvet Stick; Red-brown liner 25 Stick	046
Green	Green (for light skins) CL-3 Forest Green Creme Liner CL-2 (for dark skins)	Leaf green S-L 5	Green Foundation 102 Green Cream Blend Stick 400	Green 46 Velvet Stick Green 19, Stick liner	512
Sallow	Old Age, Creme foundation P-5	Sallow S-8 Creme Stick	Taupe 107-9	Sallow Old Age 50 Velvet Stick Sallow 11, Grease Stick	0A
Black	Black Creme Liner CL-29	Black SL 9	Black Cream Blend Stick 400 Black Foundation 102 Black Liner 107	Black 33 Velvet Stick Black 25, Stick Liner	071
Dark Blue	Blue Creme Liner CL-15	Ocean Blue Sl 2	Blue 107-1 Shado-Liner Blue Foundation Blue Stick	Blue 47 Velvet Stick (plus black) Dark Blue 10 Stick Liner	545
Dark Purple	Purple CL-18	Grey Violet SL 17	Maroon 103 Lip Rouge	Purple 21 Stick Liner	R–27
Red	Fire Red Creme Liner CL-13	Medium, true red SR4	R B Clown Red 102 and 400 Red Foundation 102 Red Cream Blend Stick 400	48 red (orangish) Moist rouge, medium	079
	*Note: Order these numbers, or specify the Ben Nye Irene Corey Makeup kit. (Includes brushes, powder, etc.)		*Note: Mehron offers a choice between *Cream Blend Sticks* and the more traditional greasepaint, *Foundation.*	*Note: Stein offers a choice between *Velvet Stick* and *Grease Paint.*	*Note: Order these numbers, or the Irene Corey Palette (#1004/IC cream)

Colors which are exceptionally good for deepening shadow on black skins are:
Ben Nye: MAROON C-L 15, and MISTY VIOLET C-L 17
Bob Kelly: GREY VIOLET
Kryolan: DARK BLUE 545
Mehron: EBONY (Base)

One ³/₁₆″ red sable lining brush, flat

One ¹/₈″ red sable lining brush, flat

These can be ordered from a theatrical supply company. If an art supply store is more convenient to you, you must designate:

#4, red sable, "bright" oil painting brush

#3, red sable, "bright" oil painting brush

"Bright" indicates a shorter bristle. You will need to shorten the handles.

Optional: #1 Round, pointed red sable, useful for eye lines and accenting fine wrinkles.

Complexion Brush: Used to brush away excess powder, it can be made of soft nylon, or natural bristles, as in a shaving brush.

Eye Liner, Cake: Used with wet brush to line the eyes. The cake form is long lasting and will not dry out.

Mascara: Usually packaged with self brush.

Powder, (Johnson's Baby): Can be used for all designs using pure color—indeed, it works well for basic makeup as well.

2-14

Translucent: light, neutral powder can be used for all regular makeup. Be aware that the highlight areas will take on the color of the powder.

Powder Puffs: The cloth velour type is preferred over those made of foam rubber; or cotton balls can be used. Zig-zag stitch the edge of the velour puff and it can be washed and dried by machine.

Q-Tips: Cotton swabs used to clean up mistakes.

Rouge, Dry, with Brush: Sometimes called a blusher, it should be a medium or dark shade—not bright.

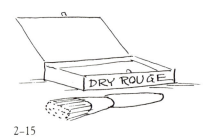

2-15

Silk Sponge: This is a small, natural sponge used to apply makeup, or, when dampened, to remove excess powder.

Soap: Bar soap to block out brows.

Stippling Sponge: A coarse, open-pored, firm sponge, used to create skin textures.

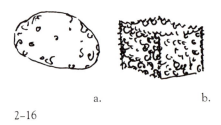

a. b.

2-16

Tissues: Used to clean brushes.

Tooth Wax, Black: Comes in liquid form and is painted on teeth to give the appearance of missing teeth, or make the edges appear uneven.

SOURCES

Makeup supply houses are located in most major cities. If none are available to you, order catalogs from companies serving your area. Think ahead and order ahead! Your needs will be met best by companies which carry many brands of makeup. See Appendix for source addresses. Except for greasepaint, most items can be found in your local drugstore, beauty supply house, or costume shop. Check Yellow Pages. Supplies needed for creating facial hair are listed in Chap. 10.

MAKING A
PICTURE FILE

2-17

Supplies

1. An accordian expanding file with 21–24 divisions, available at office supply.

2. Old magazines and newspapers

3. Perseverance. Curiosity.

It is impossible to overstress the importance of collecting a thorough selection of pictures for reference in makeup design—that is, unless you are content to go through your theatrical career playing your own face in every role. In addition to placing multiple variations at your finger tips when researching a particular role, collecting pictures will cause you to be more observant of the faces around you. As you extend your collection to include interesting animals, flowers, insects and birds, you will develop a heightened awareness of the design possibilities surrounding you. You may start seeing faces in *everything*.

Be constantly on the lookout for large, full-front, non-smiling photographs of every type and age person. Avoid tiny pictures, as they do not give you enough information. In the case of famous world leaders or celebrities, a composite of small pictures can be useful. You will soon find your file surfeited with monotonously pretty young women, and scarce in women of middle years and beyond. Start collecting early and then fill in the gaps.

In selecting pictures of animals, birds, and other such creatures, you also want full-front "non-smiling," large photos. Collect side views in addition, so that you gain an understanding of the skull structure. Include actual photos of skulls themselves, when possible.

Small pictures in the same category may be mounted on light-weight paper. Large pictures should be filed without mounting.

The following categories will serve to begin your file organization. Feel free to include other divisions. For instance, in addition to animals, you may find reptiles, fish, and birds which have makeup design potential. Or, you may prefer total alphabetizing to the following method.

PICTURE FILE CONTENTS

Artists' Concepts

CARICATURES AND CARTOONS: Cartoonists frequently reduce the essence of celebrated personalities to a few lines and planes. Satirical political cartoons can help sharpen your perception of dominant features.

JUSTICE FELIX FRANKFURTER

2-18 Caricature of Felix Frankfurter. National Portrait Gallery. Smithsonian Institution, Washington, D. C.

FICTIONAL CHARACTERS: Elves, gnomes, Godzilla, Tom Sawyer, Dracula. Try to find Santa Claus in June, and you will wish you had him in your file.

2-19 Santa Claus as portrayed by Thomas Nast, 1884,[1] in *Harper's Weekly.*

MASKS: Current, festive, African.

PAINTING AND SCULPTURE: Collect examples of how artists portray the human face. Have examples of people as seen by El Greco, Van Gogh, Bosch, Rouault, or any of the expressionists. Watch for Romanesque or Greek sculptures, Byzantine mosaics, Celtic manuscripts—the whole realm of recorded art is available to you.

2-21 Portrait of Head of the Emperor Caracalla. Roman Sculpture, III c.A.D. The Metropolitan Museum of Art, Gift of George F. Baker, 1891.

2-20 Luba painted wooden and china-clay mask, Congo-Kinshasa.[2]

Mankind

AGES: Female – Child, Youth, Prime, Advanced.
        Male – Child, Youth, Prime, Advanced

The concept of age categorization will vary, depending on your point of view. Remember that aging is not necessarily a matter of accumulating years; it is how that person has lived his life, a visible record of his experience. Find as many examples as possible in each category.

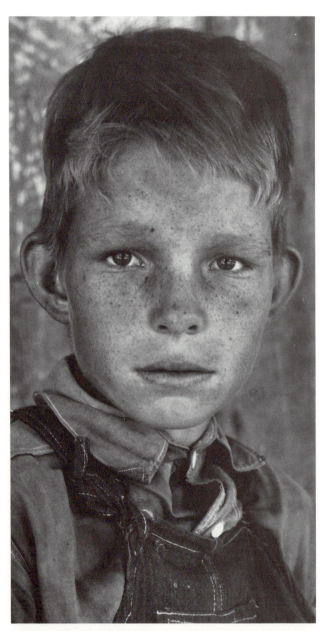

2-22a *Age Series:* CHILD, 12 years old, F.S.A. Collection, The Library of Congress. *(photographer)* Dorothea Lange.

2-22b *Age Series.* YOUTH, 21 years of age. *(photographer)* Doug Milner

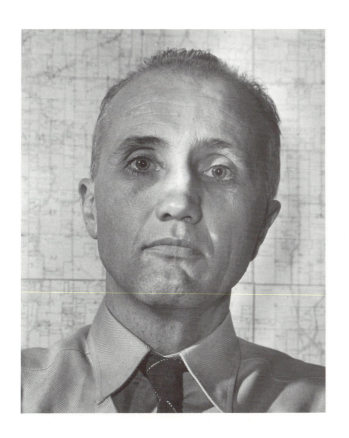

AGING PROCESS: Watch for the death of famous people. There is almost always a series of photos showing them at different periods of their lives. Or, note the change in a Presidential face from his election to the end of his term of office.

2-22c Age Series: PRIME YEARS. F. S. A. Collection, The Library of Congress.   *(photographer) Arthur Rothstein*

2-22d Age Series: Advanced years (Age 104).   *(photographer) Doug Milner*

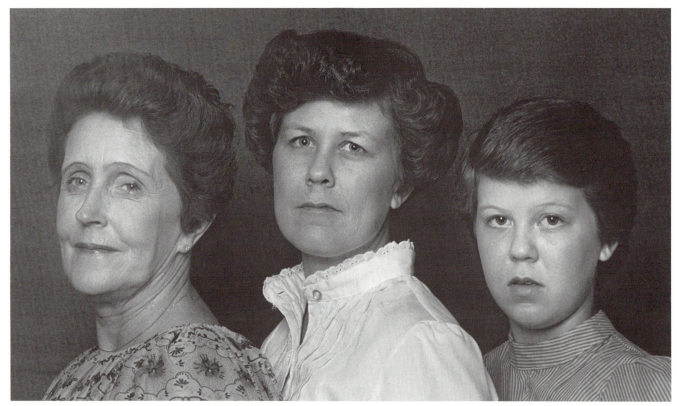

2-23 The aging process illustrated by a grandmother, daughter, and granddaughter. *(photographer) Doug Milner*

THE AGING PROCESS ILLUSTRATED BY A
GRANDFATHER, SON, AND GRANDSON

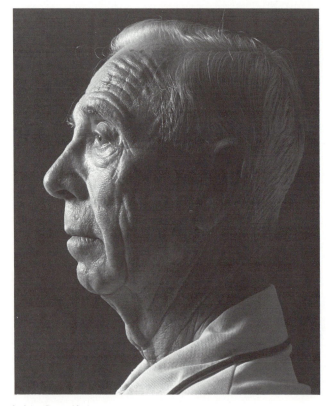

2-24a Grandfather. *(photographer) Doug Milner*

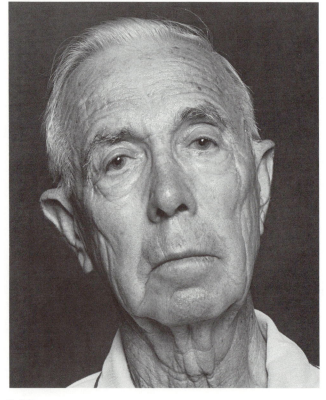

2-24b *(photographer) Doug Milner*

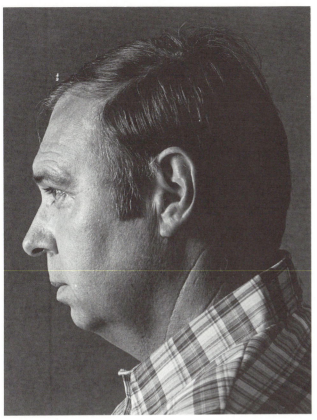

2-24c Son.   *(photographer) Doug Milner*

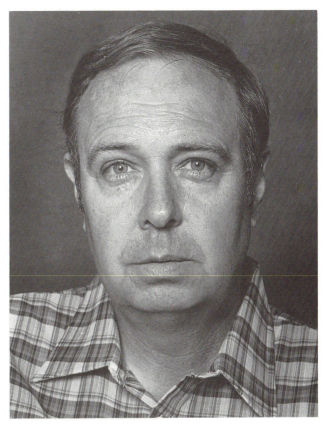

2-24d   *(photographer) Doug Milner*

2-24e Grandson.   *(photographer) Doug Milner*

2-24f   *(photographer) Doug Milner*

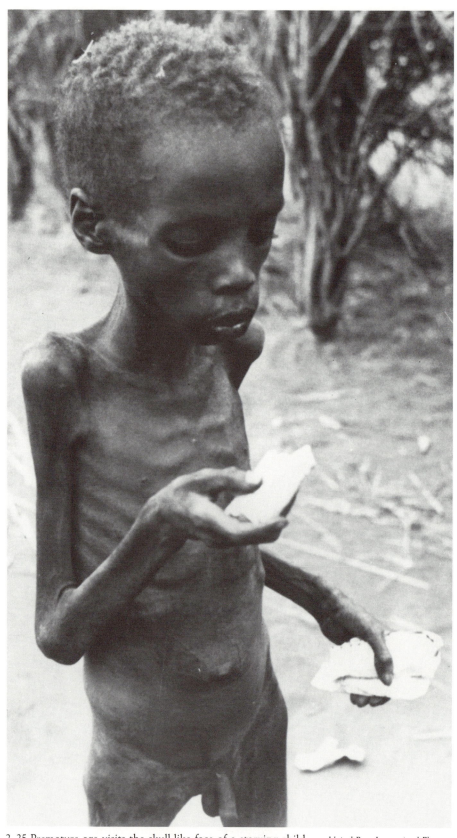

2-25 Premature age visits the skull-like face of a starving child.   *United Press International Photo.*

DEATH, DYING, SKULLS: Plays frequently require knowledge of the effects of death.

2-26 Enraged peace demonstrator, protesting the action of the police during anti-war protests in Madison, Wisconsin, December 1967.   *United Press International, (photographer) Dennis Conner.*

EMOTIONAL EFFECTS: Strong emotions mar the face. Watch for facial distortions caused by expressions of extreme hatred, fear, grief, joy, etc.

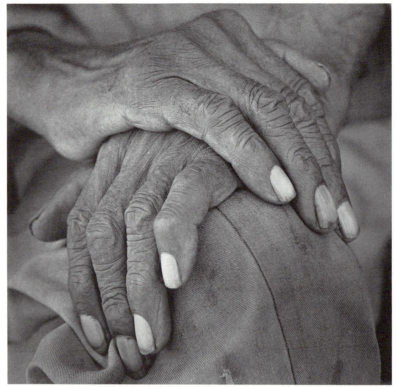

2-27a Hands of a retired farmer.   (photographer) Doug Milner

2-27b Hands of an old couple and their granddaughter. F.S.A. Collection, The Library of Congress.   (photographer) John Vachon

FEATURES: Make composite pages showing variations in eyes, hands, neck, nose, mouth, and skin texture.

HAIR, CURRENT AND PERIOD: Divide this category between male and female. Be sure to date the hair styles, as the fashions change rapidly. Hairstyles have a way of recurring. Compare the Afro style worn by Angela Davis, Illustration 10–80 and the yellow Medieval "fros" in Illustration 10–1. Collect illustrations of various styles of facial hair for men.

HISTORICAL PEOPLE:
Male: Lincoln, Hitler, Nixon, Mahatma Gandhi, Booker T. Washington, etc.
Female: Marie Antoinette, Elizabeth I, Sojourner Truth, Eleanor Roosevelt, etc.

2–28 Flourishing beard and moustache of Walt Whitman. Notice the bushy eyebrows. National Portrait Gallery, Smithsonian Institution, Washington D. C.   *(photographer) George C. Cox.*

2-29 Anna Eleanor Roosevelt, 1885–1975. National Portrait Gallery, Smithsonian Institution. Washington, D. C. *(photographer) Clara Sipprell.*

2-30 Martin Luther King, 1965.   *United Press International Photo*

2-31 Marquis de Lafayette, c. 1834. Lithograph by Nicholas Eustache Maurin. National Portrait Gallery, Smithsonian Institution, Washington, D. C.

2-32 Frederick Douglass, 1817–1895. Born a slave, he became one of the most eminent human rights leaders of the 19th century. National Portrait Gallery,[1] Smithsonian Institution, Washington, D. C.

OCCUPATION: For every presumption, there will be an exception: yet, it is sometimes expedient to rely on stereotypes to suggest certain portrayals. Collect many faces in the same profession: football players, clergy, sheriffs, etc., and see if typical characteristics emerge.

2-33 **Handyman.**   *(photographer) Doug Milner*

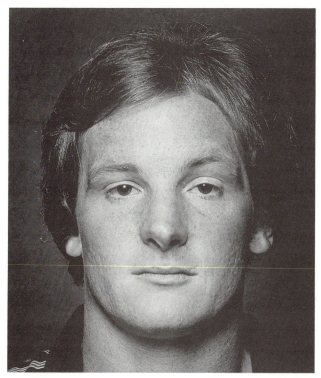

2-34 Athletic Director.   *(photographer) Doug Milner*

2-35 Sheriff.   *(photographer) Doug Milner*

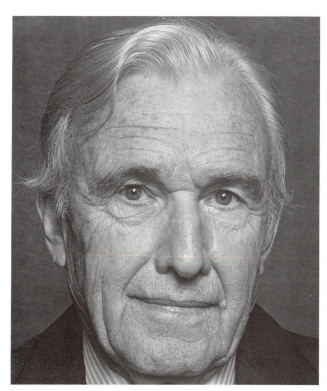

2-36a Dry goods store proprietor.   *(photographer) Doug Milner*

2-236b (profile view of 2-36a)   *(photographer:) Doug Milner*

35

RACIAL TYPES: Under each racial group, organize your pictures according to ethnic variations which might occur in each nation.

Caucasian: Could include Germans, Russians, Greeks, etc. You may find that isolating national types can only be done in the broadest sense. For instance, Greeks may be considered to be dark haired, Swedes blond and fair, while Germans may be difficult to distinguish from Russians.

Mongolian: Would include, for example, Eskimos, North American Indians, Chinese, Japanese, Korean, and Vietnamese.

Negroid: The peoples of Africa, Melanesia, New Guinea, etc.

2-37b Armenian-American. F.S.A. Collection, Library of Congress, Washington, D.C.   *(photographer) Delano.*

2-37a Italian-American. O.W.I., Library of Congress, Smithsonian Institution, Washington, D. C.   *(photographer) Gordon Parks.*

2-37c Portuguese-American. F.S.A. Collection, Library of Congress, Washington, D.C.   *(photographer) Edwin Rosskam.*

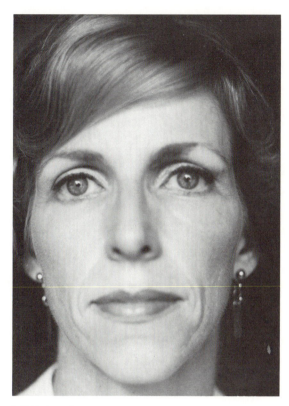

2-37d American. *(photographer) Irene Corey*

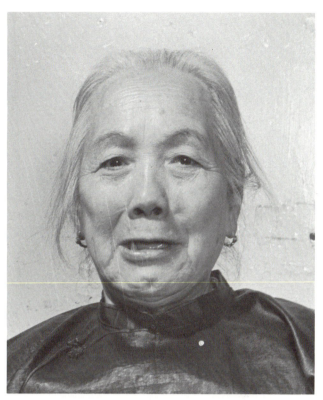

2-38 Chinese-American. OWI. Library of Congress, Washington, D. C., *(photographer) Marjory Collins.*

2-39a Negro-American. *(photographer) Doug Milner*

2-39b (profile view of 2-40a). *(photographer) Doug Milner*

2-40 Mandrill Monkey. Courtesy the Dallas Zoo, Dallas, Tx.   *(photographer) Rosa Finsley.*

Nature

ANIMALS: For makeup stylization, avoid the long-nosed animals, such as horses, giraffes, llama, etc. However, do include such illustrations should you need to make masks, or partial extensions.

FLOWERS: Enlarged close-ups of throats of orchids, pansies, lilies, roses, etc. The orchid in photograph 2–42 has a "mean face" when seen from one-direction, and a happier expression when turned upside down.

2–41 Dendrobium orchid.

2–42 Slipper orchid.

2-43a Weathered wood at Bedford Springs.

2-43b Contrast of textures.   *(photographer) Doug Milner*

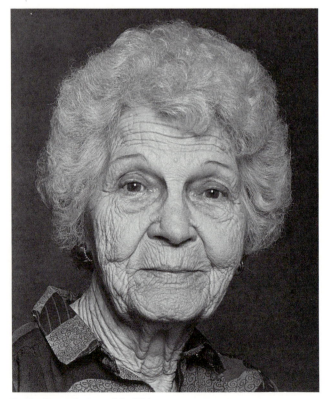

2-43c (frontal view of 2-43b).   *(photographer) Doug Milner.*

2-44 Death's Head Hawk Moth.[3]

FORMS: Collect photos in which form, as revealed by light and shadow, is of primary importance, such as sand dunes, rolling hills, clouds, and tree bark. This will aid your understanding of contouring, as discussed in Chapter 4.

INSECTS: Look for magnified enlargements, and artist's drawings. Notice the "face" on the back of the moth.

Miscellaneous

CATALOGS: Write for catalogs so you will have access to the nearest theatrical supply houses (see Appendix for addresses).

MAKEUP ARTICLES:

Corrective: Women's magazines run articles on current trends in fashion makeup, and give detailed information in how to achieve certain effects. Find old magazines and get "the latest look" for each decade. Date the pages. Fads change quickly.

Techniques: From time to time, articles appear showing an individual actor's techniques, as Hal Holbrook's transformation into Mark Twain, or Cecily Tyson's Miss Jane Pitman.

Special Effects: Science fiction creatures, black eyes, scars, bruises, prosthetics.

Stylization: Include clown makeup, mimes, Mardi Gras and Halloween faces, Punk rock, etc.

The best way to begin a serious collection is to start by making the file, and listing all the categories. Then, the moment you find your first photograph, you have a place to put it. File as you collect—and never cease observing and searching. This can be a storehouse for your imagination. As you enrich your resources, you enrich your ability as a designer.

2-45 Emmett Kelly, a famous circus clown best known for his character "Weary Willy". Donald Lee Rust. National Portrait Gallery, Smithsonian Institution, Washington, D. C.

BIBLIOGRAPHY

Mellen, James, Ed. National Portrait Gallery, Smithsonian Institution Permanent Collection Illustrated Checklist. (City of Washington: The Smithsonian Institution Press, 1980).

Boughton, Patricia, and Martha Ellen Hughes. *The Buyer's Guide to Cosmetics*. (New York: Random House, 1981).

NOTES

[1]Clarence P. Hornung. *An Old Fashioned Christmas in Illustration and Decoration*. (New York: Dover Pub., Inc. 1975.) p 45.

[2]Geoffrey Williams. *African Designs from Traditional Sources*. (New York: Dover Publications, Inc. 1971). p. 129.

[3]Jim Harter. *Animals*. 1419 Copyright Free Illustrations of Mammals, Birds, Fish, Insects, etc. (New York: Dover Publications, Inc. 1979). p. 238.

3

Learning How

The study of color can be very complex. However, if you will arm yourself with a few simple principles concerning color and value, you will understand the basis for creating the effect of three-dimensional form with paint.

Warm Colors: Those colors containing yellow or red tend to be perceived by the eye first. Therefore, they are considered advancing colors.

Cool Colors: Colors such as blue, purple, and blue-green appear to be further away, and therefore meet the eye more slowly. These cool colors are said to be receding. For example, stop signs are never blue or green; since advancing colors reach out and get your attention, stop signs are either yellow or red.

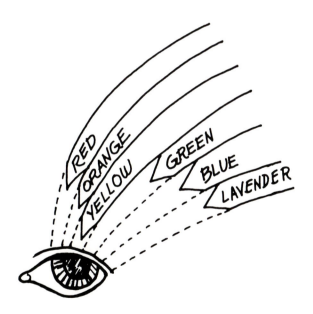

3-1

Light Values: When colors have a large amount of white in them, as in pastel tones, they are considered light in *value* and will advance toward the eye.

Dark Values: If the colors are darkened in *value* by the addition of darker colors, they seem to recede, and the eye perceives them less quickly.

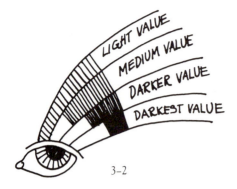

LIGHT VALUE
MEDIUM VALUE
DARKER VALUE
DARKEST VALUE

3-2

Designers, whether of costumes, settings, or makeup, are aware of these guide lines and put them to use to direct the eye. By being aware of the principle of advancing and receding colors and values, we can create the illusion of depth in facial planes. For example, (Illus. 3–3), a muzzle or fatty pouch can be made to appear to stand out from the face if it is made light in value, or warm in hue—or both. The effect is then strengthened by making the surrounding areas darker or cooler.

3–3 The muzzle and nose of the dog makeup seem to stand out because they are lighter in value than the surrounding colors. The darker values recede into the costume. Orlin Corey in makeup as Basket in *The Great Cross Country Race*. An Everyman Player Production.

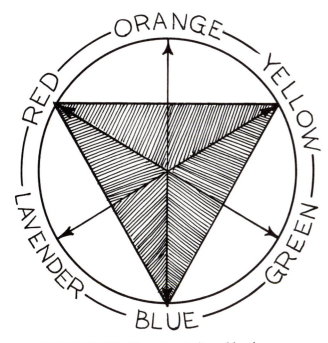

3-4 COLOR WHEEL. The colors indicated by the triangle—red, blue and yellow, are primary colors; those opposite each other are complementary. When two adjacent colors are mixed, they are considered analogous.

Complementary Colors: Those colors which are opposite each other on the color wheel (see Illustration 3-4) and will gray each other when combined. For example, red complements green, yellow complements lavender, and orange complements blue. In mixing makeup, this means that if a shade seems too red, a little green added will decrease the intensity, thus graying it down, and vice versa. If makeup appears too lavender, yellow will reduce the intensity.

Primary Colors: Blue, red and yellow are the pure pigments which cannot be achieved by mixing other colors. However, all other colors can be mixed from primary colors *if* the pigments are pure.

Browns: Before beginning to mix your skin tone, it might be helpful to learn how brown tones are made—since most skins will be a shade of brown from fair to dark. A combination of red, yellow, and blue

makes brown. If you have a water color set, experiment by making puddles of yellow, and then adding varying amounts of red and blue to each batch. You should discover colors to embrace the whole human race.

The following instructions will lead you through a step-by-step experience in mixing colors and applying makeup. *Read them through all the way* to get an overview before starting your practice.

MIXING MAKEUP

The following color mixing exercises are based on the selection of a few basic colors from which an infinite variety of skin tones can be achieved. In learning to mix your own colors of greasepaint, you will need to evolve at least three shades for Base, Shadow and Highlight.

Base: The foundation makeup which is nearest to your skin color and is applied in a *thin* film to the entire face and onto any revealed skin. This includes hands if you are creating a noticeable difference in color between hands and face.

Shadow: Makeup mixed two or three shades darker than the base. It accents hollows and structural planes related to the underlying muscle and skull structure.

Highlight: Makeup mixed two or three shades lighter than the base. It accents the protruding features, such as cheekbones, chin and nose.

It should be noted that shadows are more effective on light skins, as they have highlights "built-in", whereas dark skins have shadows "built-in", and highlighting becomes a more effective tool in modeling form. However, highlight and shadow are used on all skin tones, in order to create or reinforce form.

IRENE COREY BASIC PALETTE

Consult the Color Correlation Chart, page 19, for correlation between my generalized color descriptions and the manufacturer's brand colors. Make a selection of the grease or cream makeup of your choice which matches the following generic color names. Note that the makeup may be designated as either a base or liner by the manufacturer.

In all the instructions which follow in this book, named colors will indicate my generic color description.

Generic Palette

White
Pale Pink
Muted Yellow
Primary Yellow
Sallow (grayish skin tone)
Sunburn
Red-Brown
Primary Green
Optional colors: Hold these in reserve for later use.
Dark Blue
Dark Purple
Red, Moist rouge
Black

Makeup Color Chart: Create your own color chart by rubbing a spot of makeup directly on a white paper. Put the generic name and brand name beside each color. If you add other colors, note them on the chart.

EXERCISE TWO:

Mixing Base, Shadow and Highlight

1. In learning to mix makeup, you will first train your eye to discover which colors are needed to *match* your own skin tone. Later, you can adjust the color, lighter or darker, in order to adjust to character and lighting needs. Lightly cold cream the back of your hand to prepare it for use as a palette. If you have hairy hands, use your palm. The body temperature serves to soften the makeup to the proper consistency for application. Now, sparingly cold cream your face. Wipe off *all* excess with a soft cotton cloth.

2. If using stick grease, *scrape* off a small pile of each color with the metal part of the brush, much as you might scrape off cold butter to make it spread easier on bread. Do *not* cut off a chunk. If using cream grease, scoop out a pile with the brush. To transfer greasepaint to your hand, place the mound of makeup against your skin and twist as you pull the brush away. You will arrange small mounds of each

3–5

color between the knuckles and around the outside of the hand. Leave a space in the center for mixing. Start at the left, and apply in this order:

White
Muted Yellow
Primary Yellow
Pale Pink
Dark Sunburn
Red-brown
Primary green
Sallow
Dark Blue ⎱
Purple ⎰ For dark skins.

Be consistent in working from your hand palette. Do not try to brush makeup directly from the stick or pot. Stick makeup needs the heat of your hand to create the right consistency. It is more convenient to work from your hand palette. Make mounds of all the colors until you *know* you don't need them.

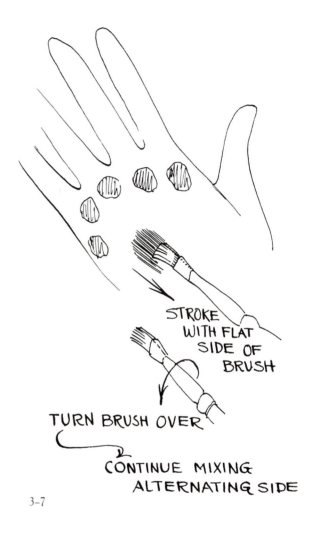

3-7

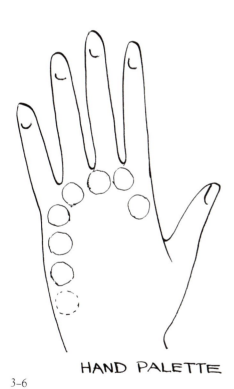

HAND PALETTE

3-6

3. To mix your base, move some of the paint which is nearest your skin color to the center mixing area. As you add other colors, mix them with the brush, stroking back and forth with its flat side. Avoid scrubbing the brush in a circular motion. Develop the habit of keeping your brush flat and knife-edged by using this flat-stroking method.

47

TEST: As you mix, you will want to test after each new addition of color. Touch a spot of the mixture to your forehead with your brush. Smooth it out with your fingers. Is it too light? Too dark? Too yellow? Too red?
Observe! Experiment!

For Light Skins:

You might start with Sallow, which is a grayish color.

If this seems too cool or bluish, add a little Sunburn.

If the mixture becomes too red, try adding Green to gray it down.

If it seems too dark, add Muted Yellow, and Pale Pink.

If it is too light, add Red-brown.

If it is too lavender, try Primary Yellow.

Be aware that *most* skins have some pure yellow and green in them.

Experiment! Observe!

MY RECIPE FOR BASE:

HIGHLIGHT:

SHADOW

3–8

For Dark or Olive Skins:

Start with a mixture of Primary Yellow and Primary Green.

Add Red-brown.

If mixture lacks red hue, add Sunburn or Moist Rouge.

If it is too dark, add more Primary Yellow.

If it is really too dark, try Muted Yellow.

If it is too light, add more Red-brown.

If a very dark color is required in order to match your skin tone, you may want to try adding Dark Blue or Purple. As a *last resort*, try a touch of Black, but be very cautious.

Black tends to make colors muddy.

Experiment! Observe! Vary the proportions.

Personal recipe: You should now have arrived at a recipe for your own skin color. List the colors that you used, and make a color splotch for later reference. You are training your eye to recognize the colors which make up the tone of your skin. Later, you may want to mix a base which is a shade darker than your skin color to compensate for wash-out caused by powdering and lighting, if you have a light skin. However, dark skins, which tend to absorb light, will depend on the highlighting to carry the structure of the face. The experience of learning to mix colors will also serve to help you choose pre-mixed colors, should the need arise.

Mix a fairly large batch of base—about one-half teaspoon. You will use part of it to cover your face with a thin coat, and the rest will be divided in half to form the basis of the shadow and highlight.

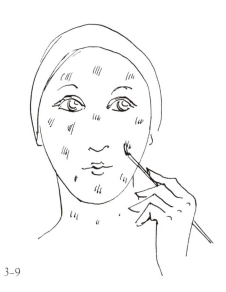

3-9

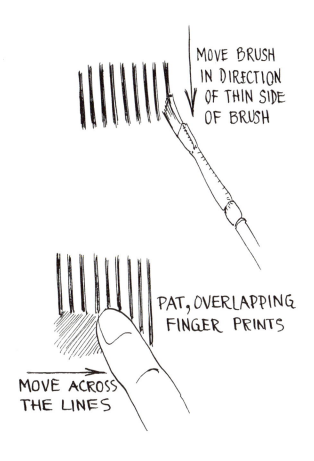

3-10 Test for value of shadow.

Applying base: Lightly cold cream your face. Wipe off thoroughly. Dot base over your face with brush or finger tip. Smooth it into a *thin* coat. With finger tips of both hands, start in the center of your face and move upward and outward. The overall skin tone is determined by the *color* of the makeup, not by the thickness of it. If it is not dark enough, change the recipe by adding darker colors.

TEST: Press a clean finger tip against the smoothed makeup. If it comes off on your finger, you have put it on too heavily.

Mixing Your Shadow: To mix shadow color, take half of the remaining base mixture and add more of each of the darker tones used in your original base recipe. Most skins will require the addition of Red-brown. If your skin is very dark, you may want to add a touch of Purple, Blue, or even a *sparing* bit of Black.

The final shadow color should be two or three shades darker than your base.

TEST: To determine if shadow is dark enough, paint several thin, closely spaced lines under the cheekbone. Don't worry about placement now. This is a test for value contrast. Blend by patting, as illustrated. Squint at it through your eyelashes. If the shadow area seems to fade into the base color, add more dark tones to the shadow mixture. The shadow should still show contrast through the squinting, but should not be so dark as to appear abrupt. You can also test to see how it shows up by backing away from the mirror 8 or 10 feet.

3-11

Mixing Your Highlight: Use the other half of your base. Add the lighter shades from your base recipe. Very fair skin may need a little white. Darker skins may require Muted Yellow in order to strengthen the highlight.

TEST: Paint small closely spaced strokes of highlight on a spot on your forehead. Blend by patting. Squint at it in the mirror to see if it appears about two shades lighter than the base.

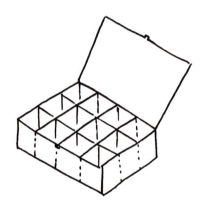

3-12

You should now have three shades of color: base, shadow and highlight. These tones will automatically complement each other, and your skin. Smudge a sample of each, side by side, on your recipe chart.

For purposes of practice or for use during the run of a show, larger quantities of the colors can be pre-mixed and stored in plastic pill bottles. However, if you are just learning, keep practicing until you can recognize color variations and are able to mix them with confidence.

Clear, plastic boxes with 12 or more molded divisions are useful for storing pre-mixed colors, and also for containing chunks of grease sticks divided for class "kits."

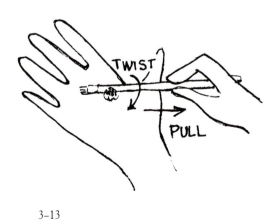

3-13

LEARNING TECHNIQUES

There are three techniques basic to the application of good makeup: *lining*, *feathering*, and *blending*. These are not necessarily easy, but they are essential if precise, detailed control is to be achieved. The following exercises are designed to prepare you for makeup application.

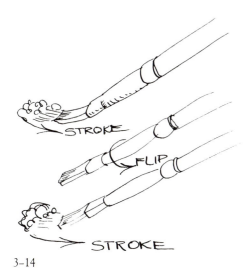

3-14

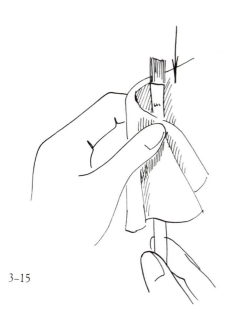

3-15

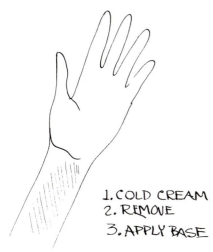

1. COLD CREAM
2. REMOVE
3. APPLY BASE

3-16 Use the wrist as a practice area.

EXERCISE THREE:

Handling the Brush

1. Lightly cold cream the back of your hand to prepare it for use as a palette. Place a small mound of your shadow color on the back of your hand.

2. Use your $3/16''$ brush. Stroke the makeup back and forth with the flat side of the brush until the paint is creamy. *Always* mix and stroke your makeup in this way. Do not scrub it around in a circular direction. The goal is to keep the bristles flat, forming a knife edge, so that the brush will make a thin line when moved sideways; however, when the brush is moved broadside, it should make a broad stroke useful for blending.

To clean the brush between colors, dip it in cold cream and wipe with a tissue. Develop the habit of pulling the brush through a lightly pinched fold of tissue to flatten the bristles each time you clean them.

EXERCISE FOUR:

Lining, Feathering and Blending

Lining Technique

It is necessary to understand how to handle "lines" on the face. Actually, lines, as such, do not occur either in nature or on the face. Folds of skin do. Repeated smiles or frowns cause raised areas next to depressions. Such contours are created with makeup by a combination of *lining* and *feathering*.

This exercise is to be done on your wrist as a neutral practice area. Later, specific directions will indicate where makeup goes on your face.

1. Lightly cold cream the underside of your wrist about six inches up your arm, and remove excess cream. Smooth base on, using any tone which approximates your skin tone for this practice, or use your pre-mixed base.

2. Using your $3/16''$ brush, stroke the shadow color into it, and maintain a sharp, flat edge. Check to be sure your shadow color is darker in value than your base, so there is a noticeable contrast.

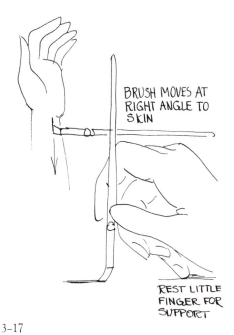

BRUSH MOVES AT RIGHT ANGLE TO SKIN

REST LITTLE FINGER FOR SUPPORT

3-17

Always hold the brush at a right angle to the surface you are painting. Make one careful stroke, leaving a narrow, clean line. You may steady your hand by resting your little finger on the skin.

Practice making many thin curved lines, each in one continuous stroke. As you end each line, reduce the pressure so that the line will fade away as the brush lifts up.

NOTE: If you put too much pressure on the brush, it will leave thick fat lines.

CHECK: Is your brush held at a right angle to the skin?

Pigment feeds off the *end* of the bristles, not the side. Remove makeup from your practice area and repeat until you have secured the technique.

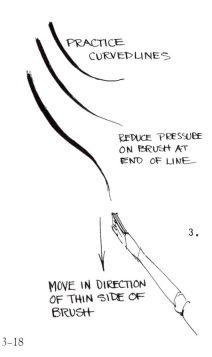

PRACTICE CURVED LINES

REDUCE PRESSURE ON BRUSH AT END OF LINE

3.

MOVE IN DIRECTION OF THIN SIDE OF BRUSH

3-18

Feathering Technique

Feathering is a technique used to achieve a gradual shading from dark to light value in order to create the illusion of depth of form. The line representing the deepest part of the wrinkle is brushed to one side so that the darkness of the crevice gradually blends into the tone of the base. Mastering this technique is crucial to creating good makeup. It calls for precision, and that calls for practice.

1. Prepare your wrist to receive makeup. Apply more base. Stroke lining color onto your brush, making sure the edge is sharp.

2. Make *one* clean, thin, curved line with a faded ending. The line should be clear and distinct.

3. Pull your brush between a pinched fold of tissue, ONCE, to remove excess makeup and to leave the bristle edge sharp. See illustration 3-15.

FEATHERING

3-19

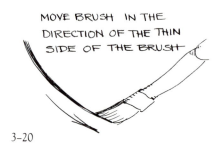

MOVE BRUSH IN THE DIRECTION OF THE THIN SIDE OF THE BRUSH

3-20

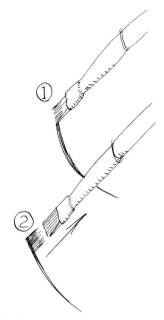

4. Place the tip-end of the brush at a right angle to the wrist *exactly on the line*.

5. Move the broadside of the brush out, up and away, like an airplane taking off. What is happening is that the makeup of the line is being dragged away from the line in a gradual shading which fades into the base color. The original edge of the line should remain even.

6. Continue feathering along the line without taking more makeup on the brush. There should be a gradual tapering at the end of the line.

7. With one finger, carefully *pat** along the feathered edge to blend it evenly into the base. The end of the line should disappear into nothingness.

3-21 Feathering a line.

3-22

DEFINITION

To pat: The tip of the finger is pressed lightly to the surface and lifted quickly up and down, making gentle contact with the skin. The "fingerprints" of the pat overlap each other as you move in a direction *across* the brush stroke. The finger tip does not lift far away from the skin.

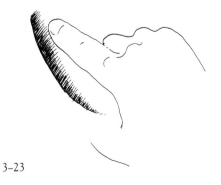

3-23

Laying In Areas

Areas of shadow or highlight are laid on in close-together, thin, parallel lines. These lines define the shapes of the shadows and highlights, and serve to distribute the makeup evenly across the area. Keep the overall shape of the area in mind as you make the lines.

Blending Technique

One of the most important techniques you must master is that of *blending*. It is crucial to the art of subtle, yet controlled and strong makeup. Added to the

3-24

techniques of lining and feathering, blending enables you to suggest endless variation in changed or strengthened forms on the face. However, to understand blending of parallel lines, review what it means "to pat": the tip of the finger is pressed lightly to the surface and lifted quickly up and down, making gentle contact with the skin. The "fingerprints" of the pat *overlap* each other as you move in a direction *across* the parallel lines. The finger tip does not lift very far away from the skin. (No kangaroo hops, please!) "To pat" is the opposite of "to rub." Rubbing greasepaint drags it off the surface onto the finger, is inaccurate, and creates muddy, unclear areas. The same applies to a dragging pat which nudges the makeup along.

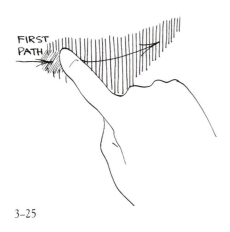

3-25

Shadow Areas:

1. Prepare your wrist with base. Lay in parallel lines suggesting a triangular cheek shadow.

CHECK: Is your brush at a right angle to the surface?

Are you allowing the paint to come off the tip-end of the bristles so that you make a thin line?

Does each line have about the same amount of makeup?

Are you watching the shape created by the lines?

Are the lines about ⅛″ apart? Too much space between will make blending difficult.

If the lines are too thick, the shadow will be too dark.

2. Place the tip of one finger at the edge of the area, and blend the lines by "patting-a-path" through the center, across to the other side. If the lines do not blend on the first path, repeat the patting on the same path a second time.

3. Pat a second path under the first one, overlapping the first path slightly.

4. Make another path under the second one. This will be a bridge between the edge of the shadow area and the base. By now, the finger tip is carrying just enough greasepaint to subtly blend into the surrounding base away from the edge of the area.

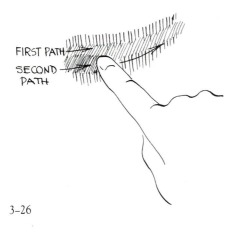

3-26

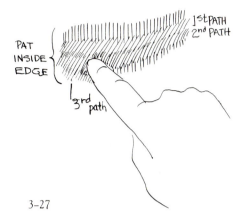

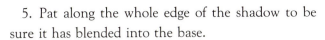

3-27

5. Pat along the whole edge of the shadow to be sure it has blended into the base.

CHECK: Are you avoiding rubbing? Hopping? Nudging?

Are you working with the tip of your finger?

Are your pats overlapping?

6. Continue the "pat-a-path" method by making new paths above the remaining area, paths 4 and 5.

CHECK: Do not overblend. Just pat until the lines fuse.

Does your shadow "disappear"? If so, your shadow mixture needs to be darker.

A well blended shadow should be darker in the center with invisible shading into the basic skin tone all around the edge. Does yours do this?

Keep practicing this technique. You will soon see the difference in rubbing and patting. If you have been known to say, "My skin absorbs makeup," it is more likely that:

*You are rubbing it off with your hands;

*Your makeup is too oily;

*Too much cold cream was left under the base.

Pigment in makeup is inert; it can't go *into* your skin—it can only go where you put it. How you put it and where you put it is what the art of makeup is all about. Clean your wrist and repeat as many times as necessary.

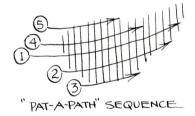

"PAT-A-PATH" SEQUENCE

3-28

The following practice will prepare you for applying highlights and shadows to the face. Highlight areas will be placed on outstanding planes of the face which you wish to accent. The shape of the highlight will be defined by laying in an area of thin parallel lines, following the same procedure as described under *Blending Shadow Areas*. All major areas of highlight and shadow will be separated by a space of base. Do not assume that the whole face will be covered in either highlight or shadow! Your ultimate goal will be a face which has a base color contoured by areas of shadow, and accented by areas of highlight. For the time being, continue to practice on your wrist.

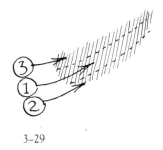

3–29

Highlight Areas:

1. Prepare your wrist with cold cream and base.

2. Use your 1/8″ brush. Stroke highlight color onto your brush.

3. With sharp edge of the brush, lay in thin, parallel lines 1/8″ apart to create a small triangular area.

4. Pat-a-path across the lines through the middle of the area (path 1).

5. Pat-a-path below the first path (path 2).

6. Pat-a-path above the first path (path 3).

CHECK: Do your second and third paths blend into the base, leaving no visible edge?

Are you using your hand as a palette?

Are your pats overlapping?

Adjustment For Contrast

Final adjustment of the amount of contrast needed between highlight, base and shadow will be determined by the following variables:

1. Powdering will always diminish the contrast of the shadow to the base.

2. A larger theater calls for stronger contrast between shadows and highlights than an intimate theater, but the blending of the areas demands the same subtle treatment.

3. Harsh, intense lights will wash out makeup, and the makeup must be adjusted accordingly. However, when gelatins of high color intensity (dark blues, teals, greens, ambers, reds) are used, they will destroy the most competent makeup illusion. Communicate with your lighting designer. Lighter ranges of these colors are a more effective aid to makeup.

BASIC PROCEDURE FOR APPLYING MAKEUP TO THE FACE

The following procedure should be followed before, and after, application of all makeup. Refer to this section after you have reached Chapter 6 on contouring.

1. *Prepare Skin*: Apply astringent with cotton pad. Apply moisture cream, or a light amount of cold cream. Moisture cream is adequate under cream bases, but cold cream should be used under stick grease. Wipe off excess cold cream.

2. *Apply Base*.

3. *Apply Makeup*. See instructions with Illustration 3–9.

4. *Powder*. Establish a powdering station at a mirror with clean puffs, nylon complexion brushes, and paper plates which have a semi-circle cut away on one side. Place powder on the plate, hold it under your chin, load the puff *liberally* with powder, and pat on all madeup areas. Fold puff in half and press edge of puff into crevices around nose and eyes. *All makeup must be covered!* When you can no longer see makeup, but only powder, you probably have enough.

Let powder stay on for two or three minutes to allow it to absorb the oil from the greasepaint. This "sets" the makeup. When properly powdered, the makeup will not smear and will withstand an enormous amount of perspiration.

Brush off excess powder with a soft complexion brush.

Be thorough. If the makeup smears, you did not use enough powder. Remove final powder with a dampened sponge or cotton pad. If the performing conditions are unusually hot, dash cold water on your face.

5. *Apply Rouge*. With a large, soft brush, such as comes with blushers, lightly dust dry rouge onto cheek hollows, along forehead at temple area, on neck, under jaw bone. The rouge is applied to add a subtle glow to the makeup—both men and women. Rouge used *as* rouge should be suited to the needs of the character. Its placement shifts with the fashion of

the times. Consult the style of the period for usage when it is to appear as rouge rather than to suggest a healthy complexion.

6. *Remove Makeup.* Work a generous amount of cold cream into the greasepaint. If you are using water-soluble cold cream, remove the emulsion with a soapy sponge or cloth. For regular cold cream, remove by wiping gently with an old T-shirt. Repeat process, if necessary, taking care around the eyes not to stretch the skin, or get cream into eyes.

Moisten cotton pads with astringent and wipe until pads come away clean. Pat water onto skin, until it is just damp. Coat skin with moisture cream.

Make this procedure an automatic part of your makeup routine!

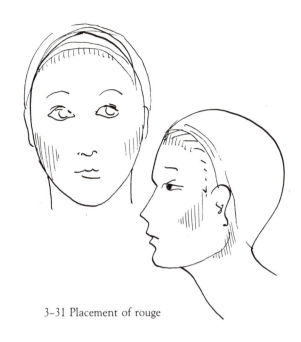

3–31 Placement of rouge

3–30a Powder Station.

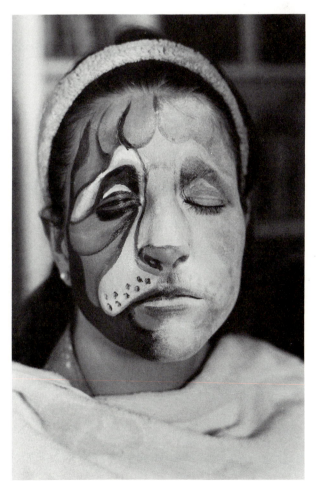

3–30b Illustration of liberal application of powder shown on one half of the face.

57

4

Understanding Form, Highlight and Shadow

FORM AND LIGHT

Form is a design element common to all the arts and is basic to an understanding of theatrical makeup. Essential to the revelation of form is light. Lighting is an integral part of theatre. It establishes mood, locale, and time. We know that changing the direction of the light changes our perception of the object lighted and reveals various forms. Consider the effect of lighting on the simple shape of an egg, the skin-like folds of drapery, and the structure of actor Nick Dalley's face.

When lighted from the front, the forms are flattened. The egg appears two-dimensional, the fabric lacks definition, and facial characteristics diffuse into an egg-shaped blur.

Lighting from the side creates shadows and models the forms, revealing the shape of the egg, the depth of the folds, and distinctive facial traits.

When the light source comes from below, different areas of the subjects are highlighted, and unusual shadows result. On the stage, this eerie effect is frequently used to heighten a sense of mystery.

Direct overhead light creates harsh shadows on the face and brings out the underlying shape of the skull.

These examples suggest only a few ways lighting is used to model and reveal form. It is through light that we come to an understanding of what form is.

FORM AND PIGMENT

Form can be *revealed* by lighting, but it can be *created* by pigment. By using shades of greasepaint varying from light to dark, the illusion of form can be created on a flat surface. In painting, this is referred to as chiaroscuro—the technique of making the flat surface of the canvas appear to have three-dimensional form, without regard for color. See the drawing in Illustration 4–5 by Annibale Carracci.

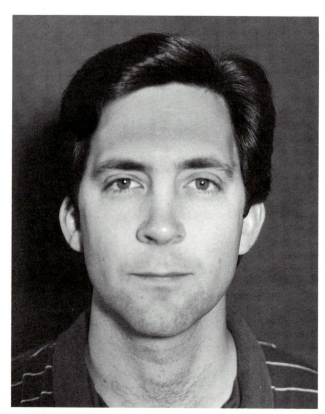

4–1a and 4–1b Egg, folds, and face of actor Nick Dalley, lighted from the front.

4–2a and 4–2b Egg, folds, and face, lighted from the side.

4-3a and 4-3b Egg, folds, and face, lighted from below.

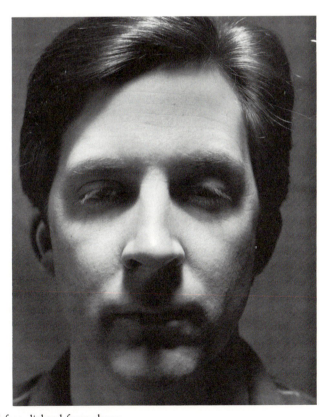

4-4a and 4-4b Egg, folds, and face, lighted from above.

4-5 Annibale Carracci creates the illusion of form by using black chalk heightened with white on blue paper. The Metropolitan Museum of Art, Gustavus A. Pfeiffer Fund, 1962.

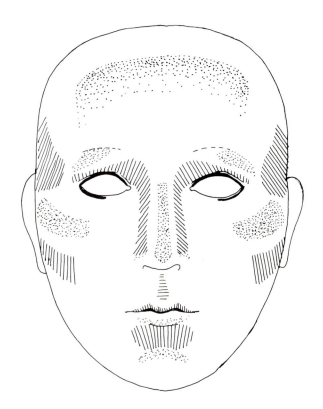

Chiaroscuro in makeup is the use of highlight and shadow either to strengthen the forms found on the face, or to create the effect of changed structure. Study the work of Caravaggio and Masaccio.

FORM AND PHOTOGRAPHS

In a photograph, the shadows fall in relation to the direction of the light sources at the time the picture is made. Yet these captured highlights and shadows give us a perception of the shapes regardless of where the shadows occur. In studying photographs for makeup purposes, we do not seek to make a *literal* translation of these shadows onto our face, but rather we establish a method which allows us to transfer the *knowledge* gained about the forms into light and dark greasepaint which describes the forms. To do this, it is necessary to establish an arbitrary light source in

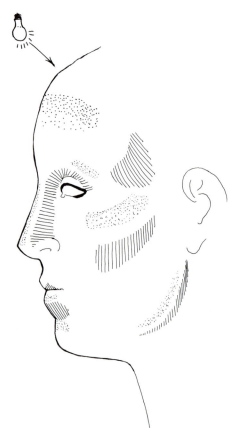

4-6a and 4-6b An illustration of how highlights (dotted areas), and shadows, (lined areas) are formed when the face is lighted from a 45 degree angle.

4-7 An enlargement of a segment of a magazine photograph reveals the chiaroscuro created by the screening process.

our makeup charts. For general purposes, consider the light as coming from above and from the front at a 45 degree angle, as in average stage lighting. Illustrations 4–6a and 4–6b show structure shadows created by such a light.

Simply stated, the arbitrary light source which you establish in your mind when creating makeup charts requires highlights to be placed above contours, and shadows underneath. This is a standard principle and applies to all realistic makeup. You will experience creating this effect in *Styling From Photographs*, Chapter 9.

To create the illusion of form on your face, the shapes which appear in a photograph are recreated with pigment. Consider the photograph. It is actually a flat sheet of paper with two dimensions. The suggestion of form comes through the ink screened in small dots which, through varying density, suggest gradation from light to dark.

By using a medium other than printer's ink, such as oil paints, pencil or greasepaint, similar illusions of form can be made. Armed with the knowledge that light, medium and dark tones create the effect of form, endless illusions can be painted on the face without the aid of putty or elaborate prosthetics.

EXERCISE FIVE:

Creating Form With Shading

The following exercises can be enhanced by doing them on a medium grey paper, so that major highlights can be accented with a white pencil.

1. Place a white ball and a white paper, fastened into a cylinder, under a *single* light source, against a light background. Sketch the outline of the shapes, and then stroke in shadows, using pencil or pen and ink. Accent the strongest light area with white pencil. Pay attention to the shadows and contrasting values which are created by the object in relation to its background. As you experience being able to create the cylinder and the shape of the sphere, you are on your way to creating similar shapes on the face.

4-8 A white ball, and paper rolled into a cylinder, or curled, provide good objects for exploration of highlighting and shadowing.

2. Cut a strip of paper 2″ wide and 10″ long. Roll it to make it curl. Reverse directions and roll several times. Twist the paper until it forms interesting curves. Place it under a *single* source of light. Sketch the outline, and then shade in the darker areas, blending as they move into highlights. Accent highlights with white.

3. Arrange one or two folds in a soft fabric which drapes easily. Use a single light source from the side and sketch the basic lines of the folds, then create shadows and highlights.

Become aware of the variation in forms around you. Notice the effects on the faces you meet. Look through magazines and find examples of photographs which stress form primarily; as a sea shell, a river rock, a snow bank or the curve of a Rolls-Royce fender. Include these in your picture file. See 2–44.

5

Discovering Your Skull and Facial Muscles

After you have mastered the preceding basic techniques, you can move on to the real art of makeup. This begins, however, with an understanding of how shading creates the illusion of depth and form. To know where this shading occurs, you must first have awareness of the underlying skull.

M. M. Gerasimov, working solely on surviving skulls of persons unknown to him, has been able to create portraits which were recognized by friends and relatives of the missing person. He finds that the face is a simplified version of the complicated skull shape which lies underneath, with no two skulls the same.[4] To further understand the surface of the face, we must extend our knowledge of what lies underneath.

EXPLORING YOUR SKULL

Consider the drawing of a skull, Illustration 5–1. It is not enough merely to look and say, "Yes, that is a skull." You must get "inside" your *own* skull by exploration, and bring it to the surface of your mind. With one eye on the skull drawing and the other looking at yourself in the mirror, explore with your *fingertips* your own bone structure:

1. Start in the center of your forehead. Follow the hard bone across your forehead until you move down into the temple area between your ear and eye. This area should feel somewhat soft and tender to the touch.

2. Move from the center of the temple area toward the eye. You will feel the bony structure at the end of your eyebrow. Follow this bone all the way around the eye socket. Get a clear sense of where that cavity is located in relation to the features on top.

3. Go back to the center of the temple and move downward. You will locate your cheekbone. Find the top of it, where it joins the lower rim of the eye orbit;

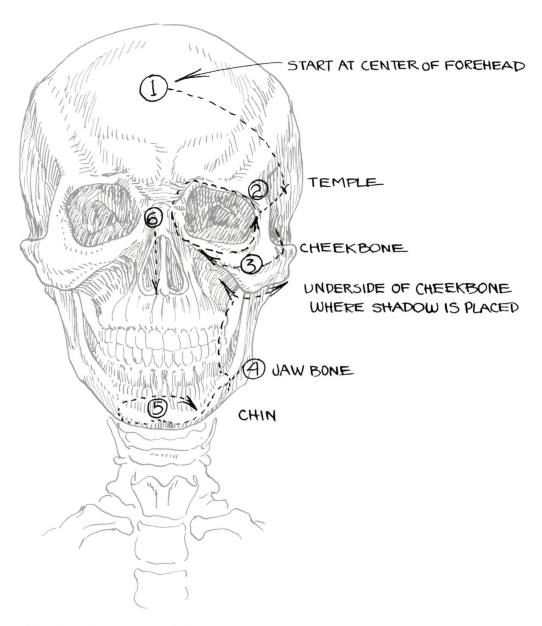

START AT CENTER OF FOREHEAD

TEMPLE

CHEEKBONE

UNDERSIDE OF CHEEKBONE
WHERE SHADOW IS PLACED

JAW BONE

CHIN

5-1 Path for discovering your skull.

follow it back toward the hairline and then forward. Decide which part of the cheekbone projects farthest outward. As you move toward the nose, realize when the bone begins to curve inward. Lay one finger flat against the front of the cheekbone and roll downward. You should be able to feel the underside of the bone. Follow this lower side toward your nose and back toward your hairline. Cheek shadows will be made beneath this bone.

4. Continue the pressing movement down the cheek with the fingertips. Find your gums and upper teeth. Feel where the lower teeth meet your jawbone. Follow the jawbone toward your ear. Feel its shape at the end, under your ear. Follow the jawbone forward until you feel the top of the chin.

5. Explore the shape of your chin. Find its front, top and sides. Feel where it meets the base of your teeth, under your lower lip.

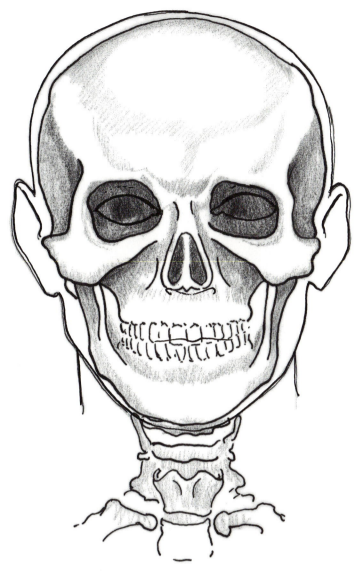

5-2 An awareness of the skull which underlies facial features provides the initial understanding of makeup.

6. Find the bridge of your nose, the indentation where your nose meets your forehead. Feel the top of your nose from the bridge down to the tip. Decide where the plane of the side of the nose stops and changes into the plane of the cheek.

7. Repeat the exercise with your eyes closed as someone reads the preceding instructions aloud. This is an important exercise. The sense of touch alone will help weld this information into your memory.

Now that you have met the substructure of your face, it will be the guide in the natural placement of your shadows, which indicate the hollows of your skull, and of the highlights, which accent protruding bones.

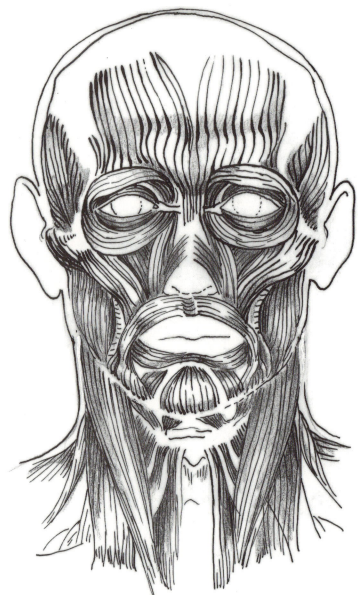

5–3a A knowledge of muscle structure lends further understanding of the outer appearance of the face.

EXERCISE SIX:

Experiencing Your Facial Muscles

Muscles, and their relation to the skull, are responsible for most of the shapes created under the encompassing skin. Become aware of these muscles by locating each one on the drawings, Illustrations 5–3a and 5–3b, while feeling it on yourself.

Work in front of the mirror and SLOWLY move various portions of your face while locating on the chart the muscles which come into use. The key to sensing the movement of the muscles is in doing it *slowly*. For example, if you try making a gradual smile, prolonging the movement as much as you can, you will become aware of the brain messages activating dozens of muscles as they begin to twitch in response to the command.

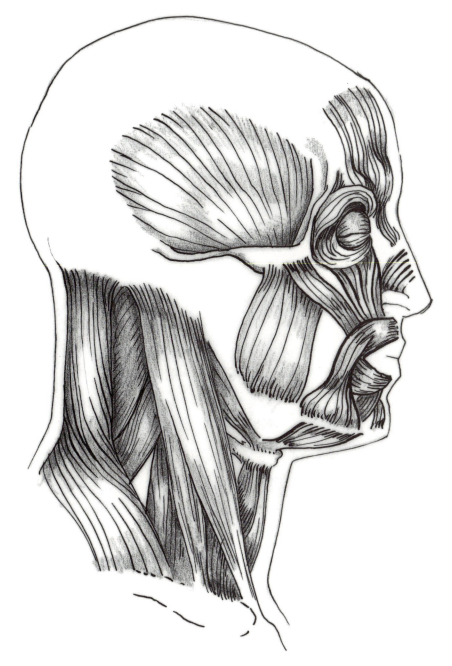

5–3b A continuation of 5–3a.

1. Raise your eyebrows.

2. Squint or wink one eye.

3. Wrinkle your nose.

4. Smile with your mouth open.

5. Frown. Fiercely!

6. Open your mouth as for a scream.

7. Purse your lips.

8. Jut out your jaw and tense the leaders in your neck.

9. Turn your head from side to side; notice the neck muscles.

Experiment! Observe!

BECOME AWARE OF WHAT GOES ON
UNDER YOUR SKIN!

Now that you have experienced your skull and
muscles, study carefully the translucent overlays in
Illustration 5-4. One half of the transparency shows
the muscles in relation to the skull underneath; the
other half shows the shadows and highlights.

Carry this awareness of the underlying structure
with you as you begin to execute makeup.

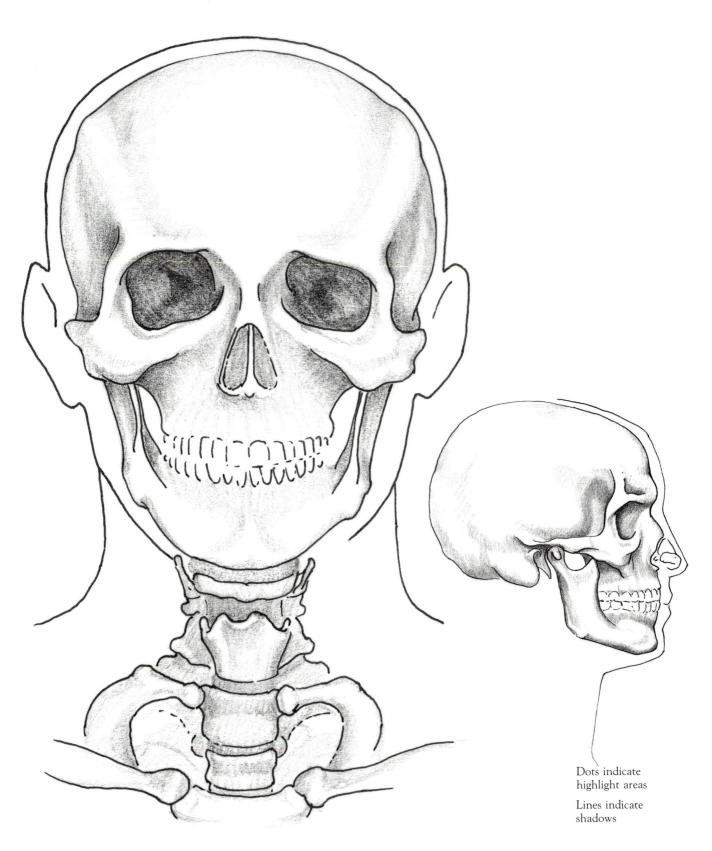

Dots indicate
highlight areas

Lines indicate
shadows

5–4a and 5–4b HIGHLIGHT AND SHADOW IN RELATION
TO SKULL AND MUSCLE STRUCTURE.

BIBLIOGRAPHY

Gray, Henry. *Anatomy, Descriptive and Surgical*. A revised American, from the fifteenth English Edition. (New York: Bounty Books, 1977)

NOTES

[4]M. M. Gerasimov. *The Face Finder*. (Philadelphia, Pa.: J. P. Lippincott, 1970)

6

Contouring

Contouring is achieved by using shadow and highlight to strengthen the natural forms of the face. It enhances the face of even the young actor because it counteracts the tendency of stage lights to wash away an individual's unique features.

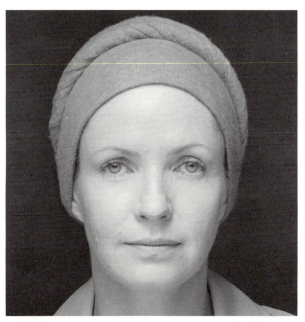

6–1a Model without makeup.   *(photographer) Suzanne Dietz*

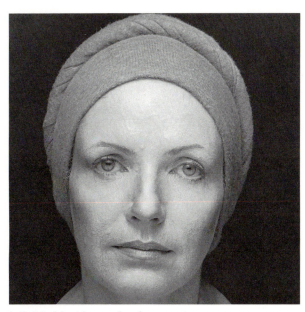

6–1b Model with completed contouring.
(photographer) Suzanne Dietz

CONTOURING
THE FACIAL STRUCTURE

Before proceeding, study the following photographs which illustrate the contouring process. The process is the same regardless of race or sex – the purpose is to strengthen the facial structure of the individual.

The entire sequence of creating highlight and shadow is shown in photographs of the Caucasian male, Illustrations 6–2a through 6–2e, and 6–3. Before and after photographs show the effects of contouring on the Negroid female, Illustrations 6–4a, 6–4b, 6–4c, and 6–4a, and on the Hispanic male, Illustrations 6–5a and 6–5b.

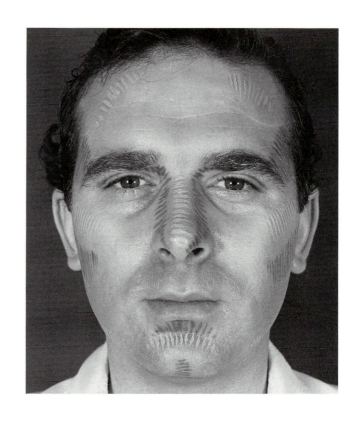

6–2b and 6–2c: Highlight and shadow lined into areas
(photographer) Bruce Wilson

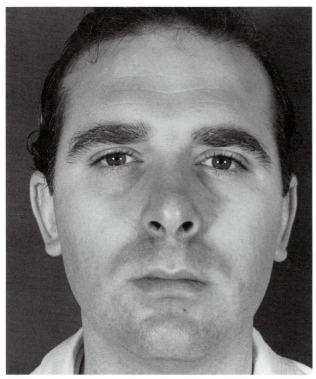

6–2a Actor, Merlin Fahey without makeup.   *(photographer)*
Bruce Wilson

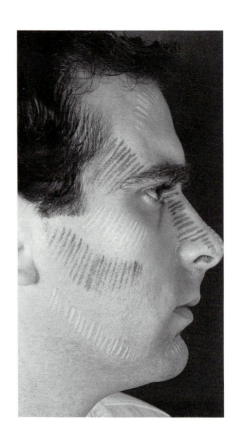

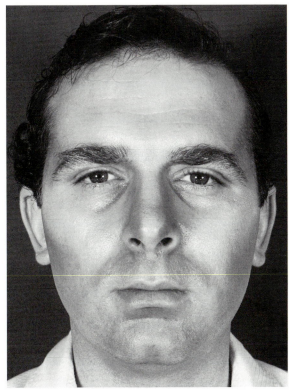
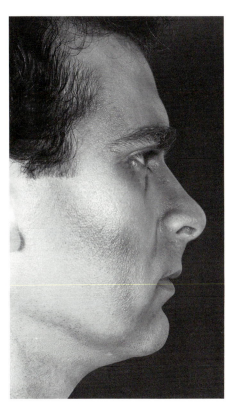

6-2d and 6-2e Completed contouring   *(photographer) Bruce Wilson.*

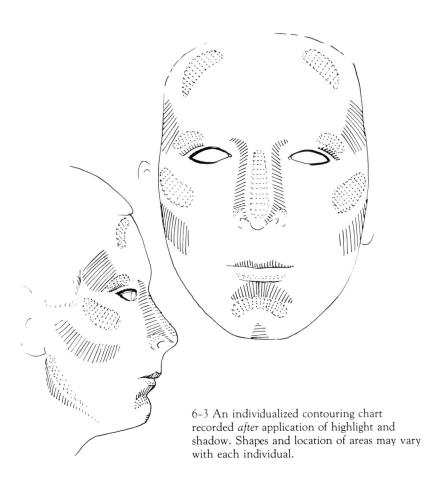

6-3 An individualized contouring chart recorded *after* application of highlight and shadow. Shapes and location of areas may vary with each individual.

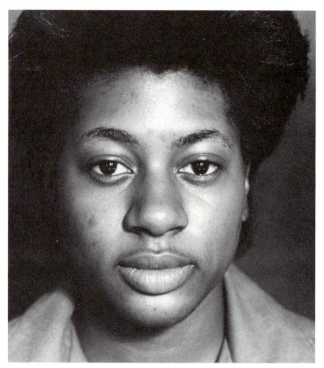

6-4a Model without makeup

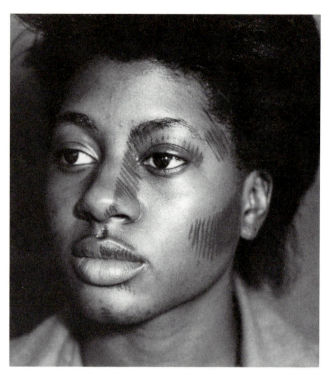

6-4b Model with shadow areas lined in.

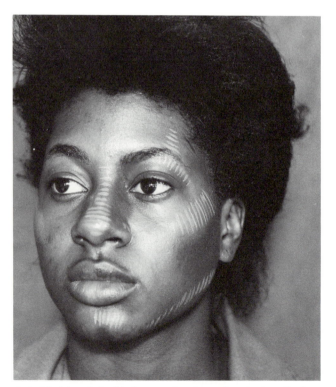

6-4c Model with highlight areas lined in, after shadows had been blended.

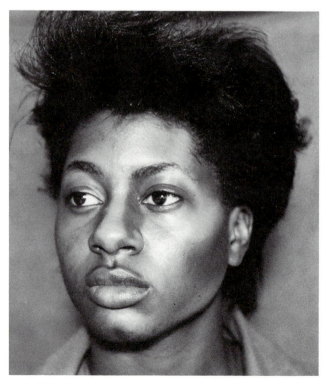

6-4d Model with contouring completed on one half of face.

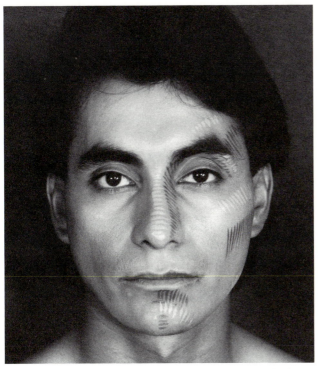

6-5a Hispanic model with highlight and shadow areas laid in.

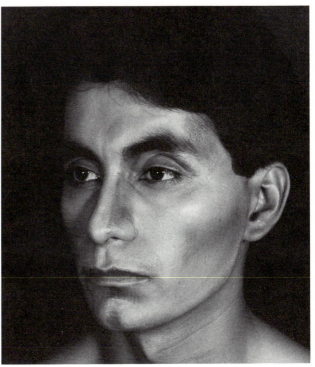

6-5b Model with completed contouring on one half of face.

EXERCISE SEVEN:

Contouring the Facial Structure

The previous exercises have acquainted you with mixing your makeup, introduced you to basic techniques of application, and familiarized you with your skull and muscle structure. Using this experience, you can now contour your own face.

1. Prepare your face for makeup (Chapter Two, *Skin care*).

2. Mix your base, highlight, and shadow colors. Have a mound of each on your hand palette.

3. Apply base color by dotting it over your face and smoothing it evenly. It should be a thin film, not a thick, sticky coat.

TEST: A clean finger pressed against your face should come away free of makeup. If the base is too thick, it will come off.

4. Recall or repeat your experience with the skull exercise in Chapter Five. Notice how the shadows relate to the skull in Illustration 6-6. Locate these areas on your face.

5. Study shadow side of *Contouring Chart*, Illustration 6-6. Pay special attention to the *direction* of the parallel area lines as drawn on the chart. Your lines should run in the same direction on your face in order to achieve the most effective blending. Be aware of the *shapes* of the shadows.

6. Use your 3/16″ brush and stroke shadow color onto it by pulling its flat side through the greasepaint. Flip the brush to alternate sides. This loads the brush, yet leaves the bristle ends straight. Lay in shadows with thin, parallel lines, 1/8″ apart. *Lay in all shadow areas before blending.* This allows you to see the overall layout and to better judge the shapes of the lined areas and the distribution of shadows. Look in the mirror, squint your eyes, and you will get an idea of the effect as seen from a distance.

7. Blend according to the "pat-a-path" method.

8. Study highlight side of Illustration 6-7. Lay in highlight areas with thin strokes. Note that there is a space between highlight and shadow areas.

9. Blend highlights by patting a path—pats close together. No hopping, please!

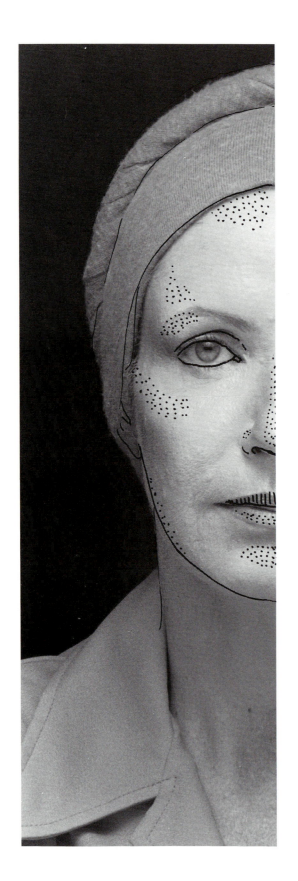

HIGHLIGHT AREAS OF CONTOURING

Forehead:

Highlight prominent part of forehead; shape will vary with each individual.

Eye Orbital Bone:

Highlight the upper outside corner, under the brow.

Nose:

Accent the top plane of the nose, and top of nostrils.

Cheekbone:

Locate the top of the bone, start about at the end of the eye, and follow the bone toward the hairline. Leave a space for base between this highlight and the cheek shadow.

Lips:

Accent shape of lower lip.

Chin:

Meet the shadow at the crease and highlight the top plane of the chin. Accent cleft, if any.

Jawbone:

Lightly accent jawline, fading as it moves forward.

6-6 CHART FOR CONTOURING HIGHLIGHTS

SHADOW AREAS OF CONTOURING

Temple:

Find tender-to-touch area. Shadow will not extend onto surrounding bony places.

Nose:

Shadow side of nose, define shape of end of nose. Do not cover nostril. Continue shadow upward to join eyebrow. Determine where the nose plane changes direction into the cheek plane.

Eye:

Shadow above eyelid and below eye-socket bone, extending slightly beyond outer corner of eye.

Cheek:

Shadow forms a triangular shape which curves slightly upward. Drop an imaginary line straight down from the outside corner of your eye—the shadow should not extend any further in than this, and should not reach the jaw bone.

Lips:

Shape the upper lip with a darker color than the lower lip.

Chin:

Shadow defines bottom of lower lip and continues down to the chin crease, or where the chin begins to jut out. Accent cleft, if any.

Jawline:

Start below the ear and extend shadow under jaw-bone. This is usually stronger on men than women.

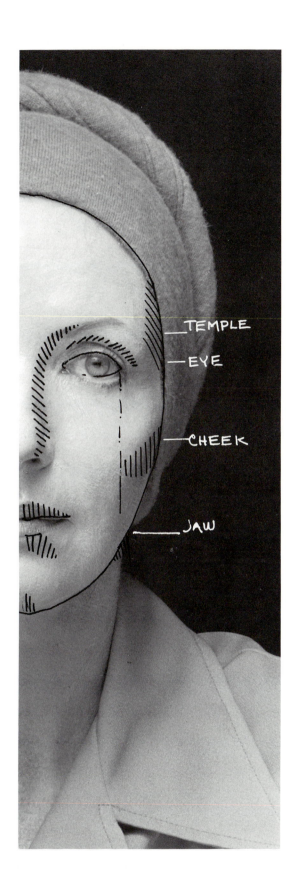

6-7 CHART FOR CONTOURING SHADOWS

This exercise constitutes basic contouring to strengthen, not age, individual features. Should your face have other distinctive features—a prominent forehead, a crooked nose, a dimple—these would be emphasized in a similar manner, using highlight and shadow. The presumption is that you wish to project *your* face, unchanged under lights, through space, to the audience.

Emphasizing the Eye

The following steps complete basic makeup, after contouring.

Eyeline: Mix a dark color which is complimentary to the skin tone; in general, black or brown-black for dark complexions, and medium brown for pale skins. The color should be darker than the tone used for shadow, since the purpose is to set off the eye. Study Illustration 6–11 in *Contouring for Crowds.* Make a thin line, directly along the lashes of the upper lid, all the way across. Draw a line next to the lashes of the lower lid, starting at the center of the eye and continuing to the outside corner. Do not extend these lines beyond the natural corner of the eye. If preferred, the eye line can be made with cake eye liner and the #1 water color brush after powdering.

If you have difficulty holding your eye steady, put a finger on the outer corner of your eye and pull the lid taut.

The eye is not totally outlined by eye liner because of a basic principle of design: an area which is partially enclosed will appear larger than a totally enclosed area. The partial outline serves to contrast the eye against the lighter value of the skin, while the opening left beneath allows the white of the eye to "merge" with the lightness of the skin and gives it an increased sense of space. This principle applies to light and medium toned skins. Although the eyes of a dark skinned person automatically receive emphasis because of the contrast of value with the white of the eye, all eyes will benefit from being accented. The more space left above the eye, between it and the brow—the larger the eye will appear. That is why the highlight of the frontal bone above the outer corner of the eye is so important, even if it means blocking out some of your natural brow.

Brows: After powdering, remove excess powder with brush, and accent the brow. Use a color slightly darker than your brow, and with small strokes of the brush, or sharp eyebrow pencil, *accent the upper portion only,* stroking in the direction of each hair's growth. See Illustration 6–11. The lower hairs of the brow need not be accented, and if left plain will give the effect of more space above the eye.

Lashes: Mascara also serves to reinforce the importance of the eyes and is used after powdering. If artificial eyelashes are needed, choose them according to the needs of your character. If the lashes are too long, they will destroy the space you are trying to create above the eye. They are generally available, along with the adhesive for attachment, at beauty supply houses and drug stores. If no mascara is used, remove excess powder from lashes with slightly oily brush.

Emphasizing the Mouth

Use two shades of color, with a darker tone for the upper lip. Men should add some red to their shadow color for the upper lip and a touch of red to their highlight for the lower lip. The shadow color on the upper lip is very important in projecting the structure of the mouth. The shape of the bottom lip is defined by the location of the shadow between it and the chin crease. Further instructions on making up the mouth are in Chapter Eight.

Correcting Mistakes

To remove a small smudge or a misplaced line, roll a Q-tip in your base color. As you erase the mistake, the base is restored. In lieu of a Q-tip, roll a small piece of tissue around the wooden end of your brush. Dip it in cold cream to remove serious mistakes.

Making A Personal Contouring Chart

After completing your contouring, and while the makeup is still on your face, make a chart. Study Illustration 6–3. If possible, use the face blank based on your life-sized mug shot. Indicate shadow areas with lines, drawn in the direction suggested by Illustration 6–6 on contouring. Using a lead pencil, indicate highlighted areas by dots, or by using a light-colored pencil. Carefully record the *shapes* of the areas. Use a hand mirror to see how your profile looks. Add any personal, helpful notes, including details of eyes, brows, and mouth. Follow this same procedure to make charts of succeeding makeup exercises, or character makeup for roles.

Perspiration Problems

Heavy perspiration can threaten the most carefully prepared makeup. Used with care, an antiperspirant in stick or cream form can be applied before makeup on the forehead, upper lip, or where excessive perspiration occurs. Avoid the eye area. The actor should use a brand to which he is not allergic. After makeup, powder heavily. Allow powder to set thoroughly. After brushing off, splash with cold water.

Powder Retouch Between Scenes

Separate a tissue into two pieces. Rub powder into a velour puff, and cover it with one layer of the tissue. It will blot, while, at the same time, powder is being restored.

CONTOURING FOR CROWDS

Dramatic productions frequently occur which feature a "cast of thousands," all of whom are inexperienced with makeup. This type of situation calls for super organization and a fast and efficient method of application. The usual solution is to quickly slap on cake makeup, which results in a stage full of flat, "egg-shaped" faces. Obviously, in such circumstances, there is not time for the "pat-a-path" method, yet the need still exists for some kind of contouring in order to preserve the structure of the face.

Contouring With Pressed Powders

An effective method of creating crowd makeup is to use dry, pressed powders for contouring. They can be applied over cake or liquid makeup, or over powdered grease and cream makeup. Obviously, the technique will not be as precise in execution as careful application of greasepaint, but it can be adequate for large crowds or choruses.

Dry, pressed powders, designated as blushers, rouge, eye shadows, or highlighters, can be purchased at the cosmetic counters of most drugstores. All of these can be used for contouring. The problem is in locating the colors which work best. Unlike theatrical makeup, such colors change names with each new advertising campaign, so that today's Dusky Rose may be tomorrow's Morning Glow. You must therefore experiment until you find the shades which work for both light and dark skins.

Although the local store may be more convenient, it is advantageous to order from a makeup company in order to have consistency of names and supply. Ben Nye Company has a large and varied color line in pressed powders for both light and dark skins. Their Toast ES 1, as highlight, and Dark Brown ES 1 are good choices for the Caucasian skin. If Mehron Cake Makeup, *Star Blend*, is left *dry* and *never* wet, it can be used for contouring with the blush brush.

See Correlation Chart, page 19, for suggested colors, but there will be no substitute for your personal experience in finding the color most effective for your skin.

Supplies

Base: Liquid makeup can be found in every shade from light ivory tones to deep sun tan, including shades prepared for dark skins, at your local drugstore. It has a less matte finish than cake makeup. Cake makeup is not always available at the drugstore but may be purchased or ordered from a theatrical supply house. The needs of your production will determine your color selection.

Highlight: Locate a dry, pressed powder eye makeup in a light cream color, *not* iridescent, to serve as highlight. Black skins may need a slightly darker tone, but it must contrast well with the skin.

Shadow: Look for a blusher which has a dark value and is not too red or too bright, more toward the brown or cool tones. Large, soft brushes, or a foam wand, come with these.

Shadow accent: Dark brown eye shadow, with small sponge wand.

Rouge: Choose a rosy color, somewhat redder and lighter than the blusher selected as shadow.

Brush: The large soft blusher brushes are preferable to sponge wands for applying shadow, highlight, and rouge.

Lipstick:

Men: A very dark, almost brown lipstick (used to accent upper lip only).

Women: Lipstick color depends on demands of production. For example, if the look is to be natural, then the color would be soft, not bright.

Eye liner: Choose a *soft* dark brown or black eye lining pencil. You may prefer liquid eye liner, which has its own brush, or cake eyeliner which moistens with water.

Eyebrow pencil: Usually harder than an eye lining pencil. Dark brown and black will meet most needs. They can be softened with a little cold cream.

Hand pencil sharpener: Do not try to sharpen lining pencils in a regular pencil sharpener; it will clog the sharpener. Soft pencils sharpen easier if cooled in the refrigerator first.

Procedure

Although the following instructions are for a group, they may also be used by an individual.

Set up "stations" with one or two members of the makeup crew manning each step of makeup. All crew members should review the principles of contouring described at the first of this chapter. The cast members file by in an assembly line, eliminating the need for individual makeup tables and mirrors. The number of makeup crew members at each station will be determined by the size of the cast. Skin care procedure should be followed, as described in Chap. 2.

Base station: If using liquid makeup as base, apply it with tips of fingers or with a sponge. For cake makeup, keep a water supply handy. Add water to the top of the cake. Blend with the sponge until a thick, creamy consistency is reached, then squeeze the makeup into the lid of the container. More water can be added to it until it tests out on the skin as a thin film of color. It should *not* create a thick paste-like mask.

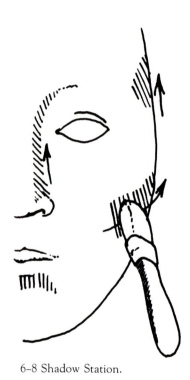

6-8 Shadow Station.

Shadow station: Use the large blush brush, or large sponge wand, and lightly stroke in the shadow areas, using Illustration 6–6 to locate shaded areas. If using wand, hold it parallel to the face. Do not overload; flip it and use the reverse side to blend the edges. Dust the brush or wand on a tissue to avoid overloading. Keep aware of the skull structure.

6-9 Highlight station.

6-11 Eye Station.
1. Accent the upper portion of the brow with small strokes.
2. Shadow under orbital bone above eyelid.
3. Line next to lashes across top and half way underneath.

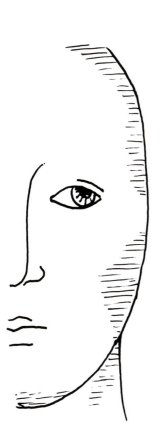

6-10 Rouge Station.

Highlight station: Follow Illustration 6-7 and highlight all areas indicated. On dark skins, the highlight will be the most effective means of reinforcing structure.

Rouge station: Lightly apply rouge over the cheek shadow area, along temple, and under jaw bone to lend a little glow to the face.

Eye station: With eyebrow pencil, draw small strokes along the hairs on the top part of the brow, in the same direction of the hair growth.

With small wand or brush rubbed in *dark brown eye shadow,* shade in under the bone which is above the eye—start a little beyond center (toward the tear duct) and continue outward to the outside corner. See Illus. 6-11. Blend edges.

Ask the performer to look downward toward outer corner of eye, and draw a line with *soft liner pencil*, next to lashes, all the way across the top. Ask him to look up toward the ceiling, and draw line next to lower lashes from outer corner to halfway underneath. Liquid eyeliner may be used instead of pencil.

Mascara may be used on women and men, particularly blond men.

Colored eyeshadow should be used only if the character demands it.

Mouth station:

Women: Apply lipstick in colors indicated by the designer.

Men: Gently touch the dark reddish brown lipstick with the finger, and *sparingly* smudge it on the upper lip only. The edge should be soft and indistinct, suggesting a shadow and should not look like lipstick.

Hair station: This station should be equipped with a large mirror, brushes, combs, hair pins, and hair spray. Many cast members will be able to dress their own hair. If, however, it is a period show, more hair dressers will be needed, with all the paraphernalia necessary, such as: wig stands, spirit gum, alcohol, toupee tape, hair rollers, curling irons, setting gel, and possibly hair whitener.

7

Getting Older

Usually, aging is considered simply the accumulation of years. However, it is obviously also a record of the happenings in our lives. We record our experience with sun or cold, health or illness, responsibilities and pleasures, and perhaps most revealing of all, we record how much tension, fear, laughter or serenity our lives hold. All are key factors in aging, but ultimately it is the habitual repetition of our emotional attitude which hardens the muscles into tell-tale messages. A lifetime of disapproval is expressed by thin compressed lips, perpetual anxiety creates indentations in the brow, and laughter leaves lines radiating from the eyes. More people collect messages in their faces than not.

The inevitable aging process is clear in the evolution of the skull.

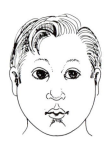

Baby fat melds into distinctive features;

7-2

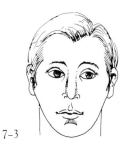

the adolescent glow gives way

7-3

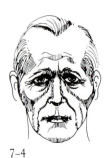

to middle aged sags and puffs,

7-4

and finally, a corrugated skin stretches over bones and sags into deepening hollows, where, lurking underneath it all, your skull awaits its final appearance.

DETERMINING AGE

What is "age"? Since age is relative to your point of view, a person of twenty years is already considered ancient by a five year old, and even though tolerance seems to accumulate along with years, there still remains a tendency to pigeon-hole age groups. There are potent exceptions to the age stereotypes we tend to project. The octogenarian, who is vital and active, can seem much "younger" than the 60 year old who has retired and lost the motivation of life. Therefore, it is misleading to assign a definite span of years to indicate "young," "middle," and "old" age. Perhaps the designations—youth, prime, and advanced—suggest divisions, yet leave room for exceptions. For the sensitive theatre artist, the look of the aged character will be determined, not by the accumulated years, but by those characteristics which suggest where and how he has lived.

AGING PROCESS

To understand aging in terms of your own features, it is useful to progress from the contouring exercise into aging. The treatment of the various planes of the face communicates age more than an intricate tracery of lines. In fact, do not think of "lines," as such, in relation to aging. What you are attempting to create is a change from the smooth face of youth to the undulations caused by sagging muscles. The resulting creases and crevices are sculptural forms and must be created by modeling with light and shadow. So, a laugh "line," or a frown "line" is actually an indentation beside a fold in the skin.

7-5 Underlying skull begins to appear in photograph by Theodor Jung, F.S.A. Collection, Library of Congress, Washington, D.C.

(photograher) Theodor Jung

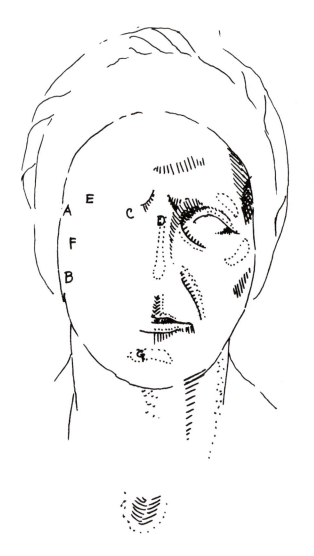

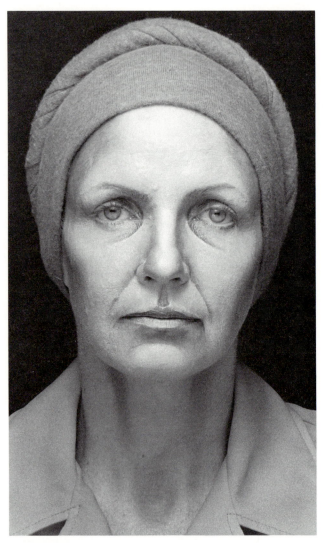

7–6, 7–7a and 7–7b Basic Contouring makeup extended into aging.   *(photographer) Suzanne Dietz*

EXERCISE EIGHT:

Getting Older

Deepening Contouring for Aging

1. Repeat the contouring exercise through Step 9. Do not powder. Review the techniques for blending and for feathering. Study Illus. 7–6, 7–7a, and 7–7b.

2. Add some of the dark colors from your shadow recipe to make a color two or three shades darker than your basic shadow. To determine darkness, stroke a line of base next to a stroke of shadow. Squint at it. Is there a good contrast? You may also experiment with adding a little red to the shadow to give more color vitality.

3. With thin lines, lay in an area in the center of the shadowed temple area (A) and the shadowed cheek area (B).

4. Darken the area at the corner of the eye, under the brow, next to the nose (C).

5. Blend these tones into their surrounding shadows by patting-a-path.

6. Mix a highlight color a shade or two lighter than used in contouring.

7. Create accent areas with small strokes in the center of major advancing planes:

   (D) bridge of nose

   (E) bone above outside corner of eye

   (F) cheekbone

   (G) top of chin

8. Blend areas by patting-a-path.

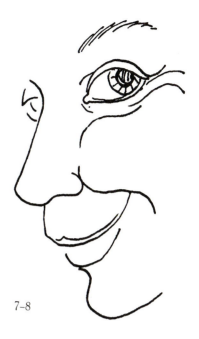

7–8

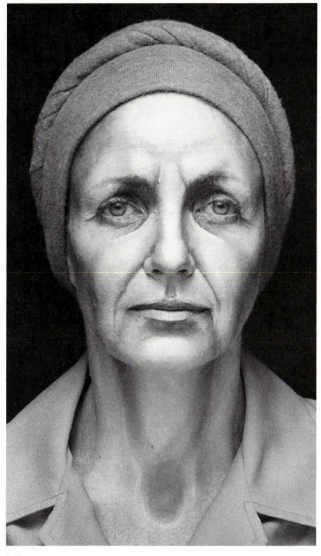

7-7b   (photographer) Suzanne Dietz

Creating Laugh Line (Nasolabial fold)

1. Look in the mirror and smile. Note where your cheek creases into your laugh "line." Relax. You will still be able to see it. Note where it begins beside the nostril. Stroke your brush into the shadow color. Keep the edge of the bristles flat and straight. Place brush at right angle to skin where crease meets nostril. With one stroke draw the line, tapering at the end, as in instructions for feathering.

2. Wipe brush *once* and feather the line. The shadow should gradate from dark at the line to light, or until it blends into the base. The goal is to suggest the curve of the side of a cylinder, as you did in Chap. 4. The lower end of the fold should not end abruptly but should be patted out until it disappears.

3. Highlight with a row of small strokes which run parallel to the feathered line, almost touching the edge of the feathering.

4. Pat, following the area of highlight from nostril, downward.

Creating Eye Bags

1. With shadow, use the thin edge of the brush to draw in eye bag. Let it begin near the inner corner of the eye, linked to the shadow beside the nose. If you are over twenty, you can probably see it. It follows the eye socket, starting near the tear duct. It will extend about halfway under the eye for aging to 35–40 and become more prominent with greater years. See illus. 7–9. Genetic tendencies or excessive dissipation may cause a more distinctive eye bag.

2. Wipe brush once. Feather line upward. Let outside end of line fade away.

3. Make a narrow highlight line under the eye bag line and feather downward. If the contrast is too sharp, pat along the line where highlight joins shadow to soften.

7-9 Puffy eye bags. *(photographer) Doug Milner*

Lower Lip:

1. To thin lower lip, paint a line higher than normal lip line, using your darkest shadow color. Do not extend line all the way to mouth corner, particularly for men. Let the line fade at ends.

2. Feather downward from new lip line into shadow underneath. Pat outside corners to blend into base. Shadow corner of mouth.

3. Highlight on lip *above* the newly indicated lip. If lip color is required, add after powdering.

4. If puffy bag is desired, highlight an area between the lashes and the eyebag and shadow under lashes.

5. For "hollow-eyed" look, blend shadow upward all the way to lashes.

Thinning Lips

The first step in introducing age to the mouth area is to thin the lips. In the last stage of advanced age, wrinkles may begin to appear, as in Illus. 7-10.

Upper Lip:

1. Lips frequently become thinner with age. To show this compression, use your darkest shadow color plus red to draw a new line on the upper lip, lower than your natural lip line. (See Illus. 8-3a,b,c,d,e)

2. Paint base on lips above the line, and blend upward.

3. Shadow the convex crevice on the upper lip.

4. With highlight, accent the edges of the crevice down to the new lip line. Paint a narrow highlight against new lip line and blend upward.

7-10 Compressed lips and mouth wrinkles. Detail: F.S.A. Collection, Library of Congress, Washington, D. C. *(photographer) Delano.*

90

Aging Forehead

The forehead, too, will record aging, but not in the all too common stereotype of flying a flock of crows across it! It is a mistake to assume that breaking up the smooth surface of the skin stretched across your skull by drawing lines to suggest those created by raising your eyebrows will automatically create age. It is not mandatory that these lines remain dominant in a face except for skins which retain wrinkles constitutionally, or skins which are subjected to climatic extremes. For example, Illus. 7–11 shows more deeply etched forehead lines on a man 39 years old, than on the man in Illus. 7–12, who is 95 years old. It is far more important to suggest the underlying *shape* of the skull and, over that, the ridges and furrows brought about by repeated emotional use of the muscles.

1. To determine how your forehead may age, look in the mirror and compress the muscles of your brow into a frown or a look of anxiety. You will note that there are, in addition to possible frown folds between

7-12 Forehead lines of man 95 years old.
(photographer) Doug Milner

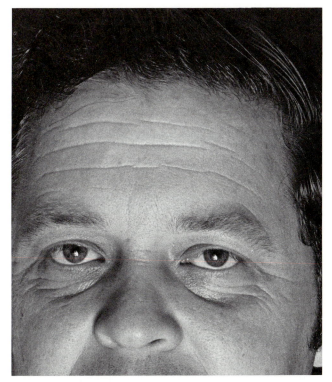

7-11 Forehead wrinkles, man 39 years old.
(photographer) Doug Milner

the brows, certain indentations and ridges above. These are wonderfully varied with each individual. Locate the hollows, treat each depression as an area of shadow, and blend.

2. Highlight and blend any raised ridges adjoining the hollows.

3. Frown again and see if any furrows, commonly called crow's feet, are formed between your eyes. Note that they generally grow up out of the shadow beside the nose, and fade away at the top. They do not abruptly start and stop, and are sometimes unequal in length. Create these furrows with the same procedure used for the laugh line: frown, observe the crease, relax, draw the line and feather it. The direction of the feathering is arbitrary, but if you think of the light source as shining on the center of the face, the shadows will move away to each side. A central crease may be shaded away from the line in both directions. Re-accent the line after feathering.

4. Highlight the ridge of each furrow.

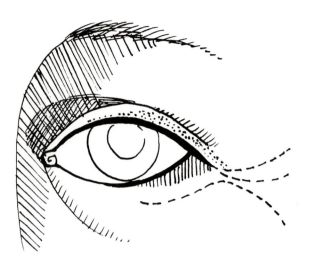

7-13 Chart for aging eyes. Dotted lines suggest development of "laugh wrinkles".

Aging Eyes

1. All eyes age differently, but it is most usual for the skin above the outer corner of the eye to begin to droop. Suggest this by extending a dark line down and outward from the corner of the eye, following the line of the lashes. Feather downward, under this line at the outer corner of the eye.

2. Highlight above, and next to, the dark line. Ignore your own eyelid. Study eye variations in your picture file.

3. Depress the inner corner of the eye socket by making it darker than the shadow between the eye and nose.

4. Laughter frequently causes a radiation of wrinkles from the corners of the eyes. Like the forehead "lines," they gain permanence in a face at varying ages. They are common among those working and squinting in the sun. To locate such wrinkles, squint in the mirror. Be very selective and create the major wrinkles with the same technique used for all skin folds: a line which is feathered, and then highlighted, tapering to nothing at the end. Be sure the lines grow out of the shadow at the corner of the eye.

Eyebrows

Aging Brows: Past middle years, the hairs in the brows become more unruly. This is particularly true for men; women tend to grow fewer or keep theirs plucked. For the bushy brow, confuse the hairs by brushing grey greasepaint backward, against the direction of growth, after powdering. For a slightly less shaggy look, paint irregular strokes leading out of the brow line. See examples in Illus. 2–28, and 8–12.

Blocking Out Brows

1. To relocate the brow, first soap or wax your own. If using soap, rub a bar of wet soap against the grain of the brow and then separate and flatten the hairs, pressing down with the bar of soap. Continue until the hairs are stuck to the skin. Illus. 7–14. Allow to dry thoroughly. Keep your face immobile while drying. If perspiration is a problem, you may prefer to block the brow with wax.

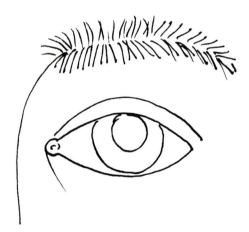

7-14 Soaping to block out brow: 1. Rub wet bar of soap backwards into hairs of brow. 2 Separate hairs up and down to flatten; rub them in place with the bar. 3. Keep face immobile till dry. Brows can also be blocked with derma-wax.

2. Load a brush with base color and paint over the brows.

3. A new brow can now be created. If your character is a woman past middle age, who would wear obvious makeup, the eyebrow should be penciled in after powdering. Otherwise, brows are created by a series of short brush strokes going in the natural direction of growth, indicating hairs. Let the color, or colors, be dictated by the shades of color present in the character's hair.

Contouring Larger Areas

Having now experienced the precise technique of laying in shadow and highlight shapes with fine lines, and then blending them with careful patting and feathering, you may want to explore a looser technique for the larger areas of the neck and hands. This method does not, however, give you the specific control necessary for the subtle variations demanded by the multi-faceted contours of the human face.

Think of this technique as an extension of the "patting" method in which you lightly tap one finger into your shadow color, and after pre-determining the shape and placement of the depression area, pat the makeup onto the skin in overlapping pats. Without adding more makeup to your finger, come back with another path-of-pats to blend either side of the shadow into the base. The same procedure is used for highlights.

Aging the Neck

1. Feel your jawbone under your ear. Pat a shadow under this bone, bringing it forward under the chin.

2. Review the muscle chart. Study the neck. Turn your head all the way to one side and see and feel the leader which goes from behind your ear down to the center of the hollow at the base of your throat. Shadow down each side of this muscle.

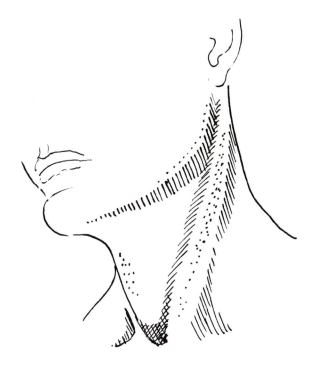

7-15 Shadow and highlights indicating aging for neck.

3. Highlight the top of the muscle. Swallow and watch for the indentation made by the voice box—the prominent part of the front of your throat. This will be more obvious on men.

4. Feel the hollow at the base of the neck and shadow it; highlight the bones on either side. Study variations of necks in your picture file to determine the degree of aging you wish. The same principles of contouring apply to the collar bones or to any part of the body which is exposed.

5. For the look of a heavier neck, do not accent the jaw line. Tuck your chin tightly downward and observe the folds which are created. See Illus. 8–13. The transverse areas which appear can be shadowed and highlighted. A deep crevice would be lined and feathered upward. Jowls are formed by continuing the highlight from the cheek down onto the neck. Again, look for examples, and experiment. Use your hand mirror for profile view.

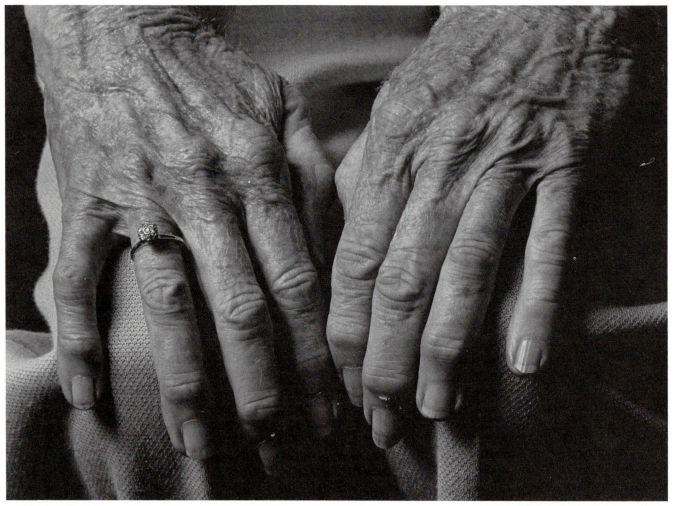

7–16 Aging Hands. *(photographer) Doug Milner*

Aging Hands

If your character has aged sufficiently to require a change in the appearance of the hands, some modeling will be necessary. Of course, the hands should *always match the coloration of the face*. Relate the amount of hand aging to the life of the character. For example, a 50 year old woman, who has worked with her hands, may require more changes than someone of the same age whose hands have been mainly decorative extensions. Hands of overweight people tend to show less age. The following exercise is a fast and simple way to arrive at the overall look of aged hands.

1. Apply base to hands, matching the face.

2. With shadow color on thumb and forefinger, smudge shadow on sides of fingers of opposite hand, by pinching between knuckles. Pat to blend edge of shadows.

3. Spread fingers, and with shadow color on tip of finger, pull the color between the knuckles along the line of bones onto the back of your hand.

4. Accent any hollows on the wrist.

5. Bend fingers and, with brush or finger, touch highlight to knuckles and along the top of the bones. Blend edges.

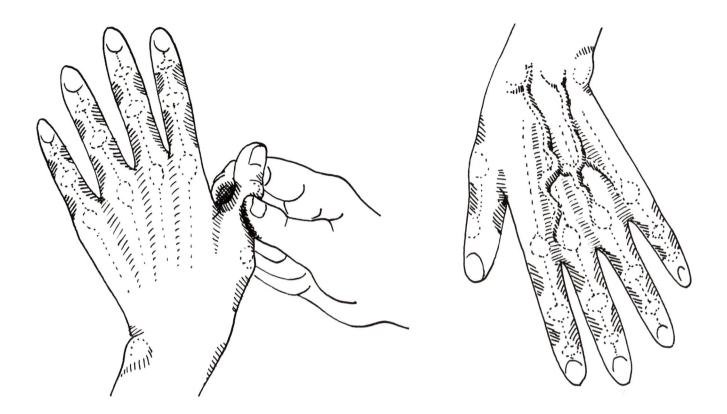

7-17 Chart for aging hands: highlight knuckles and bones; shadow between bones; accent veins.

6. More details can be added with the brush to accent wrinkles on the knuckles.

7. With aging, veins begin to stand out on the hands of thin people and hands that have done a lot of work. To see the veins in your hands, hold your elbow up and let your hand hang down to let the blood flow into it. Choose dominant veins and paint the line of the vein with the brush, using your shadow color, with perhaps a touch of blue. For a very fair skin, a greyed blue-green might be used.

Study the people around you for the veining your character should have. See Illus. 2–27b.

8. Highlight one side of the veins, arbitrarily. Note how the vein becomes more rounded when crossing over a bone. Pat to blend highlights, and shadow to create a cylindrical look.

9. Your picture file should also show you the random placement of yellowish-brown age spots, which begin to appear at middle years and increase thereafter.

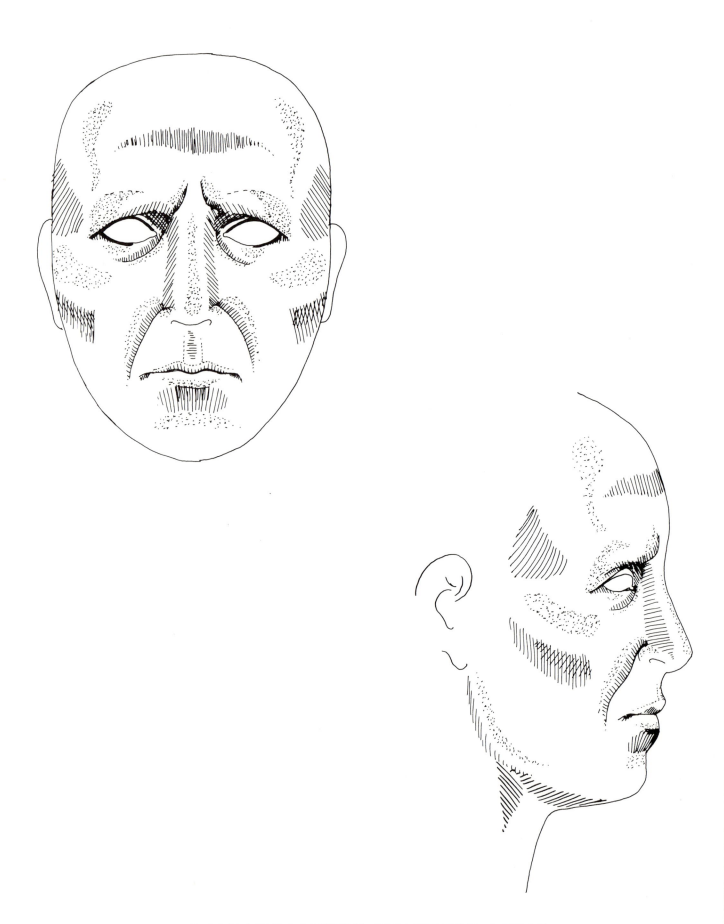

7-18 BASIC MAKEUP CHART FOR AGING

7-19 Migratory worker's wife whose skin shows effects of exposure to sun and wind. F.S.A. Collection, Library of Congress, Washington, D.C.   *(photographer) Arthur Rothstein.*

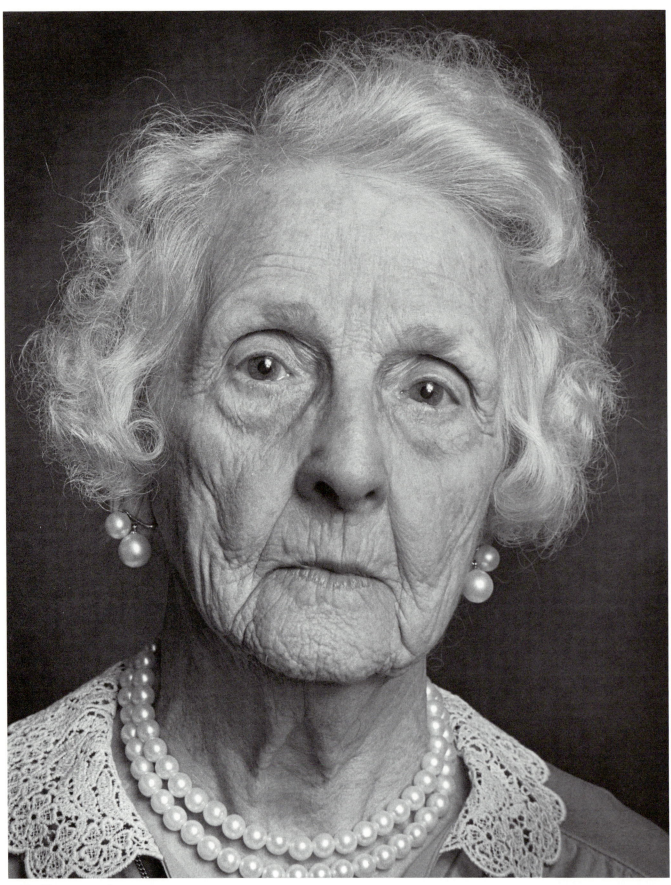

7–20a Character study.   (photographer) Doug Milner

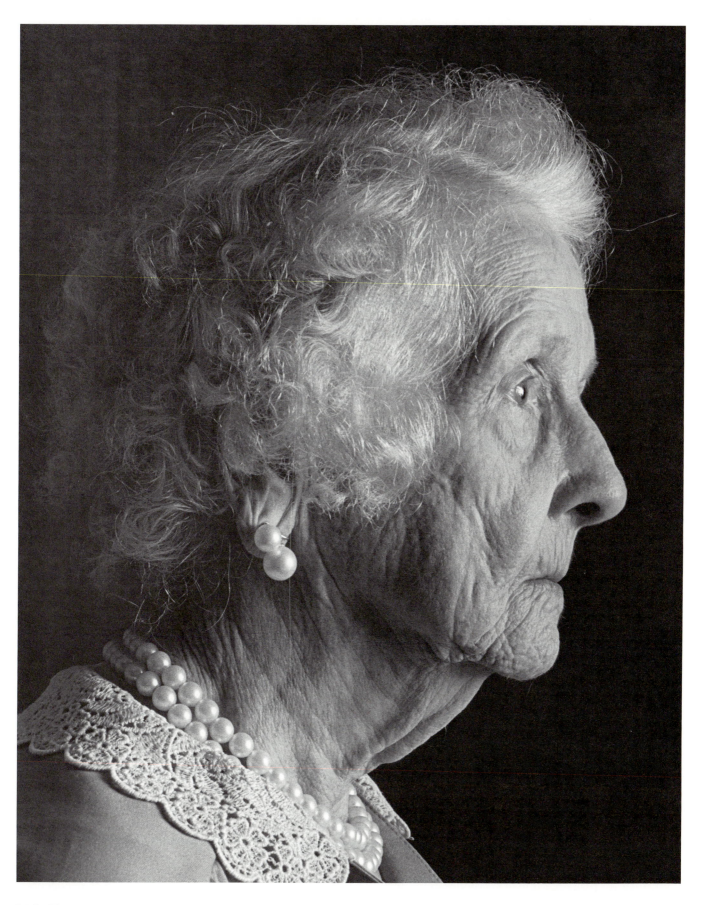

7-20b Character study, profile.   (photographer) Doug Milner

ALTERING SKIN COLOR

Many factors can influence the colors used for base, highlight and shadow. Having learned to mix colors compatible with your own skin tones, you may find the genetic, climatic, or physical condition of a character requires other hues. For example, an elderly frail person might use a greyish base with some blue (*not* black) added, carrying the same colors through the shadow and highlight. For a suggestion of sickness, experiment, but don't go berserk, with the addition of yellow or green. A black skin might become more grey. Robust old age may call for more red in the basic colors.

Record your age makeup on your own chart. Add any special notes which are helpful to you. Refer to Illus. 7–18 for basic aging approach.

OBSERVE! EXPERIMENT!

For real insight into colors used to create shadows on the face, study portraits of the great artists, such as Renoir, Cezanne, Rembrandt, (Color Plate Two) Jawlensky, (Color Plate Six) and van Dongen, (Color Plate Five.) There you will find a rich palette used to create the effect of light and shadow. An attempt to match such colors should inspire the creative use of color in your use of makeup.

TEXTURING

The surface of the skin will change as the aging process continues. The result may be a mesh of pores dried into a leathery network, as in Illus. 7–20, or simply developed into a crepe-like texture as in Illus. 7–21a,b.

In aging, the skin not only loses its underlying youthful fatty tissue but it may become thinner, making tiny blood vessels more visible.

Excessive alcohol intake may also result in discoloration caused by a fusion of tiny broken veins. On the face, as on the hands, random, irregularly shaped brown spots begin to appear, called age spots. See Illus. 7–22.

Weathered, or crepe-like skin texture can be suggested with the stippling sponge, or with a brush with which you cross-hatch first with shadow color, and then with highlight. For a tracery of broken blood vessels, mix Red-brown with Moist Rouge, brush the color across a stippling sponge and lightly press it against the skin. Stress the areas of the nose and cheeks. Use discretion in adding such texture. Not all aging requires it.

GRAYING HAIR

Observe the variety of patterns in which gray appears in hair and beards. If only a suggestion of graying is needed, paint liquid hair whitener on a comb, and comb it evenly through the hair. Or, cut alternate bristles out of a toothbrush, and dip it into hair whitener poured into a shallow dish. Apply to the hair. Let the whitener dry, then brush thoroughly. Ben Nye liquid silver can be brushed in for accent highlights. Silver mixed with liquid white works well for a whole head. Should the whitener tend to powder after a liberal coverage, spray with hair spray. Always try not to blotch the color on, and remember—a little silver goes a long way. If you are using one of the many colored hair sprays, beware of a heavy metallic look.

Substitutes for hair whitener are off-white cake makeup, or in an emergency, white greasepaint or white shoe polish. Powdering the hair with white powder can result in embarrassing cloud puffs on stage; moderate powdering can be somewhat secured with hair spray.

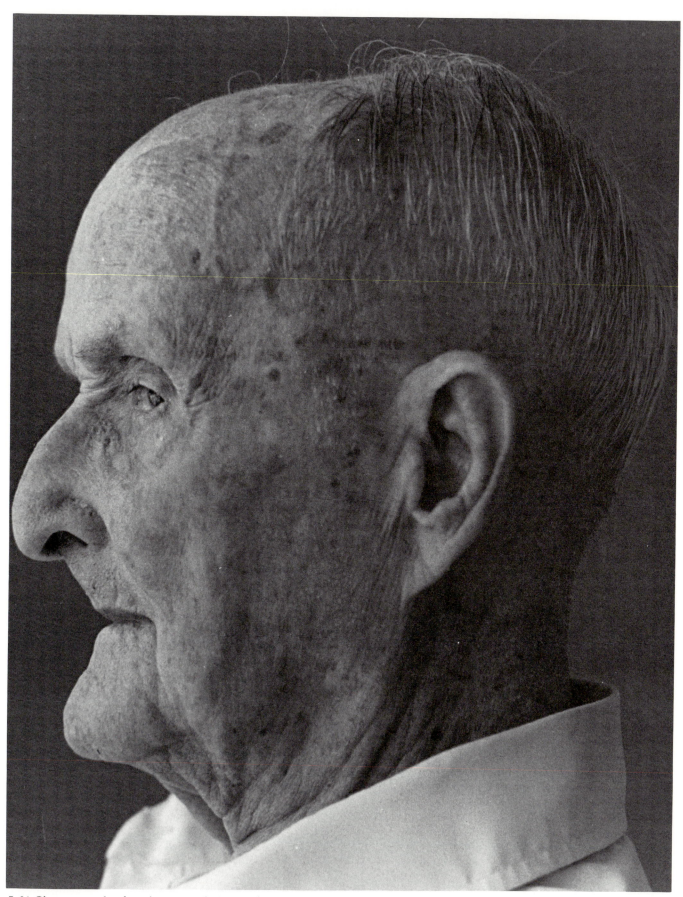

7-21 Character study of gentleman, aged 104. See frontal view 2-22d. *(photographer) Doug Milner*

AGING WITH
PRESSED POWDER

It is possible to use pressed powders for aging by following the same instructions given in Chap. 7. However, the results will not be as precise. I would suggest you perfect your aging technique with greasepaint first, then experiment.

You will find you need a larger, round watercolor brush, #6, to blend edges of shadow contour. In addition to the basic aging achieved by creating laugh lines, eye bags, and skull shape, there are several quick effects which can be made with pressed powder. To form the frown lines between the brows, forehead wrinkles, or lines at the corners of the eyes, compress the face into these gestures, and pat compressed powder highlight over the top of the formed ridges. This will accent the top, leaving the effect of wrinkles in the crevices. Further careful accenting can be done with a sharp lining pencil—Maroon or Red-brown.

AGING AND
FASHION MAKEUP

Makeup which is meant to *look* like makeup is always applied *after* basic contouring, for the young and beautiful, as well as for the carefully aged. Complete the basic substructure of the face and then add the fashion or street makeup. Colored eye shadow, rouge, lipstick, mascara, false eyelashes and eyebrows follow the establishment of the forms underneath. They can be applied carefully with greasepaint before powdering, or after powdering, with dry rouge and eye colors. The latter is an easier method.

You have now experienced the basic techniques for introducing aging to your face. The results will vary with each person. The number of years added is determined by the amount of contrast you use to suggest the hollows and highlights of structural change. In all cases, the blending should be subtle, good for the *front* and the back row of the audience.

Further age explorations are illustrated in the following pages. Study them. There are as many variations on this aging theme as there are faces in the world. They await your discovery and exploration.

7-22a and 7-22b Age progression as seen in the photograph of Alice Roosevelt Longworth with her daughter Pauline, c. 1932, and as she appeared in later years. (See her portrait as a young woman, Illus. 10-39)   *United Press International Photos.*

7-23a and 7-23b John C. Calhoun, c. 1834, and later in 1850.   *James Barton Longacre. National Portrait Gallery, Smithsonian Institution, Washington D. C.*

7–34 and 7–35 Mattie Garret Odle, Age 40. *Photo courtesy the Odle family.*

7–32 and 7–33 Mattie Garret Odle, age 24. *Photo courtesy the Odle family.*

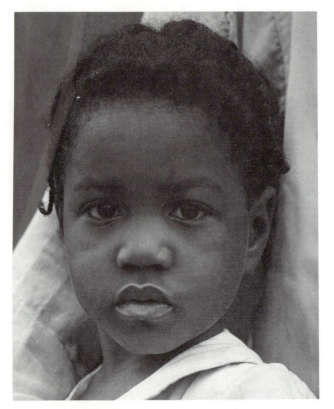 

7-24, 7-25, 7-26 and 7-27 Age progression, Negro. *(photographers:) 7-24, John Collier, F.S.A. Collection, Library of Congress Washington, D. C.;*

7-28, 7-29, 7-30, 7-31 Age progression of the American Indian as captured by Edward S. Curtis: Mosa, a young Indian child (7-28),

7-40 and 7-41 Age progression, Hispanic. *The San Antonio Light* collection University of Texas, Institute of Texan Cultures at San Antonio.

7-36 and 7-37 Mattie Garret Odle, age 74.   *(photographer) Beth Odle*

7-38 and 7-39 Mattie Garret Odle, Age 101   (photographer) Beth Odle.

7-25 Doug Milner; 7-26 Doug Milner, 7-27, Jack Delano, Library of Congress, Washington, D. C.

an Indian brave (7-29), wife of On High (7-30), and Big Head (7-31). Library of Congress, Washington, D. C.   *(photographer) Edward S. Curtis*

BIBLIOGRAPHY

Berliner, Bert, Ed. *Fifty Famous Faces in Transition.*
(New York: Simon and Schuster, 1980).

8

Creating the Illusion of Changed Form

If you are not possessed with what you consider perfect features, or if for some reason you want to suggest changes, contouring with light and shadow provides the method. Once you have mastered careful application and blending of shadowed and highlighted areas, and the feathered line technique, the suggestion of changed form or corrected form is available to you. The viewer's eye will accept the forms you create, just as he accepts the faces and figures an artist places on a flat canvas.

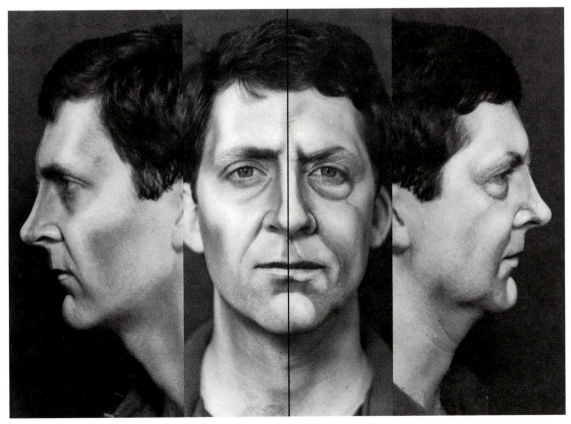

8-1a, 8-1b and 8-1c

OVERVIEW OF CHANGED FORM

The following exercise will give you an overview of changed forms for all your features. It involves making the planes of your face appear thinner on one side and heavier on the other.

EXERCISE NINE:

Fat/Skinny Face

Study Fat/Skinny Chart. Illus. 8–2 indicates shadows by means of lines and highlights by dotted areas; one half creates the illusion of thinning and the other half that of increased volume.

Transferring Information From Chart to Face

Transference involves comparisons, by means of perpendicular lines at right angles to horizontals. It is very important that you experience how this works in the Fat/Skinny exercise, so that you can use the same principles when working from any photograph. Establish the relationships and positions of features for the thin side of the face first; then, use the same procedure to establish the other side.

Note that the transference of feature position from the chart to your face is done in relation to the eye, first on the eye of the chart and then on your eye.

Looking at the Fat/Skinny Chart, note the horizontals created by lines drawn through the corners of the eyes, and across the mouth opening. Study the lines, a, b, c, d on the skinny side:

Line a: A perpendicular line extending from the corner of the mouth upward. Make a mental estimate of where it intersects the eye. Half way? Less than half way?

Line b: A perpendicular line extending upward from the widest part of the laugh line toward the eye. Where does it intersect the eye? Estimate.

Line c: A horizontal line extending from the lowest portion of the eye bag toward the nose. Estimate where it strikes the nose. Half way? Less?

Line d: A horizontal line at the tip end of the laugh line. Where is it in relation to the mouth? Above? Below? How much?

Create and letter corresponding lines on the fat side of the chart. You are now ready to transfer this information to your own face.

Correlating Chart Information to Face

Look in the mirror with the chart nearby. To recreate the vertical and horizontal lines visually, hold the handle of your brush against your face and move it from feature to feature to simulate lines a, b, c, d, as seen on the chart. For example, note where line a meets the eye on the chart; find this point on your eye, align the brush with it, follow the line of the handle downward, and establish a point opposite the corner of your mouth. If the mouth in the chart is wider, you will extend your mouth to that point. If it is less wide, you will let the lip shapes stop before the natural corners of your mouth. Continue to orient your features using this comparative method, working through lines b, c, and d.

More thorough instructions for creating your own charts using spatial relations of features can be found in Chap. 9. However, working from the pre-planned Fat/Skinny Chart, you should be able, with careful observation, to execute this exercise.

Makeup

In addition to your regular base, highlight, and shadow, mix a medium tone, somewhat darker than your base with which to sketch the major lines and planes as seen on the chart.

Creating the Skinny Side

Sketch onto your face all the major lines which indicate planes, using the medium shade. Repeat the same techniques which you used in contouring and aging; lay in shadow areas and feathered lines with shadow color, as indicated by parallel lines on the chart. Blend. Lay in highlights, indicated by dotted areas on the chart. Study makeup on Illus. 8–1a, b, and c.

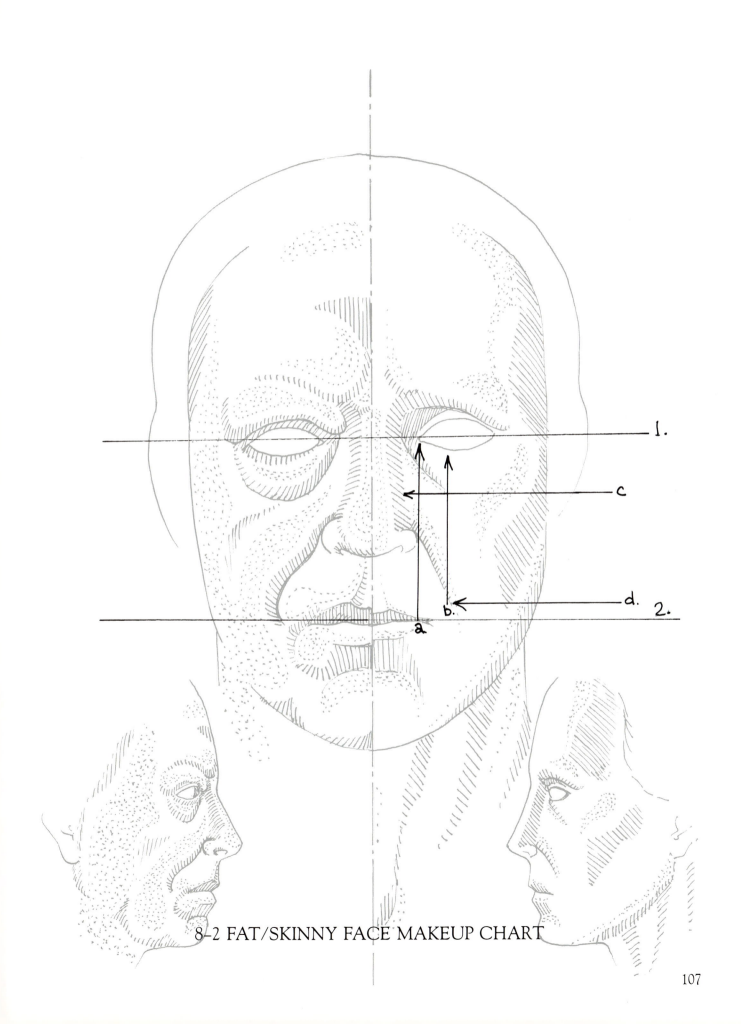

1.

c

d. 2.

a

b.

8-2 FAT/SKINNY FACE MAKEUP CHART

Thinning Lips: Although the changing of the mouth was practiced in the *Aging* exercise, more detailed instructions follow:

1. Cover lips with base.

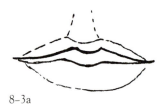

8–3a

2. Ignore your natural lip shape and outline the new thinner upper lip with a dark red-brown. Take the line all the way to the corners of the mouth, or further, if the mouth needs to be wider.

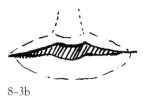

8–3b

3. Fill in beneath the line with the same red-brown. (In the future, you may wish to alter this color for other characterizations, but the upper lip should remain a darker shade than the lower lip.)

8–3c

4. Shadow the indentation above the upper lip and highlight the ridges on either side of it. Bring shadow and highlights all the way to the newly created lip line.

8–3d

5. Ignore the shape of your lower lip and, with a dark shadow color, draw the thinner lip line across your lip, but do not take it all the way to the corners. Feather downward beneath the lip line, blending into shadow between lip and chin crease.

8–3e

6. Highlight lower lip directly against, and above, the newly established lower lip line. Feather highlight upward.

7. Make a slight shadow at the corner of the mouth.

Accenting Jaw Bone and Neck:

1. Study profile view on chart.

2. Accent jaw line by shading beneath it and highlighting above. Continue the highlight toward chin.

3. Shadow between leaders on neck.

4. Highlight outstanding muscles.

Creating the Fat Side

Study lines *a*, *b*, *c*, and *d*, which you made on the fat side of the chart. Simulate them using the handle of the brush, and continue the entire process of laying in lines and planes and contouring.

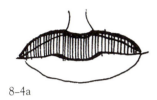

8-4a

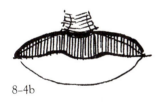

8-4b

8-4c

Thickening Lips:

1. Ignore your lips and outline new shape above natural lip line, using dark red-brown. Coordinate the line with the corners of mouth. Fill in beneath the line.

2. Shadow and highlight the indentation above the lip. It can be made somewhat wider than natural.

3. Draw new, fuller lip line beneath natural lower lip, with dark shadow color. Do not carry it all the way to the corners of the mouth. Feather downward from lip line into shadow area between lip and chin crease.

4. Highlight lower lip, exactly against the newly established shape of the lower lip. Feather highlight upward.

5. Shadow indentation at corners of mouth and add a touch of highlight above to create a fat pouch.

Fattening Neck:

1. Notice profile view on Chart 8–2. Study composite of heavy profiles, Illus. 8–5 through 8–12. Tuck your chin, to see where your natural folds occur, as in Illus. 8–13.

2. Let highlight continue from fat of cheek onto neck to break up jaw line.

3. Shadow under jowl.

4. A ruddy look can be introduced on a fat Caucasian face by mixing red into the shadow color, or by brushing dry rouge into temple, jowl, and neck shadows after powdering.

CHECK:

*Do your shadows need to be deepened (that is, darkened) in the center of the areas? Note cross hatch areas on chart.

*Do your highlights look flat? Do you need to accent the center of them with a slightly lighter color?

*Cover one half of your face with a piece of paper and study the other side.

*Look in the mirror at each profile for contrast.

*If possible, record with photographs.

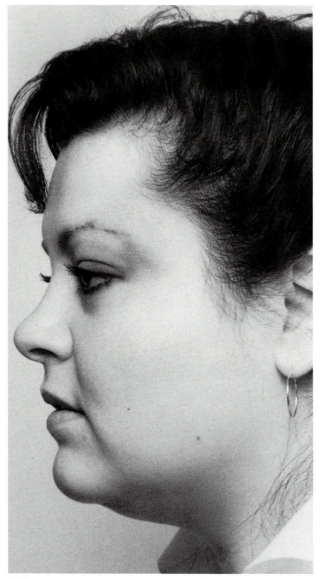

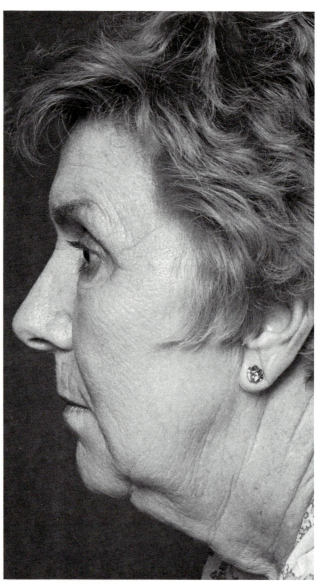

CHARACTER STUDIES FOR HEAVY FEATURES

8-9   (photographer) Doug Milner

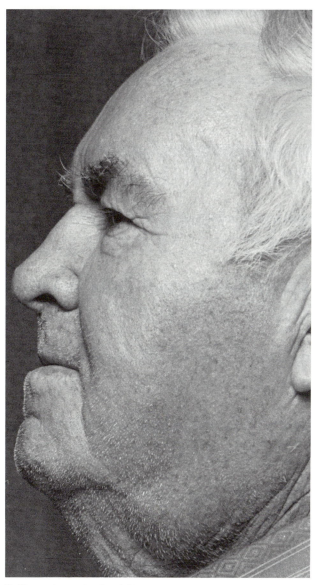

8-10   (photographer) Doug Milner

8-11   (photographer) Doug Milner

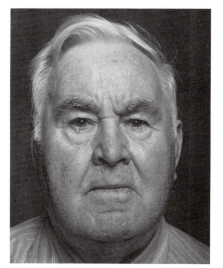

8-12   (photographer) Doug Milner

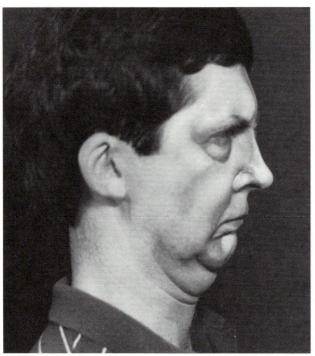

8-13 Tuck your chin toward your neck in order to see where the natural folds occur.

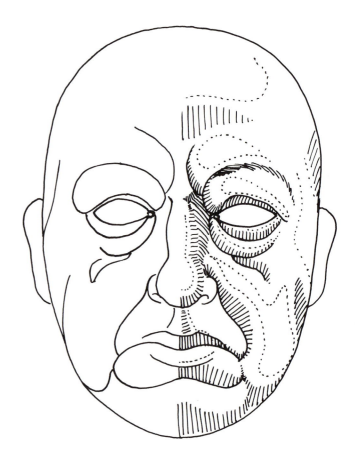

8-14 FAT FACE MAKEUP CHART

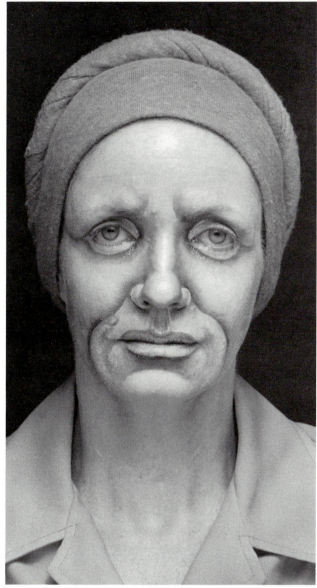

8-15 The illusion of heavier features created on a thin model. See 6-1a for contrast without makeup. *(photographer) Suzanne Dietz*

Make Your Own Personalized Face Chart

While the makeup is still on your face, record what you have discovered. A sample of a fat face chart is seen in Illus. 8–14. If time permits, repeat, doing an entire face, first fat, and then thin. Choose a face from your picture file, or select from faces in Illus. 8–5 through 8–12, or work from basic Fat Face Chart.

LOOKING GOOD

Correcting for good looks is a highly personal thing. We all seem to carry some ideal face in our minds which we do not match. Heaven forbid we should all look alike or pursue some bland prototype presented by advertisers, such as the look-alike people of fashion magazines, but it seems reasonable to focus on one's best features, while minimizing others.

After experiencing the Fat/Skinny Exercise and feature alteration, you may want to create your most attractive face, correcting the faults as you see them. Make the corrections on one half of the face only, so that you can see the effect of changes. Be free to experiment with "changing" a crooked nose to a straight one, shading away a square jaw, etc. You now have the techniques with which to create such illusions. Just remember the basic principle of creating form: darker tones recede and lighter ones advance.

8-16

8-17

EXERCISE TEN:

Experiencing Changed Form of Nose, Eyes, Mouth

CHANGING NOSES

Think of the nose as being divided into planes: the bridge, top, bulb (or end), side, and nostril. The arrangement of highlights and shadows will determine the corrections.

To Widen a Narrow Nose

1. Extend highlight further onto side of nose, shown by dotted lines.

2. Let shadow start next to the highlight and continue down side of nose, stopping where plane changes to cheek area.

3. Pat to blend where highlight meets shadow.

To Narrow a Nose

1. Place highlight in desired width on top of nose.

2. Bring shadow up to the highlight, and pat-a-path between them to blend.

3. Paint highlight on the nostril, creating a smaller nostril.

4. Place shadow next to the highlight and feather away from the line.

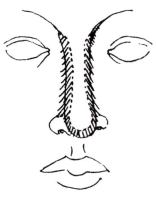

8-18

To Straighten a Crooked Nose

1. Ignore the wayward direction of the top of your nose and create a highlight which makes the top of your nose straight in relation to the horizontal line of the eyes.

2. Support this correction with the shadow on the side of the nose.

3. Blend edges.

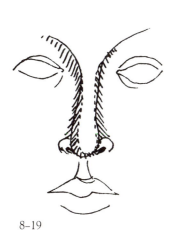

8-19

To Take a Break Out of a Nose

1. Highlight the depressed area.
2. Bring shadow straight down the sides.

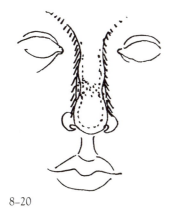

8-20

To Lengthen a Short Nose

1. Take the highlight area further than usual up on the bridge of the nose and extend it under the bulb.

2. Support with shadow.

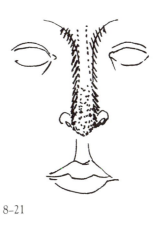

8-21

To Shorten a Long Nose

1. Shadow the lower tip of the nose.
2. Stop the highlight before you reach the tip and do not carry it all the way to bridge.

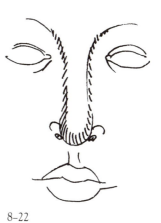

8-22

115

Character Noses

The same principles used for correction serve to create character noses. For instance, see how far you can go to create the illusion of a Cyrano nose without the use of nose putty.

Making an Extra Large, or "Cyrano" Nose

1. With shadow color, draw the nostril slightly larger at top and sides, onto cheek plane. Increase the size of the nostril hole, using very dark color.

2. Leave a wide area across the top of the nose and place the shadow down the side, stopping at the line of the newly drawn nostril.

3. Highlight a broad area across top of nose.

4. Highlight top of nostril directly against the line of the new nostril, leaving the line distinct.

5. Blend highlight and shadow on sides of nose.

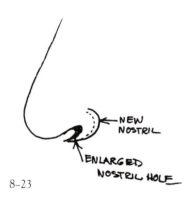

8-23

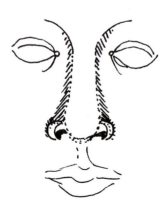

8-24

Making a Crooked Nose

1. Let the shadow encroach on one side of the nose, and diminish it on the opposite side.

2. Create highlight area accordingly.

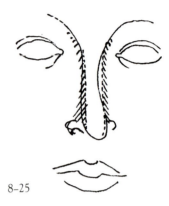

8-25

Making a Grecian Nose

1. Drop shadow area in a straight line from the level of the brow down the side of the nose.

2. Disregard the natural bridge of your nose and highlight a straight plane down the center of the nose. Blend, letting it fade into the forehead area.

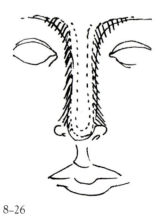

8-26

116

Making a Bulbous Nose

1. With shadow, indent about halfway down the nose and then widen to encircle the end of the nose.

2. Nostrils may be enlarged as in directions for *Extra Large Nose.*

3. Highlight the round shape in the center of the bulb and top of nose and nostrils.

4. Shadow under rounded bulb.

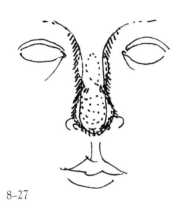

8-27

A similar approach would create a broken nose. Your picture file will suggest many other variations for noses. Once you have practiced the preceding examples, you will be able to create others.

CHANGING EYES

Eyes are the most important of all facial features. The eyeball itself does not vary much from person to person. The expressiveness occurs in the details of the area around the eye and in their placement in relation to the rest of the face. Corrective makeup can work its magic on eyes, suggesting changes in size and placement.

Making Eyes Further Apart

1. To give an impression of greater space between the eyes, reverse the usual shading procedure and apply highlight from the bridge of the nose down in the hollow by the eye. Fuse edges.

2. Block out inner corner of eyebrows with soap. Cover with base.

3. Make a shadow at the outer corner of eye, starting out of the crease made by eyelid fold. Extend shadow outward and upward, but do not join it with brow.

To better see the effect of the following examples, complete one eye only, so that you can compare with the unaltered eye. Stand back from the mirror and check it from a distance.

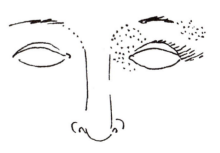

8-28

117

Making Eyes Larger

1. Shadow under the upper orbit bone, between the bone and the eyelid. Let the shadow extend slightly out to the side.

2. Extend the space between the brow and the eye by highlighting the bone directly under the brow. If the hairs of the brow are too low (and you aren't inclined to pluck them), cover the lower ones with highlight. Men may need to block out the lower part of the brow in order to cover it with greasepaint.

8–29a

3. Accent brow along top edge with short strokes made in the direction of the hair growth. Do not bring the outside brow line too low or it will enclose the space around the eye.

8–29b

4. Line next to lashes on upper lid and halfway only along lower lid, using dark brown or black.

5. Mascara can enhance the framework the lashes provide for the eye. Apply to the tips and separate lashes with dry brush. False eye lashes should be used in relation to the needs of the character.

6. Very small eyes may require white, barely tinged with blue, painted on the inner surface of the eye lid *between* the lashes and the eye. Believe it or not, this surface is dry.

8–30

Lifting Out Deep Set Eyes

1. In addition to Steps 2 and 5 under preceding *Making Eyes Larger*, highlight the entire area between brow and eye, including eyelid. Add a touch of white to the eye lid.

2. Very carefully, make a fine dark line next to the lashes on the upper eyelid and extend it $1/8''$ beyond corner.

3. Under the eye, paint a thin line of white next to the lashes, starting at outside corner and fading out about halfway under eye.

4. Extend dark eye line from outer corner halfway under eye, next to white line.

5. Accent the upper hair of the brow only and extend slightly at outside end.

6. Extend highlight under brow toward outside.

7. Paint white on inner surface of eye lid, between lashes and eyeball.

8–31

118

Making Eyes Smaller

Characters sometimes appear in a script who need mean, beady eyes, or perhaps the penetrating gaze of a Svengali. The process is almost the reverse of making eyes appear larger.

1. Shadow to bridge of nose and under brow, making it darker on inner corner. Continue shadow all around eye, blending edges; include eyelid.

2. Use a very dark brown, or black, and totally outline the eye, next to lashes.

3. If desired, black can also be painted on the surface between the lashes and the eyeball.

4. Accent brow more strongly next to the bridge of the nose.

5. Aged eyes will appear weak if not outlined at all.

8-32

CORRECTING LIPS

The directions for thinning or enlarging lips under *Fat Face/Skinny Face*, Illus. 8-3a through 8-4, are valid for making corrections in lip shapes, as well as for creating new ones. The same method is used when it is only one lip which needs to appear thicker or thinner. Usually, the upper lip will be darker because it is in shadow, but if the lower lip protrudes, use a darker tone on it. Also, the lips themselves can be contoured to suggest more fullness, such as for a "bee-stung" mouth.

Sensuous or "Bee-Stung" Lips

1. Outline the upper lip and fill it in with desired color. Use a slightly lighter color and fill in the lower lip.

8-33a

2. Use a shadow color, such as red-brown, and shade on either side of center on the upper lip and on center of lower lip. Part lips and extend the shadow to the inside.

8-33b

3. Highlight center "pouch" on upper lip and on either side of shadow on lower lip. Pat to blend.

8-33c

4. Shadow the indentation above the lip; highlight on either side and continue highlight along rim of upper lip. With basic skin shadow color, line underneath central part of lower lip.

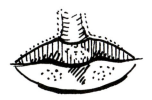

8-33d

119

This process can be used for men or women. If it is used for women wearing lipstick *as* lipstick, a tiny outline of red-brown can be drawn around the lips to make them more definite.

Lips Which Are Too Full

Paint lip color just a little way inside natural lip line.

8–34

EXPERIMENT! COLLECT PICTURES!

FASHION MAKEUP

The most contemporary style may not necessarily be the most complimentary. Fads can entrap. The actress who wants to look her best will first utilize corrective and contouring principles, and then choose eye shadow, rouge, and lipstick as it relates to the character to be portrayed and the costume to be worn. Current fashion magazines usually provide more than you need to know about what look is "in."

GETTING YOUNGER

There are several techniques which can be used to give the illusion of reducing age, within reason, that is. In general, highlights are used in place of shadows so that all depressions and creases are lightened. The following exercise, while somewhat extreme, will introduce other ideas which might be used to take off a few years.

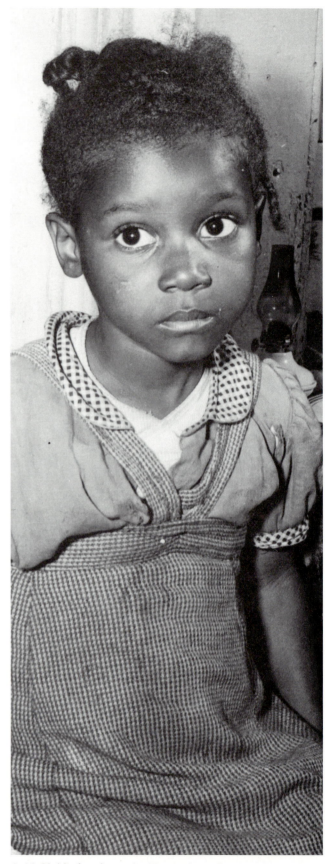

8–35 Child's face for study: Notice the wide set eyebrows, full cheeks, short nose and narrow chin. F.S.A. Collection. Library of Congress. *(photographer) Gordon Parks.*

120

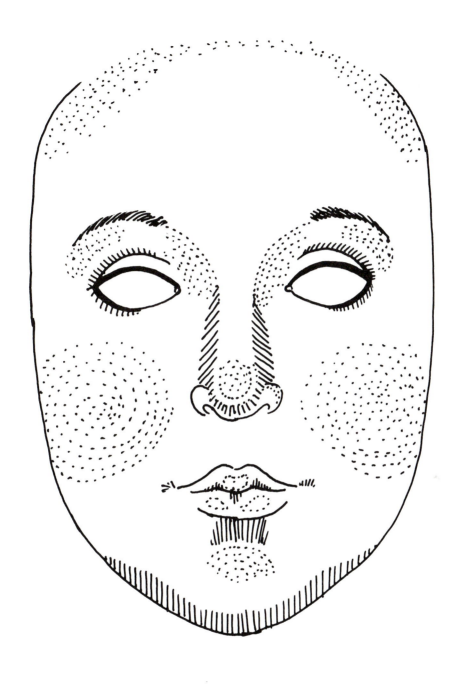

8-36 CHILD-LIKE MAKEUP CHART

Note: *Highlight applied to cheeks to create fullness
   *Highlight between eyes to increase space
   *Block out inner corner of natural brows in order to space them further apart.
   *Shadow under nose to shorten; accent round "button" tip
   *Rose bud lips
   *Shadow lower part of chin to shorten face.

EXERCISE ELEVEN:

Creating a Child-like Face on an Adult

Select several photographs of small children from your picture file and observe how their facial proportions differ from that of an adult. Notice the large forehead, small chin area, short nose, fat cheeks, wide-set eyes, and slight, wide-set brows. If you have a beard, audition for a gnome.

1. Soap out brows. (See Illus. 7–14.)

2. Apply base. If necessary, mix lighter shade of base and apply to brow with brush.

3. Highlight from nose bridge toward outside of eye.

4. Highlight cheeks under cheekbone where contour shadow normally goes.

5. Highlight temple area.

6. Shadow under tip of nose to shorten it.

7. Start shadow area half-way down chin and blend underneath.

8. Shorten width of mouth. Create a "rose-bud" mouth, a shorter version of *Sensuous Mouth*.

9. Make eyebrows far apart and higher than usual, using small, delicate strokes.

10. Line eye, all the way across the top, next to the lashes, and half-way underneath. Experiment with feathering out from eye line to make the eye look larger.

8–37

11. Optional effect: Do not feather eye line. Ignore fold line of real eyelid and use dark red-brown to paint a higher line on the skin above the lid, to give the effect of a higher lid. Feather upward from this line. Highlight from false eyelid line to lashes. Line next to lashes; all the way on top, half way below.

12. Highlight forehead all across the top. Pull hair back to increase importance of this area.

SPECIAL EFFECTS

The use of prosthetics is not handled in this book. Since they involve techniques which are required in such a small percentage of roles, as special effects, they can be researched in the many excellent books available through your library. Among these, offering advanced techniques and information on dimensional makeup, are *Techniques of Three-Dimensional Makeup* by Lee Baygan[5] and *Stage Makeup*, by Richard Corson.[6]

Nose putty can be useful but is usually overdone, creating more the look of a Proboscis monkey, than simply that of an enlarged nose. Putty can also be used to shape an outstanding wart. Work it into a pliable ball, using a little cold cream to keep it from sticking to your fingers, and apply to a clean skin, free of grease. Secure along the edges. Remember, however, that even a wart can be created with paint, since it is nothing more than a sphere which can be indicated by highlight and shadow, as in your sketch of the white ball in Chap. 4.

Scars are frequently made with collodion, a substance which draws and puckers the skin but can be peeled off, or with rubber latex, built up into several coats and attached with spirit gum. However, a line of red-brown shadow, bordered by a reddish pink and highlighted irregularly, will also give the illusion of a type of scar. As in everything else, scars should be researched; is it fresh? with stitches? old and faded to a pale, puckered pink? Similarly, a black eye or bruise changes colors day by day. You can probably observe these first hand, noting how the first deep purple discoloration slowly gives way to blues, greens, and then yellow. If you know how they look, bruises will be simple to paint. For missing or irregular effect on teeth, use black tooth wax.

RACE AND
ETHNIC GROUPS

In considering different facial characteristics, the subject of race must be considered. Major structural differences between races are found among groupings categorized as Caucasian, Negroid, and Mongolian. Further divisions take the form of ethnic groups, those peoples who have achieved a certain distinctiveness through physical and cultural traits.

As we seek to establish, for purposes of makeup, visual facial differences of various races, the dangerous ogre of stereotyping arises again. A vivid example is the racial stereotype perpetuated by the minstrel shows which toured this country for 100 years parodying the entire black race as joking, rolling-eyed comics.

To avoid caricature in selecting characteristics of any ethnic group, consider that if you count back five generations, you have had 1,024 grandparents; and further back to ten generations, over a million grandparents, all individuals, and all of whom have contributed to your own unique combination of traits. Surely, therefore, a single *look* cannot be assumed for any one group of people. When designing for a specific role, in addition to guidelines provided by the author, remember that the uniqueness of the individual should stay preeminent in your thinking.

The photographs, Illus. 2–37a through 2–39b serve to illustrate the basic racial types. Obviously, when you create designs based on these faces (which are, after all, individuals), and then recreate them on your own face, you will automatically have made variations on the theme of race.

8–38 Sharp Nose, an Arapaho Indian. National Archives, Washington, D.C.

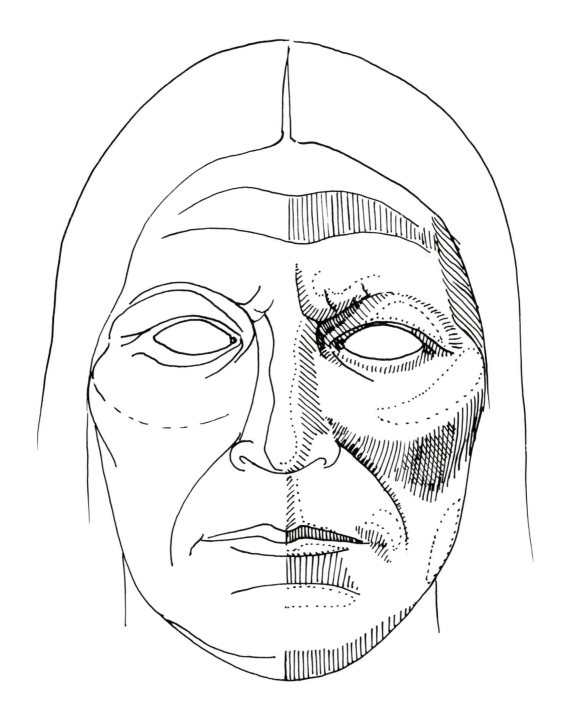

8–39 AMERICAN INDIAN MAKEUP CHART

Note: *Shape of the eyes
*Wide, high cheekbones
*Strong jaw line; accent
*Shadow on lower part of chin

In this chart, notice the shape of the eyes, the wide, high cheekbones, and the strong jaw line. By shadowing the lower part of the chin and accenting the jaw, the face appears shorter and more square.

8–40 Indian makeup worn by actor Tim Green for a role in Mark Medoff's *Firekeeper*.

8-41 Herman Wheatley in role as a half-breed in Mark Medoff's *Firekeeper*, exemplifies Indian makeup applied to a Negro. Compare to 8–42, and 8–43.

8-42 Actor Herman Wheatley before makeup.

EXERCISE TWELVE:

Capturing Racial Characteristics

To create a racial type, select a photograph (or composite) which seems to capture the psychological qualities of the character at hand, as well as racial features, and then utilize the necessary methods of giving the illusion of changed form. For example, a Plains Indian and a chart for his makeup is shown in Illus. 8–38 and 8–39, while Indian features executed on a Caucasian is shown in Illus. 8–40. It is interesting to see similar makeup applied to a Black actor whose role demanded Indian characteristics, (Illus. 8–42 and 8–43), in comparison with the photograph of a Negro man (Illus. 8–43) one of whose grandparents was an Indian.

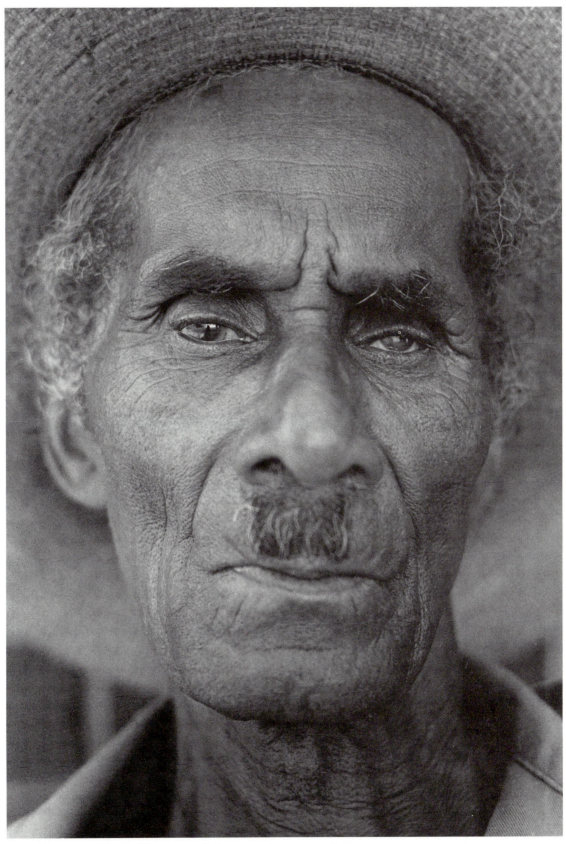

8-43 Character study of a Negro, one of whose grandparents was Indian.   *(photographer) Doug Milner*

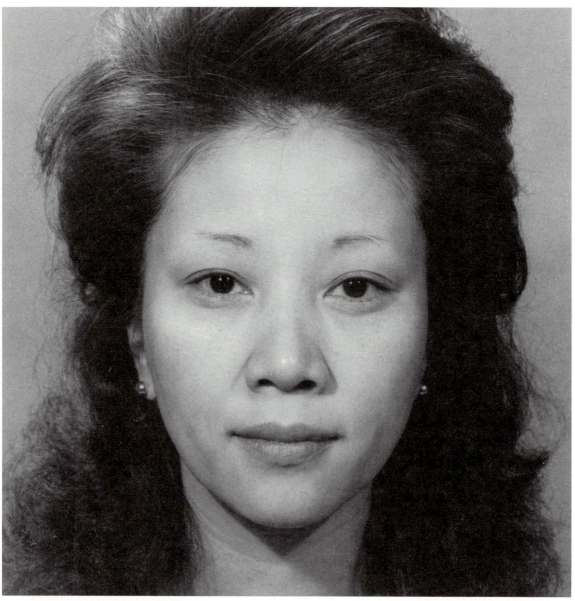

8–44 Character study, Japanese female.   *(photographer)* © *Linda Blase, 1983*

Creating Oriental Makeup On Non-Orientals

Contouring and aging for the Oriental follows the same principles already presented. Make a thorough research for faces which embody the racial characteristics and the kind of experience and age your particular character demands, before proceeding with techniques of light and shadow which suggest the sags and bags of aging.

The primary problem is that of creating the illusion of an oriental eye on a non-Oriental. The challenge is to create the effect of the fold of skin over the eye, (called the epicanthic fold,) which seems to narrow the eye, to flatten the orbital area, and to suggest high, wide, cheek bones. The following exercise and charts, Illus. 8–46 and 8–47 should provide the experience necessary for such productions as *The Mikado* or *Madame Butterfly*. Because such productions have large choruses, the makeup used is water based, combined with pressed powders for ease in application. A "mask" of white grease serves to flatten the area beside the nose and under the eye. Contouring is done with dry, pressed powder makeup.

128

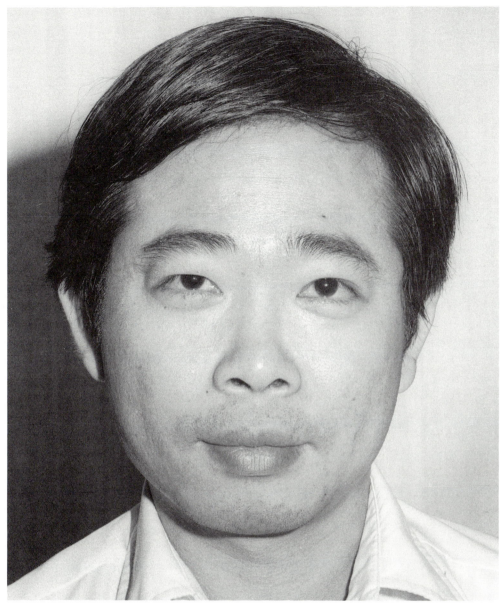

8-45 Character study, Chinese male. *(photographer)* © *Linda Blase, 1983.*

Supplies:

Base: Kryolon Aqua Color #521, or Mehron #4B

Shadow: Brown, dry pressed eye shadow (Ben Nye's 'Shadow', Mehron 7C*)

Highlight: White, dry pressed eye shadow (Ben Nye's white, or white Mehron*)

*These water based cakes must be used dry, having *never* been wet.

Mask Area: White, grease

Liner: Red-brown, grease

Black, grease

Dry Rouge, with brush or wand

True red lipstick, or Moist Rouge

Misc: Bar of soap, baby powder, sponge

*Available at cosmetic counters or through catalogs.

See chart on pressed powder makeup in Chap. 6.

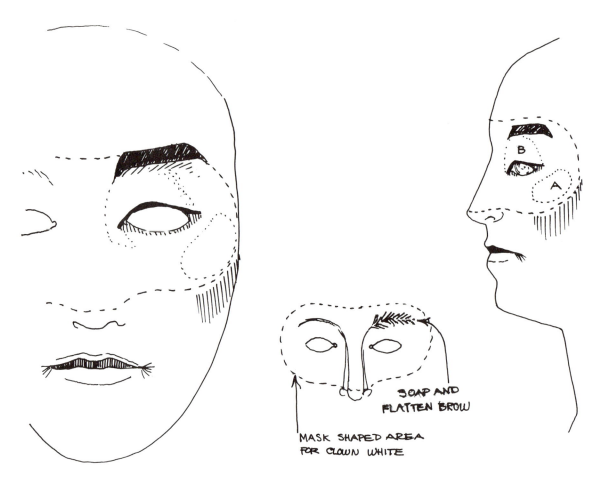

8-46 ORIENTAL MAKEUP CHART, MALE

Men

1. *Brows*: Block out, separate and spread hairs to flatten; they need to be very smooth.

2. *Mask area*: Pat white grease onto mask-like area around eyes, over brows. Blend edges. If brows don't cover, paint white on with brush.

3. *Powder*: Be *liberal* with white baby powder.

4. *Base*: Apply thin coat of cake makeup with sponge over all areas, including "Mask."

5. *Eyes*: With lining brush and brown liner, paint thin line along lashes of upper lid; *study chart*—the line straightens at outer corner and should extend beyond the corner, but no more than one-fourth inch. Drop the line one-eighth inch downward at tear duct. Wipe brush once and feather eye line downward. Drag some shadow along lower eyelash line. Edge of shadow should fuse into base.

6. *Highlight*: Apply pressed powder highlight with wand immediately above the brown eye line and

extend over to nose and up to brow (Area B). Highlight top of cheekbone—wide and far to the side (Area A).

7. *Cheek shadow*: With dry, pressed brown shadow, use wand to brush shading contour under cheek, no further forward than the corner of the eye. Blend edges.

8. *Mouth*: With brown liner, paint the upper lip only. For thick lip, create mouth only half-way up. Smudge shadow at corners of mouth.

9. *Brow*: Study shape in chart. The brow should be short and *slightly* slanted. Paint it with black grease liner. Suggest the hairs with strokes along the bottom.

10. *Eye line*: Go over the brown eye line with black liner.

11. *Powder*: Cover brow, eye, mouth and brush off excess.

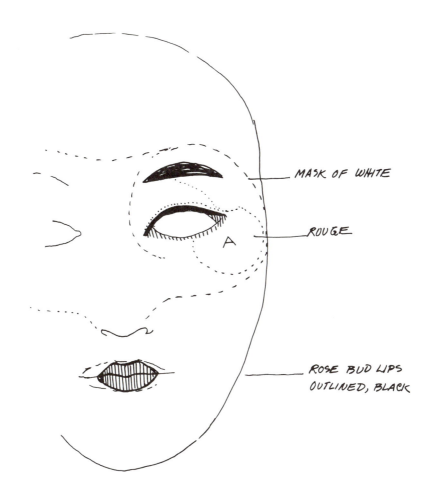

MASK OF WHITE

ROUGE

ROSE BUD LIPS
OUTLINED, BLACK

8-47 ORIENTAL MAKEUP CHART, FEMALE

Women

Follow the same directions as for men, steps 1 through 6.

7. *Cheeks*: With blush brush, apply dry rouge in cheek-eye area (A) about half-way from the center of eye to outer corner. Fuse edges.

8. *Eyebrow*: Paint with black liner. Start above your natural brow, right along the top edge of it. The shape is straight on the bottom and curved on top.

9. *Liner*: With black liner, go over the brown eye line above the eye to accent it.

10. *Lips*: With red lipstick or #3 moist rouge, paint small cupid's bow lips within your natural lips. Outline lips with tiny black line.

11. *Powder*: Apply liberally and brush off.

Black Skin and Oriental Makeup

1. Coat the skin with Stein's #1 pink.
2. Powder.
3. Proceed with rest of the instructions, on top of this base.

Creating the Caucasian Effect
on the Oriental

The oriental eye can be made to look more round by reversing the techniques just explored, should that effect be desired.

1. Create a shadow from the bottom of the brow down the side of the nose, stopping at the nostril. Extend the shadow slightly beneath the inner corner of the eye, in the eye bag area.

2. Introduce a shadow where the fold of the eyelid would be, and extend outward and upward toward the temple, under the orbital bone.

3. Shadow the outside of the cheek bone to reduce the width.

NOTES

[5]Lee Baygan. *Techniques of Three-Dimensional Makeup.* (New York: Watson-Guptill, 1982)
[6]Richard Corson. *Stage Makeup.* Sixth Edition. (Englewood Cliffs, N. J.: Prentice-Hall, Inc., 1981)

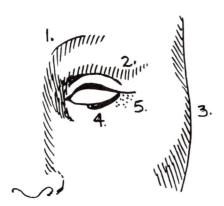

8-48 Creating Caucasian features on an Oriental face.

4. With a dark brown liner, paint a solid eye line next to the lashes, from the inner corner of the eye, and stop at the corner of the eyeball. Do not extend beyond. Round this line upward in the center. Under the eye, paint a line halfway, from center of the eye to outer corner, not beyond. Paint false eyelid line, again creating a curved shape.

5. With highlight, paint out the natural shadow which is formed by the overlapping epicanthic fold.

9

Styling from Photographs

By now your picture file should be burgeoning with variations in facial features which differ from your own. A careful study of these photographs can inspire you to an enriched and subtle portrayal of the character you are creating. The goal is to be able to select information from the photograph and incorporate it in your makeup.

9-1   *(photographer) Karl Stone*

Working with a Photograph

In working from a photograph it is important to make this distinction: *you are not copying the photo*, you are studying it to gain information about the shapes of the features of the face. These are revealed by the shadows cast by the light sources at the moment of the shutter click. They are not necessarily the shadows you will be using. Do not confuse yourself by making a literal translation of the shadows. The light on one side of the face may give more information than the other side. Study both. The important thing is to *observe the shapes*. Learn to look at a face as if it is chiseled into planes or facets. Think of the features as having a top, base, and sides. For example, the nose has a top (which suggests its shape) a base (the lower form of the tip of the nose) and sides (delineated by the change in direction of planes into the cheek). In other words, you must decide where the nose ends and the cheek begins.

Many masks offer perfect illustrations of facial features translated into planes. Study Illus. 9–3 where the emotional content implodes behind the chiseled features.

Once you have discovered the forms, you are ready to translate them, first into a makeup chart, then onto your face, using the application techniques you have already learned.

EXERCISE THIRTEEN:

Styling From a Photograph

Analyzing the Photograph

Study overlays 9–5 through 9–7. Turn the overlays back to see how the planes are selected in relation to the underlying photograph. This is an example of working with a photograph to discover the forms. (Translation of the forms to *your* face comes later.) Refer to the overlays as you do the exercise.

1. *Select a Photograph:* From your collection, choose a large, full front, non-smiling face. The size and frontal view is crucial, particularly for this first experience. Do *not* work from a small, insignificant photo-

9–3 Facial features structured into planes. *Head of a Heavenly King*, 12th century Japanese. Dallas Museum of Fine Arts, The Eugene and Margaret McDermott Fund.

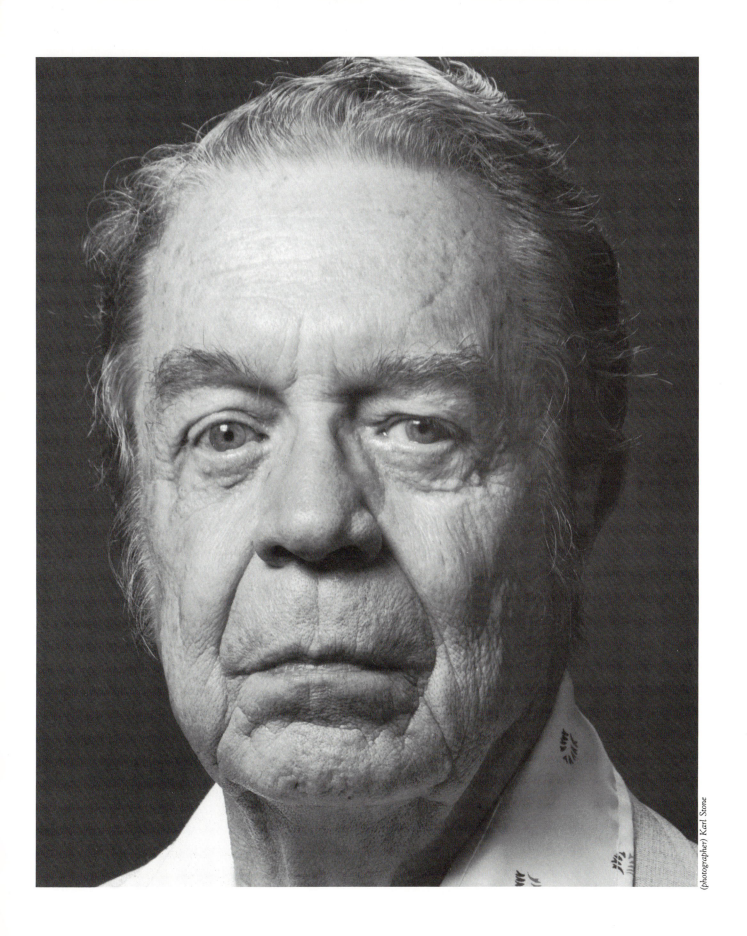

(photographer) Karl Stone

WORKING FROM A PHOTOGRAPH

graph, a smiling face, or one with glasses. Such studies will not give you the information you need, and will compromise your experience with this exercise. Choose a middle-aged face with interesting features, rather than a young or "made-up" face.

2. *Tracing*: Lay very transparent paper over the photograph. Work with a lead pencil and eraser, so that you can make changes. Trace the shape of eye openings, eyelid, brow line, top of nose, nostrils, mouth, and dominant creases. Ignore tiny lines. Search until you have determined the basic shapes. You may lift the tracing paper from time to time to see more clearly. You now have a basic line drawing of features. Compare your drawing to the line drawing in Illus. 9–4.

3. *Shadow Areas*: Continue working on your shading, and indicate areas of depression and sides of projecting forms with close-together parallel lines. Again, remind yourself that you are using shadow to indicate the *form* you *know* to be there. If the shadows which occurred the moment the photograph was taken do this—good! If not, ignore them and be your own sculptor. As you indicate the shadows, stay aware of their overall *shape*. If the face in your photograph seems to have unusually deep depressions, such as sunken eyes, indicate such areas with cross-hatch lines opposing your shading lines. Compare to Overlay 9–6.

4. *Crevices and Folds*: Draw any remaining crevices or wrinkles. Shade away from the crease lines with close-together parallel lines to indicate dimension. *This will always indicate the use of the feathering technique*, both on the charts which you make for yourself, as well as for all of the charts in this book.

5. *Highlight Areas*: Study the highlight areas illustrated in 9–7. Look for the bony structure or the parts of the face which protrude. Try to imagine the skull which exists beneath the face. Decide on the *shape* of each highlight. Define these areas with small dots. The nose, cheekbones, chin, and forehead are obvious protrusions, but as you may discover, there are variations within these features. The nose may have a lump, a hook, or a round bulb. Indicate the shape of the top of the nose and the top of the nostrils with a dotted line. Many foreheads also have

distinctive ridges; accent these with highlight. Clefts, dimples, bags, or any strong muscular forms will require a highlight.

As you create the highlights, remember to leave appropriate space for the base; the entire face is *not* divided between highlight and shadow!

Translating Photographic Information to Your Face

1. *Comparing*: Hold the photograph beside your head while looking in the mirror and study its features in relation to your own. Is the mouth wider? Are the lips thinner or thicker? Is the nose longer, shorter, fatter, knobbier? Are the eyelids heavy or do they disappear behind overhanging flesh? Examine and compare.

2. *Spatial Relation of Features*:
Review instructions in Chap. 8 on transferring and correlating chart information to the face. Refer to Illus. 8–2 and establish horizontal and perpendicular lines on the drawing you just finished. Draw a horizontal line across the face through the corners of the eyes (1) and at the center of the mouth opening (2.) These lines will be nearly parallel with each other. In the following steps you will make vertical lines at *right angles* to these parallel lines in order to determine spacing of features.

  a. *Corner of Mouth*: Extend a perpendicular line from the mouth upward. Where does it intersect the eye? Half-way? Three fourths?

  b. *Laugh Line*: Draw another perpendicular line upward from the widest part of the laugh line toward the eye. Where does it intersect the eye? Half-way across? Less?

  c. *Eye Bag*: Extend a horizontal line from the lowest portion of the eye bag toward the nose. Does it intersect half-way down the nose? Three-fourths? Estimate. Are they the same on both sides?

d. To determine how a laugh line extends, intersect the face with horizontal line *d*.

Notice the flesh above the eye. Does it sag, causing a fold which continues below the corner of the eye? Such seemingly slight differences contribute to the uniqueness of each face. Number and letter each of the horizontal and perpendicular lines as in Illus. 9–8.

Makeup Chart Layout

Transfer the information you have now discovered onto your personal makeup chart or face blank, as in Illus. 9–8, which is made from the photograph, Illus. 9–5. Again, work with a lead pencil. *Always* start with the mouth.

1. Study the correlation lines which you established on the tracing of the photograph. Note where line *a* intersects the eye on the photograph. Find that point on the eye of your face chart and drop a line down opposite the mouth opening. This establishes the width of the character's mouth; disregard your own.

2. Locate the laugh line in the same way. Note where the right angle line *b* meets the eye of the photo. Find this point on the eye of your chart. Drop a line downward; this is how wide the laugh line will be.

3. Continue until all major features are in place. OBSERVE! Use this method as a tool toward recognizing spatial relationships. You will soon have a line drawing of the face transferred from the photograph to your own chart. Think of the chart as an elevation map showing peaks and valleys.

Creating the Face with Makeup

You are now ready to transfer the information contained in your personal chart to your face. If you prefer, you may work from Illus. 9–1 and 9–2, or 9–8, or 9–10 for the purposes of this exercise, regardless of your sex or race. The information will give equal experience. However, the process will become more established in your mind if you develop your own chart from the beginning.

1. Apply base.

2. Mix a tone just darker than your base to copy the lines of major features onto both sides of your face. Refer to the line drawing side of the makeup chart.

3. To recreate the vertical or horizontal spatial relation lines on your face, hold the handle of your brush against your face to visually establish a similar line. For example, start with the mouth; note where line *a* meets the eye on the chart. Find this point on your eye, follow the line of the brush downward, and establish a point opposite the corner of your mouth. You now know whether the mouth in the photograph is wider, narrower, or the same as yours. Disregard yours. Let the paint create the illusion.

4. Eyes and eye bags should be your second point of orientation. Continue to watch for relationships between features. Locate the droop of the eyelid, the height and width of the brow, the depth of the eye bag, etc.

5. Continue, until you have drawn in all major lines with medium tone.

6. Lay in shadow areas with fine lines, 1/8″ apart, using your basic shadow color. Lay in all shadow areas before blending.

7. Blend shadow, using the pat-a-path method.

8. Draw in major lines—laugh lines, eye bags, etc. with shadow color. You will be going over some of the original layout lines. Feather as you go.

9. Stroke in highlight areas with fine lines. Be sure there is a space of base left, where appropriate, between highlight and shadow areas. You will learn the exceptions as you go along.

10. Blend the highlights with the pat-a-path method.

11. If your chart calls for very deep shadow, mix a darker shade to stroke into the centers of those areas already blended. Use this darkened color, also, to deepen crevices, repeating the line and feathering technique where needed. For extra projection of features, a lighter shade of highlight can be applied and blended into the center of the highlight areas.

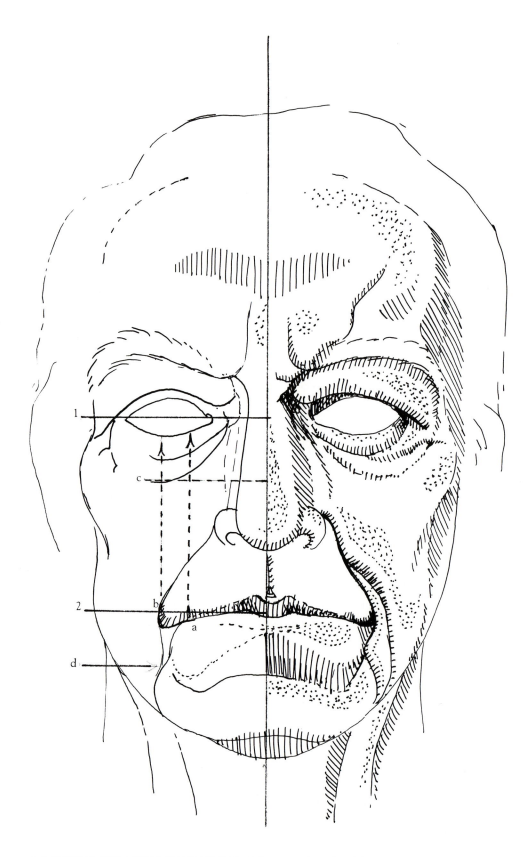

9–8 SPATIAL RELATION OF FEATURES: *Information Transferred from Photograph to Makeup Chart.* Parallel lines indicate shadow areas. Dots indicate highlight areas.

12. Powder.

13. Add brush-on dry rouge, if required. If texturing is indicated, it should be done before powdering.

To further refine your skills in utilizing photographs for theatrical purposes, repeat the process of styling from photographs, using different facial types, with varied ingredients of race and age. You may not necessarily achieve an exact "look-alike," particularly if your face is greatly different in shape, but you will learn to manipulate your features and capture the dominant characters found in the photograph.

A further example of working from a photograph is seen in a study of the features of Samuel Beckett. Illus. 9–10 provides the features translated onto a generic face chart.

NOTE: Subsequent exercises and charts will presume that you have all the techniques presented thus far well in hand. They will not be repeated.

9–9a Line drawing taken from a photograph of Samuel Beckett.

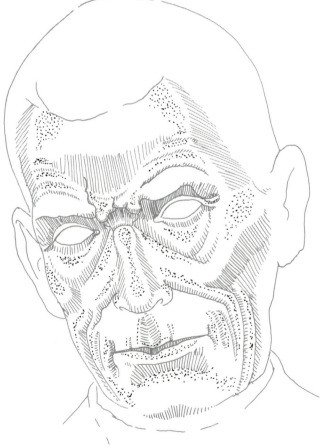

9–9b Highlight and shadows areas indicated by parallel lines and dots.

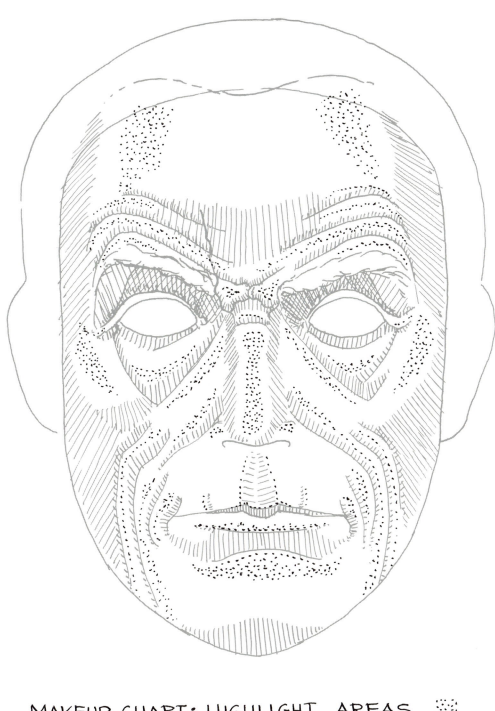

MAKEUP CHART: HIGHLIGHT AREAS
SHADOW AREAS
FEATHERED LINES

9–10 BECKETT MAKEUP CHART

Information taken from analysis of Beckett photograph and applied to generic face chart.

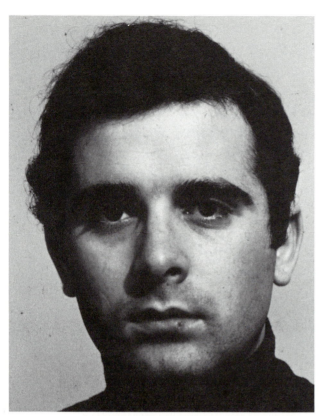

9–10a Merlin Fahey, actor, without makeup.
(photographer) Bruce Wilson

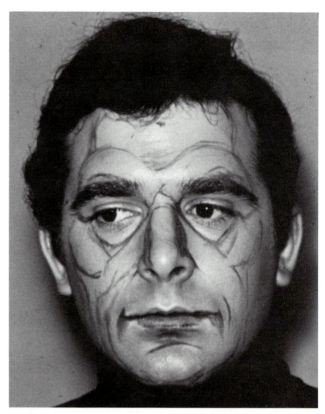

9–10b Lines indicating basic areas.   *(photographer) Bruce Wilson*

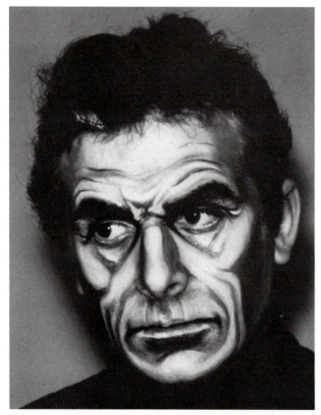

9–10c Completed Beckett makeup.   *(photographer) Bruce Wilson*

FACE CHARTS WITH INTERCHANGEABLE FEATURES

Facial patterns are created from seemingly similar components: two eyes, a nose, a mouth, etc., yet the essential individuality of a face depends on the inter-relationship between features taken as a whole. We experience the face in context with the whole perceptual framework of the moment. Slit the pages of Illus. 9–11a through 9–11e, on the dotted horizontal lines so that by flipping one nose, mouth or eye section at a time, you can become sensitized to how the quality of the face alters with the slightest change.

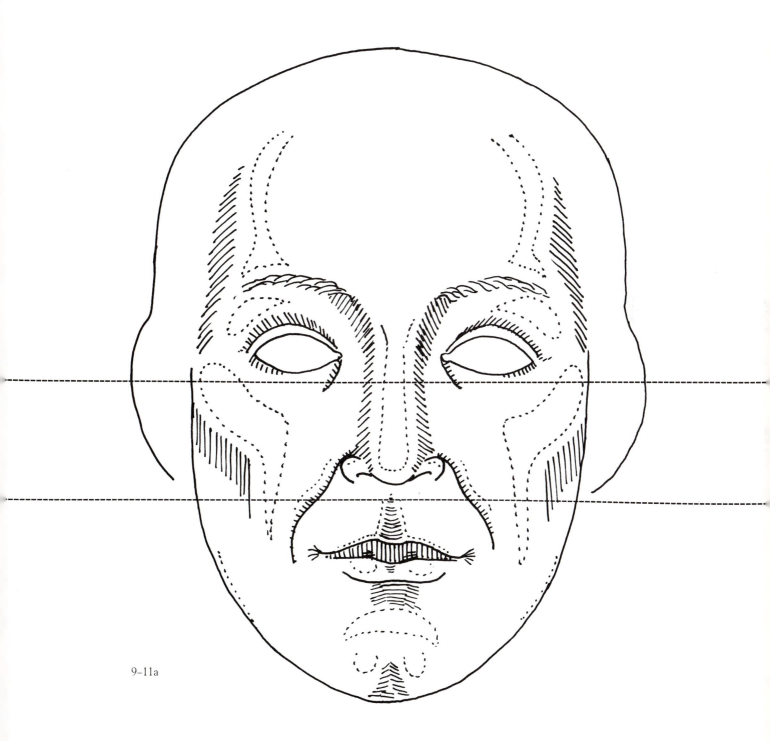

9–11a

FEATURE EXCHANGE

Cut the pages on the dotted lines and flip the sections to observe how exchange of features changes the characterization.

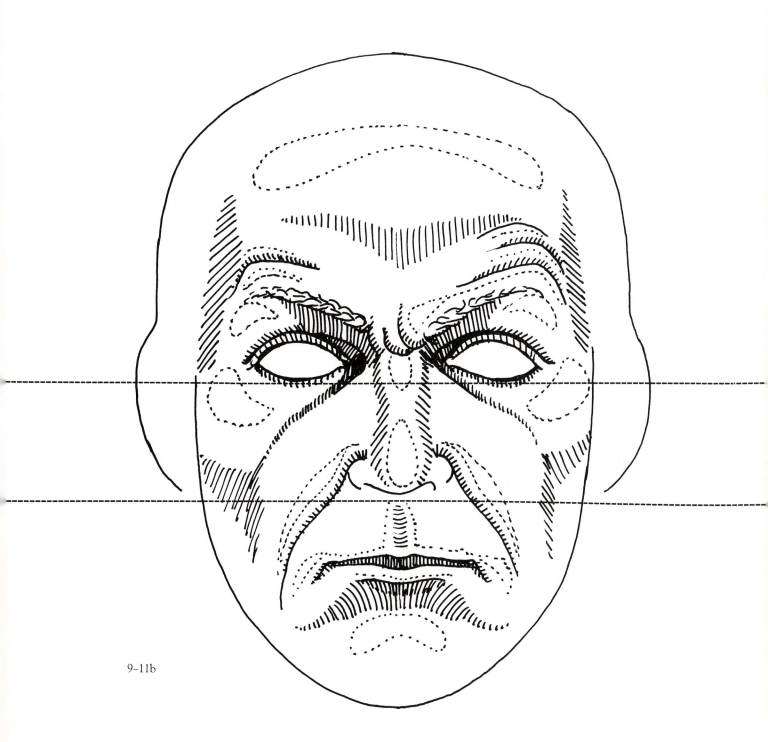

9–11b

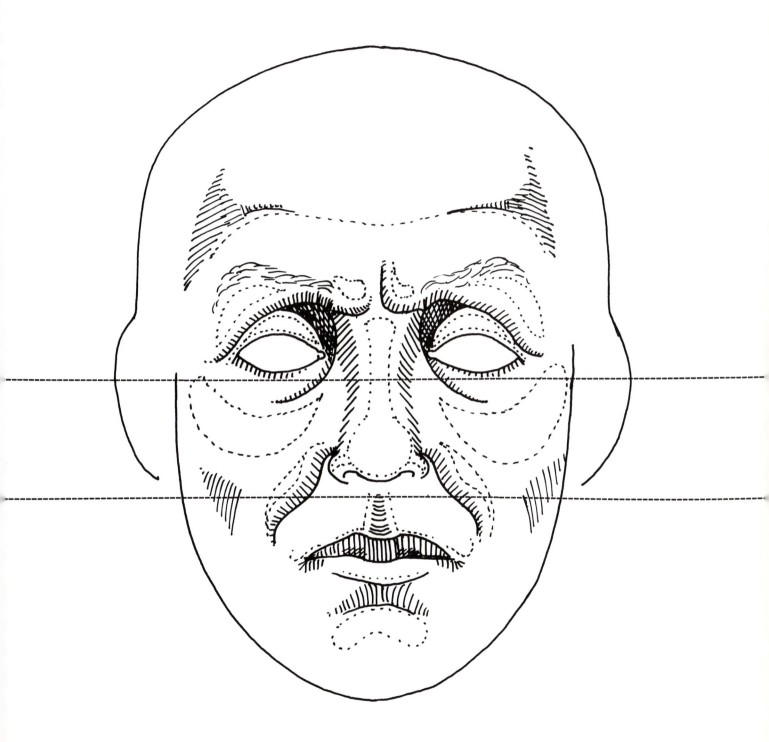

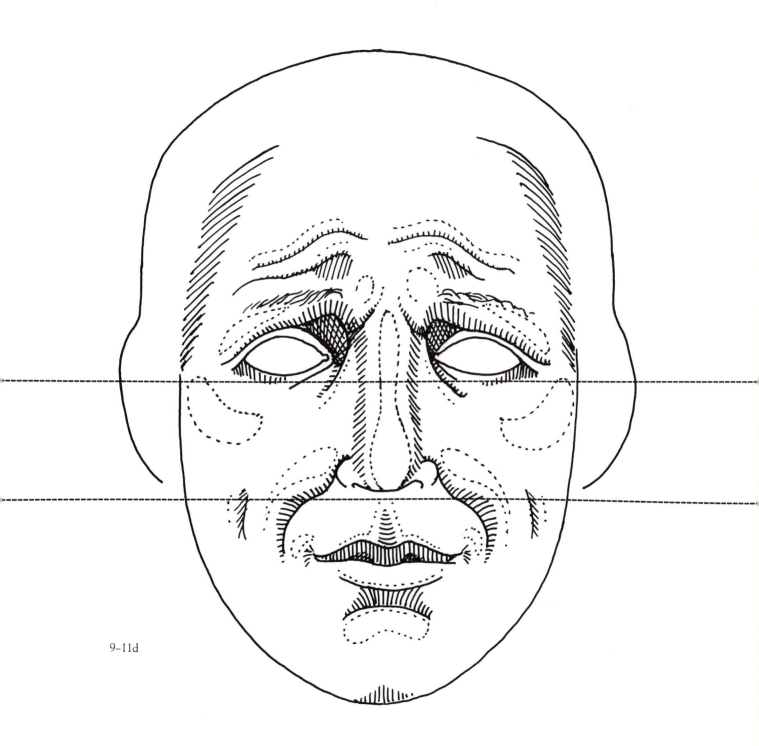

9–11d

149

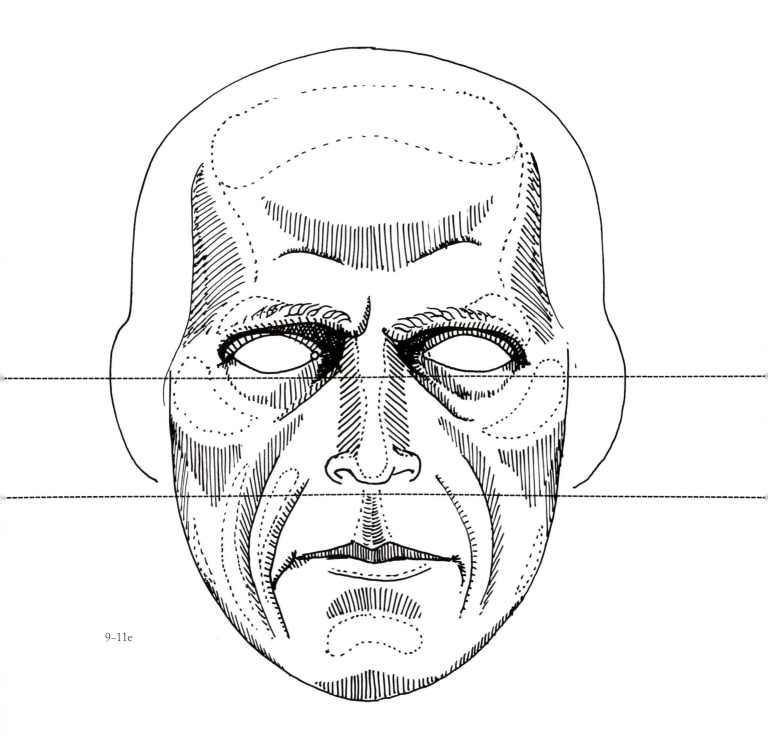

9-11e

151

Photographic Research and Characterization

The photographs in Illus. 9–12a through 9–12g found in *The Appalachian Photographs of Doris Ulmann*[7] have been correlated with some of the characters in *Dark of the Moon*, a play written by Howard Richardson and William Berney, and set in the Smokey Mountains. They serve as an example of how photographic research may enrich character presentation.

These sensitive portraits were made by Doris Ulmann in the late 1920's and early 1930's. She respected those proud mountain people, and captured for us much of their life attitudes, revealing their strengths, sadness and isolation. She said, "I have been more deeply moved by my mountaineers than any literary person. A face that has the marks of having lived intensely, that expressed some phase of life, some dominant quality or intellectual power, constitutes for me an interesting face."[8] There could be no better advice to guide the search for faces appropriate for character revelation in the theatre.

9–12a Character study for Conjur Woman. Sitter unknown.   *(photographer) Doris Ulmann*

9–12b Character study for John, the Witch Boy. Sitter unknown.   *(photographer) Doris Ulmann*

9-12c Character study for Miss Metcalk. Mrs. Bird Patten.   *(photographer) Doris Ulmann*

9–12d Character study for Preacher Haggler. Mr. Ritchie.   *(photographer) Doris Ulmann*

9–12e Character study for Mrs. Summey. Orlenia Ritchie.   *(photographer) Doris Ulmann*

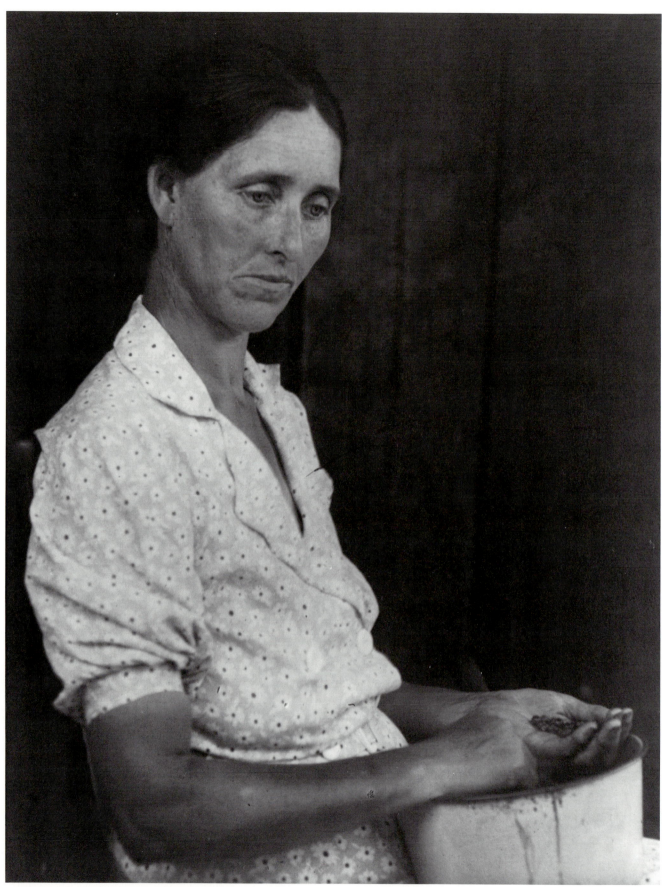

9–12f Character study for Mrs. Allen. Mrs. Stewart.   *(photographer) Doris Ulmann*

9-12g Character study for Smelique. James Duff, fiddler, (and John Jacob Niles). *(photographer) Doris Ulmann*

NOTES

[7]Lee Baygan*The Appalachian Photographs of Doris Ulmann.* John Jacob Niles, Introduction. Jonathan Williams, Preface. (Penland, N. C.: The Jargon Society, 1971).

[8]Ibid.

10

Capturing Periods

When reference is made to "period" makeup, keep in mind that what is meant is the *look* of a specific time, which may, or may not, include the use of cosmetics. To recreate a specific look, we must first discover the *ideal* of beauty prevalent at the time. For instance, during the age of Chivalry in the Middle Ages when the position of women was elevated, this romanticizing was reflected by creating a look of purity and innocence. The hair was pulled back (or shaved) from a high serene forehead (Illus.

10-1 Detail from *The Chess Players*, Girolamo da Cremona, c 1467–1473. The Metropolitan Museum of Art, Bequest of Maitland F. Griggs, 1943. Maitland F. Griggs Collection. There is a constant cycle of change and repetition of hair styles which presents surprising similarities across time. This "Afro" hair style of Angela Davis in the 1960's parallels those found in the mid 15th Century Italian painting by Girolamo da Cremona.

10–11).Contrast this youthful Madonna-woman image with the preference for a more voluptuous type of beauty at the turn of the century, as seen in the Gibson Girl (Illus. 10–42). At this time the stress was on a natural healthy glow, fostered by the use of the proper soap, by pinching the cheeks, but not by the use of cosmetics. However, with the coming of motion pictures, pounds were lost, locks shed, and glamour and cosmetics were in.

For men, also, ideals of handsomeness change from time to time, often in the emulation of a dominant personality of the day. Consider the contrast of the powerful silhouette of Henry VIII, the quiet sensitivity of James Dean, or the urbane slickness of Valentino. To create a period, we must set out to discover and entrap those qualities which create the ambience of a space in time. Larger generalizations can be made about historic periods preceding the development of mass communication. Today, no single voice can dominate. No single role model can dictate. Each segment of society goes its own way, making it more complicated, but no less important, when designing a contemporary play, to know where each character comes from and why he or she chooses to look the way they look.

The Director

Starved for attention, makeup is too frequently an orphan to the theatre arts, existing on an occasional glance, or a scrap of time. The overall quality of makeup for any production depends on the attention—and time—given it by the director and the actors. If the director has no eye for makeup, and cannot discern the possible presence of different styles of application resulting from the varied backgrounds of his actors, he is likely to end up with a visual mulligan stew. If, however, the director and designer consider makeup a valuable extension of character, it can make a cohesive contribution to the production.

Character Analysis

Before designing makeup for a production, the designer should have a thorough understanding of the characters as presented by the playwright, and as comprehended by the director. "Designer" can refer to the one in charge of makeup, the costume designer, or the individual actor. An understanding of characterization in plays is fundamental to the design process, not only for the makeup artist, but also for the setting, costume and prop designer. On what else should such aesthetic decisions be based?

An effective way to gather and organize analysis information is to label a separate page for each character. Having first read the play, go back and respond to the script line by line. Copy out all action and dialogue which gives insight into the personality and physical attributes of the character. The person speaking will not only indicate his own personality, but may also reveal information about others and his relationship to them. Look for emotional tones "between the lines." A careful study of Shakespeare, for instance, will reveal that he emphasizes psychological motives rather than physical and social attributes. The following check list might be helpful in discovering qualities of your characters:

Age, health, occupation
Physical characteristics
Position in society
Financial condition: newly rich? casually rich? genteel poverty?
Down and out?
Religious restrictions, convictions
Awareness of style: appropriate? fashionable? faddish? conservative?
How they see themselves; how others see them
Belief system: what motivates them?
Attitude: conformist? free spirit?
What the character has been, is now, hopes to be.

Research

The next step involves research into the Historical aspect of the play. The time span is usually indicated by the author, but may be changed by the director. The designer must plunge into a sea of information concerning the elements that indicate the aura of the period in order to select the most effective styles of hair and makeup for each character. People are products of their societies, their environments. Information of the more remote periods of the past comes to us in various forms. For times preceding the printing press, the most immediately useful sources are visual recordings by contemporary artists. However, fascinating details are also found in letters and diaries of travelers eager to convey newly observed manners of dress and custom to those at home. Sometimes such information is sandwiched between the political intrigues reported by historians. To experience the feel of a specific period, it is always best to refer to such original sources . . . contemporary paintings, sculptures, or photographs, via books, magazines, or museums. There one finds the observations of the artist shaped in manner and style by the social expectations of his time. To modern eyes, the portraits may seem formalized or unnatural, but by studying the original works, the designer can choose to interpret the style literally, or to freely re-state the essence in his own manner. Be cautious in relying on illustrations which have been sketched from original sources by other artists in later periods, for that means that they have been filtered through another set of eyes. Let *your* eyes be the first-hand observers.

Stereotyping

In choosing facial components to create character makeup, inevitably one will need to consider the problem of stereotyping. The artist's need is to give definition to his art. If a specific type of character is to be suggested, the element of stereotype will enter into the choices, because it is a reality in our thinking. Our ideas about what is beautiful, what is ugly, what is terrifying—are brought about by our conditioning. Memories and experiences of the past carry over in our current attitudes and responses. We have precon-

ceived concepts of such types as villains, heroes, mothers, prostitutes, or preachers, and we carry pigeonholes in our minds into which to stuff such people. Yet, even though we know there are vast exceptions to these generalizations, there is enough potential force in the shared recognition of such concepts that we cannot ignore them.

Heavy reliance on stereotypes bespeaks a deadly repetition and can lead to boring character interpretations, whether in theatre, art, or literature. A good writer does not try to relate a total description of a landscape or character, but knowingly chooses specific details which will evoke a certain response—a common response shared by many. Likewise, the makeup artist can select certain characteristics to deliberately evoke a type of personality. Such associations as these may come to mind:

High, wide forehead: Strong intellectual capacity. (Double that if wearing glasses.)

Small, receding chin: Weakness and timidity.

Large eyes, wide space between: innocent, childlike.

Small eyes, close together: Meanness and suspicion.

Downward slanting brows: Threatening.

Such presumptions could continue, endlessly, to include even categorization of race by the size of the nose, and nationalities by the color of the hair. Nonetheless, regardless of a desire to avoid such conformity of thought, it may be difficult to justify, for example, a blond, fair-skinned Italian, when our "instant recall button" calls for an olive skin and dark hair.

The makeup artist should take such generalizations into consideration and use them, but not lean on them. Or, the actor-artist can deliberately pit the qualities of the character against unexpected images, if the script allows. Stereotypes can be used as a point of departure from which to launch a character, and to spark instant recognition on the part of the audience. Thus activated and developed by the actor, it moves from stereotyping into individuation. Individuation is the essence of art, and the projection of the individual is the ultimate goal of makeup.

163

Hair

It is impossible to recreate the look of a particular time period without giving attention to hair style, or facial hair. Although hair is a common natural commodity, through the years we have managed to alter its natural state. We have oiled it, lacquered it, decorated it, straightened it, curled it, covered it, wigged it—or shaved it off.

Hair forms change according to the capriciousness of fads and the pressures of fashions. Styles are frequently an extension of the inner attitudes of the wearer and can communicate how he feels about himself, and his position in the world. Hair is used as a tool to attract attention or conform. In recent history, as a weapon of revolt, it has registered the protests of minority groups against the short-haired establishment, erupting into such shapes as duck tails, Beatlemops, corn rows, and Afros, until, in a kind of follicular perpetual motion, the hair of the establishment evolved into side-burns, blow-dry cuts, and long hair—at which time the fringe groups began to shave their heads.

Such vagaries of expression are reflections of the society at any given time, and must be taken into consideration by the designer. Whatever the arrangement of each lock of hair, always be aware of the overall silhouette. Think of hair as providing a frame for the face. Facial hair can decorate, accent, or obscure the face, and its cut and shape will suggest period style. Techniques for applying facial hair follow at the end of this chapter.

Collecting Visual Information

The researcher's work is complicated by the fact that there is never one specific look for any particular place and time. There are always overlapping styles caused by such factors as differences in wealth, slowness in communication, adherence to tradition, or just simply desires to be "different." Frequently, religious dictums affect segments of the people, as exemplified by the Puritans, or currently, the unadorned look of the Amish sects in America. At times, deprived of permission to wear makeup, the women of certain conservative religious groups burst the bonds of restraint and flaunt elaborate arrangements of their hair. It is true, too, that it is far easier to find examples of the preferred look of the rich and handsome, than it is to find the appearance of the average or the poor. As a rule, the less privileged mimic the style of the upper classes—a little late, and with less subtlety. All of this is said, not to discourage research, but rather to suggest the rich possibilities available.

After the Renaissance, the predominant look of an age was usually established by the monarch of the most powerful country of the time. Thus the pendulum of style swung from country to country, even during periods of sluggish communication. Queen Elizabeth I's taste for the Spanish style established ruffs around the necks of the fashionable of Europe, but during the reign of Louis XIV, the English looked to France for their models.

From our vantage point today, it seems that past fashions stagnated for long periods of time before yielding to freshets of change. In Egypt, where the priests dictated the representations used by artists, the customs of adornment stretched across centuries. Only the recent, almost accidental, discovery of King Tutankhamen's tomb, showing details of Akhnaton's iconoclastic reign, informs us that there were variations even in that sea of repetition.

As contact between peoples increased via easier travel and communication, the life span of a dominant style became shorter and shorter. There was an acceleration of information and a compression of time. Even the lingering styles of the Middle Ages finally gave way to new influences as East met West via the Crusades. Dramatic advancements in communication affected style changes to a great extent. The printing press compressed the process to a mere decade or less. Another major catalyst can be seen in the industrial revolution. During the early years of the 20th century, newly emancipated women found that they could stop by the dime store on their way home from their factory jobs, purchase a ten cent lipstick, and mimic the pouting lips of the movie stars. By the 1920's, one woman's bobbed hair could cause an avalanche of fallen tresses. The "latest look" had been released from the exclusivity of the upper classes.

Today, movies and television can catapult a fad into instantaneous recognition, and by the same token, make it passé almost as soon as it is seen. Ours is a time of multiple variety. Fad succeeds fad so quickly that the pendulum barely has time to swing.

HOW THIS CHAPTER WORKS

The illustrations in this chapter are selected to suggest a method of research for designing makeup and hair styles of past periods, not as a definitive history. It is impossible within the framework of one chapter to cover the entire range of period makeup. Ideally, each period would be represented by the most influential figure of the time, male and female, illustrated by the observations of contemporary artists and accompanied by examples of possible variations in hair styles which might be worn by people of a similar class in a similar time. Further examples would illustrate variations within other strata of society. As an example of this method of selecting information, refer to the illustrations of Henry VIII, and the accompanying variations in hair and beard styles, (Illus. 10–16, 10–20). Similar choices would need to be considered for any other class of character, such as a workman, a peasant, or an up-and-coming merchant. Obviously, the same research would be done for the women. Please note that the examples in earlier periods rotate between men and women in order to provide makeup exercises for both sexes.

Such a process would be followed by the designer for collecting information on all members of the *dramatis personae* until a wide range of choices for each character has been copied or sketched. Watch for styles which indicate differences in social position, wealth, religious restrictions, personal attitudes or affectations, etc. It is presumed . . . no, it is *mandatory* that you have your character analysis in mind and in hand, so that it will guide all your choices. It is the observation, collection and *selection* of details which define an historic period, and enlighten a character.

Another period which illustrates the variations within a certain time frame is found in the decade of the sixties, (Illus. 10–75–10–85.) For many, this era has come to be characterized by the memory of the "Hippies", with their anti-establishment revolt and preference for the long-haired natural look. However, at the beginning of that same decade we find the sophisticated influence of Jacqueline Kennedy, with her bubble cut, the asexual image of Twiggy with her little boy hair, and the Afros and the cornrows introduced by the "Black is Beautiful" revolution.

In this skeletal overview of the changing image of the ideal male and female beauty, I have played leapfrog over the years, stopping at only a few periods before the turn of the century, and at each decade up to the present time. By alternating between men and women, makeup exercises are provided for both sexes.

The actual execution of makeup based on the following makeup charts should enrich your understanding of the silhouette of the hair, the placement of rouge, shape of lips, or accent of eyes, all providing subtle differences which vary from time to time, giving each period its own special look. Within that "look," further details delineating age and character can be expressed.

THE EGYPTIAN WOMAN

Paintings and art objects left in the Egyptian tombs leave no doubt that elaborate makeup and wigs were part of the daily life of the Egyptians, particularly of the ruling classes. Artists usually portrayed woman lighter than men, either to show that they stayed out of the sun, or that they used a light foundation before applying red to the lips and rouge high on the cheekbone. The eyes were given great importance, perhaps relating to their belief in the Eye of God as an emblem of protection. Lines of black kohl liner

10–3 Head of a Canopic Jar representing Princess Mert-Aten. Egyptian Dynasty XVIII. The Metropolitan Museum of Art, The Theordore M. Davis Collection, Bequest of Theodore M. Davis, 1915.

10–2 Wig of Princess Nany, Egyptian Dynasty XXI. The Metropolitan Museum of Art, Museum Excavations, 1928–29.

encompassed the eye, enlarging it and extending the shape on both ends; a straight line extended at the outer corner, Illus. 10–4. The eyebrows were reinforced in black and drawn down toward the temple. A line of green malachite was placed above, and sometimes below the eye lines.

Wigs were often worn by both men and women. They were frequently coated with beeswax and woven into string, which then formed the cap. The wigs were massive, hiding the ears, and extending to the shoulders or below. If a woman chose to use her own hair, she added false braids to it. Later, both sexes preferred to shave their heads, to make wigs more comfortable. Headbands, jewels, or crowns of flowers adorned the wigs. The Egyptians used perfumes abundantly, and oiled their bodies to protect their skin against the dry climate.

10-4 EGYPTIAN MAKEUP CHART

Note: *Eyelids, peacock blue or green
   *Eye Shadow extends higher than normal lid
   *Black brows extended at outside
   *Black eye line extended at sides
   *Contouring for structure

THE GREEK MAN

Greece was a male dominated society. Physically, men were preoccupied with strength in battle and success in sports, while philosophically they sought balance and proportion in all things. This accent on natural beauty left them uninterested in the use of cosmetics which had been practiced by the Egyptians. Only Greek courtesans indulged in makeup. Before battle, the Greeks performed the ritual of bathing, and then anointing their bodies with oil.

Long hair and beards were dominant until the fifth century B.C. when younger men were shaved, Illus. 10–5, and beards indicated older men and philosophers, as in Illus. 10–6. Many ways were invented to control hair during physical activity. A simple head-band secures the short hair seen in Illus. 10–5, while in Illus. 10–7, the longer hair is pulled up and tucked under the band. Illus. 10–8 shows an arrangement of curls around a fillet. Longer hair was pulled back into braids on either side, criss-crossed at the nape of the neck, and knotted together in the front. The shorter hair was combed down over the forehead, Illus. 10–9.

The sculptors have left us with many examples in which the human face has been idealized into a serene arrangement of features, which we have come to call "classic". Dominant among these is the classic nose which extends in an unbroken plane from the forehead. The makeup chart, Illus. 10–10, suggests how this sculptural illusion might be achieved.

10-5 Head from a fragmentary statue of The Diadoumenos, Roman copy of a bronze statue by Polikleitos, c. 430 B.C. The Metropolitan Museum of Art.

10-6 Male Deity, Zeus or Dionysos, Roman copy of Greek work, V century B.C. The Metropolitan Museum of Art, Rogers Fund, 1913.

10-7 Sketch after the Apollo, West Pediment of Temple of Zeus at Olympia, 460 B.C.

10-8 Sketch after the Kritian Boy, circa. 480. Athens, Acropolis Museum.

10-9 Sketch of Omphalos Apollo. Circa 470 B.C. Athens, National Museum.

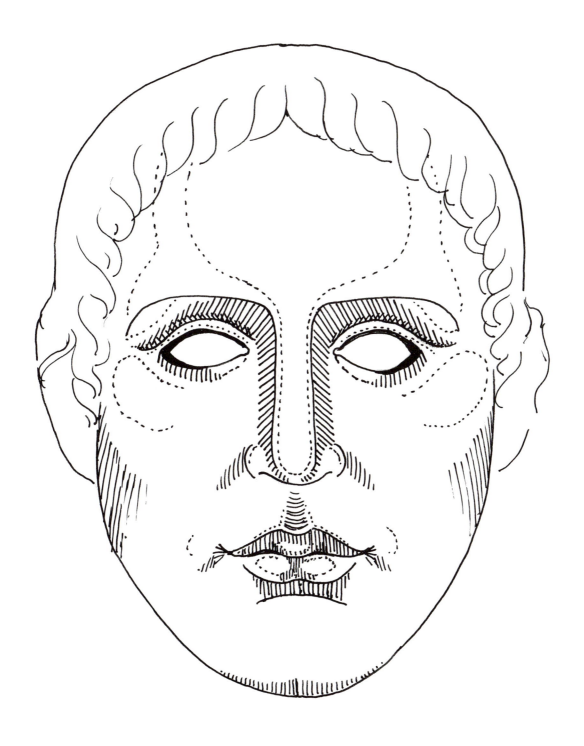

10–10 GREEK MAKEUP CHART–MALE

Note: *Forehead and nose are highlighted as one plane
     *The Nose is shaped by straight shadows on the sides
     *Sculptured lips
     *Clean brow line

THE RENAISSANCE WOMAN; FIFTEENTH CENTURY

In the Middle Ages, the church denounced decadent Roman ways, including cosmetics, yet ironically, the Christian Crusades reintroduced the very things condemned. Women of the upper classes welcomed the treasures from the East—perfumes, hair dyes, and recipes for beauty potions, thus opening the door for the re-entrance of cosmetics. However, their use remained minimal during the fifteenth century.

During the age of chivalry, the code of the knights included among its noble qualities a readiness to protect women, thus elevating them to a position of romantic adoration that had not existed before. The ideal beauty of the age is typified by the Ghirlandaio Madonna, Illus. 10–11 and Color Plate One. Her skin is pale and transparent, her eyebrows plucked, and the hair shaved away from her forehead. The stress is on facial structure and delicacy of features—the idealized woman of the Chivalric Age. The overall effect is of unblemished paleness, with slight touches of color in the cheeks and lips.

Hair was worn pulled away from the forehead in styles ranging from the simplicity of the braided or twisted rolls, to the intricate braids and curls depicted by Botticelli in Illus. 10–12. Sometimes the head covering becomes an integral part of the arrangement of the hair, as in Illus. 10–13 and 10–14. For a surprisingly divergent style of the same period, see Illus. 10–1, in which the ubiquitous "fro" appears, worn by both sexes.

10-11 The idealized beauty of the Chivalric age is portrayed by Domenico Ghirlandaio in *Madonna and Child*. The National Gallery of Art, Washington, D.C. Samuel H. Kress Collection, 1961. (See in color, plate one).

10-13 Sketch after *Madonna and Child* by
Pietro Perugino. Umbrian, early 1500
National Gallery of Art, Washington D.C.
Samuel H. Kress Collection. 1939.

10-12 Sketch after *Young Woman*, by Sandro Botticelli.
Gemäldegalerie, Berlin.

10-14 Sketch after *Ginevra Bentivoglio*, Ercole Roberti, c.
1480 The National Gallery of Art, Washington D. C.
Samuel H. Kress Collection. 1939.

10–15 RENAISSANCE WOMAN MAKEUP CHART

Note: *Hair pulled back (or shaved) from forehead
*Forehead highlighted
*Brows soaped out (Same treatment can be used on hair at top of forehead)
*Small rose bud lips
*For coloration see the Ghirlandaio painting in color, Plate One

THE TUDOR MAN; HENRY VIII, 1509–1547

Men had returned from the crusades with hair and beards grown long during neglect in battle, and thus started an era of long hair. But when Francis I of France accidentally caught his hair on fire, his short hair became the model and was imitated by even Henry VIII in England, who ordered all his male subjects into the new style.[9] Francis I also grew a beard to hide a burn scar, and soon all Europe was bearded, despite the outcry of the church fathers. Henry's square cut beard echoed the horizontal silhouette of the period. Illus. 10–16.

The short hair was usually covered by a hat, worn both indoors and out. For an exception, see Illus. 10–17. Variety in the period lies largely in the shape of the beard. The curly beard of Frederick the Wise of Saxony, parted in the middle and pulled to either side, is preserved for us by Durer, Illus. 10–18. An even more flamboyant style is presented by Lucas Cranach, the Elder, in Illus. 10–19.

Members of the rising merchant class sought means to express their equality with the nobility. Their new wealth allowed them to purchase and refine a similarity in dress and appearance. Although cosmetics were

10-16 Henry VIII, king of England. Artist unknown. National Portrait Gallery, London.

known at this time, it remained for Henry's daughter, Elizabeth, to establish their popular use after she became queen.

10-17 *Phillip Melanchton*, by Albrecht Durer, 1526. Rosenwald Collection. National Gallery of Art, Washington, D. C.

10-18 *Frederick the wise, elector of Saxony*. Engraving by Albrecht Durer, 1524. Rosenwald Collection. National Gallery of Art, Washington, D.C.

10-19 *Portrait of a Man with a Gold Embroidered Cap*. Lucas, Cranach The Elder. German., 1532. The Metropolitan Museum of Art, Bequest of Gula V. Hirschland, 1980.

10–20 HENRY VIII, MAKEUP CHART

Note: *Unusually high brows, (soap out actor's brows before beginning makeup)
*Effect of weight is suggested by patterns of highlight and shadow
*Greater width is established by building beard out to the sides

THE ELIZABETHAN WOMAN; QUEEN ELIZABETH I, 1558–1603

Elizabeth I of England was a forceful personality with an independence characteristic more of the twentieth century than the sixteenth. Such was her influence that her preferences became the preferences of all women of consequence. Her use of cosmetics spread to both men and women in her court. She augmented her rather plain face with a mask-like coat of white paint which contrasted with a frame of frizzy red hair. Although in her later years, she banned all mirrors from her presence, she continued to have her face, neck, and breasts painted, and her hair (or wigs) dyed red.

The pursuit of the fountain of youth via cosmetics often led the Elizabethan woman to decayed teeth and bones, and an early death. After "clarifying" the skin with a lotion based on mercury, and glazing it with egg white, it was covered with a paste called ceruse; a mixture of white lead and vinegar. Red mercuric sulfide supplied color for the lips. All of these ingredients were poison, except the eggs! No price was too high to pay for the lily-white complexion, free of all blemishes, especially freckles.

Characteristics of the previous century continued.

10-21 M. Gheeraerdt's portrait of Elizabeth, captures much of her strength and character, c. 1592. National Portrait Gallery, London.

The forehead retained its importance, and eyebrows were de-emphasized. In Illus. 10-21, Queen Elizabeth's hair is brushed up and over a pad. Back hair was either plaited, coiled, or swept up to help form the front roll as seen in the side view, Illus. 10-22. A French version, Illus. 10-23, shows a triangulation of the roll built to the sides. Small ringlets form a halo on the head in Illus. 10-24.

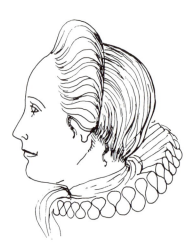

10-22 Sketch after tomb figure in Pershore Abbey, Worcs. England.

10-23 Sketch of hair style variation, French.

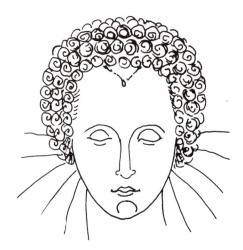

10-24 Sketch after Margaret, wife of Sir Peter Legh, tomb sculpture in Church of All Saints, Fulham, England

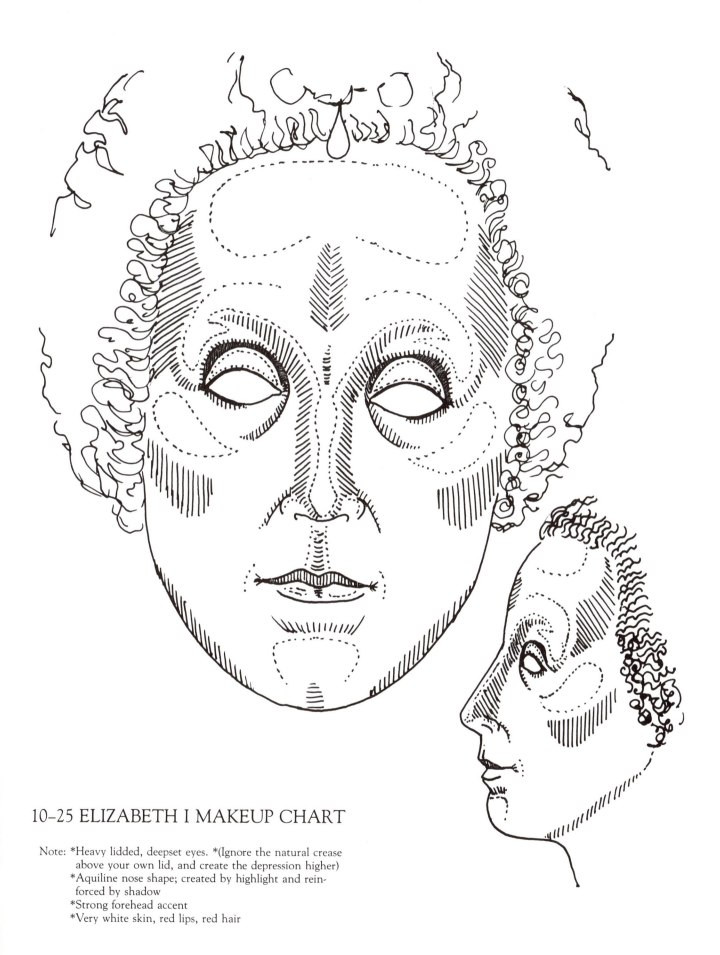

10–25 ELIZABETH I MAKEUP CHART

Note: *Heavy lidded, deepset eyes. *(Ignore the natural crease
above your own lid, and create the depression higher)
*Aquiline nose shape; created by highlight and rein-
forced by shadow
*Strong forehead accent
*Very white skin, red lips, red hair

RESTORATION MEN
1660–1685

At the time of the Restoration, when Charles II was restored to the throne in England following the stringent years of the Puritan "Roundhead" government, men's hair became long again. The upper classes wore waves and curls cascading to the shoulders, and the young men frequently wore their own hair, as seen in Largilliere's portrait, Illus. 10–26 and Color Plate 3. The length of men's hair continued to be denounced by the church in the same manner in which it had condemned short hair during the reign of Henry VIII. It is always upsetting to conservatives to witness changes in style . . . *their* style.

Lavish use of makeup by women had survived despite Puritan restrictions. Men who preferred to use cosmetics had them at their disposal. Monsieur, brother to Louis XIV of France, was notorious for his elaborate dress and painted face; as were the fops so caricatured by the Restoration playwrights.[10] However, most men, such as Samuel Pepys, the noted diarist, chose wigs and perfumes as a primary means of expression. Perfumes had gained a necessary popularity in the centuries following the demise of the Roman bath.

When Louis XIII, 1610–1643, wore a wig to hide his baldness,[11] the trend for wearing wigs was begun. After the style was adopted by Louis XIV, the use of wigs over shaved heads or closely cropped hair spread through most of Europe, and continued until the end of the eighteenth century.

The middle classes recognized the wig as a badge of acceptance, even though it required money to buy it, time to keep it, and restricted activity to wear it. The styles and shapes from which to choose were varied and complicated. Illus. 10-27, shows the hair built high on either side of the part and flowing in curls to below the shoulders. Louis XIV preferred the large wig which was full at the bottom, Illus. 10-28. In America, although the leaders of church and state protested and passed prohibitive laws, styles generally followed those worn in England.

10–26 Detail from Nicolas de Largillière's *A Young Man with his Tutor*. Samuel H. Kress Collection. National Gallery of Art, Washington, D.C.

10–27 *Game of Billiards*. Antoine Trouvain, French, 1694. The Metropolitan Museum of Art, The Elisha Whittelsey Collection, The Elisha Whittelsey Fund, 1949.

10–28 Louis XIV. Sculpture, French school, after Bernini. National Gallery of Art, Washington, D. C.

10–29 RESTORATION MAN MAKEUP CHART

Note: *Study color plate *Three* for coloration.
*Flushed (or rouged) cheeks
*Rosebud lips, in shape and color
*Plump, rounded features

THE EIGHTEENTH CENTURY WOMAN; MADAME DU BARRY, 1743–1773

Madame du Barry became successor to Madame Pompadour as mistress to Louis XV of France when she was officially presented to court in 1769. She represents a beauty greatly admired in that day. Drouais' portrait of her, Illus. 10–30 and color plate four shows hair swept up into a row of curls, a child-like face, large heavily-lidded blue eyes set against a fair skin, and glowing cheeks. It is unlikely that her beauty was unaided by paint. By this time, cosmetics had become a matter of commercial importance and were readily attained, not only by the court, but by the newly leisured middle class.

According to Maggie Angeloglou in her excellent book, *A History of Makeup*, in researching makeup, one should note that, while the French artists who painted portraits of the eighteenth century woman actually recorded the makeup worn, the English portraitists seem to have had an unwritten agreement not to reveal the use of artifice and therefore portrayed their subjects as paragons of natural beauty.[12]

Whereas Elizabethan ladies had once shocked the French with their exposed breasts, now, in France, necklines plunged to expose lightly covered charms; charms frequently marred by the pockmarked skin caused by continued use of the deadly ceruse, and aggravated by greasy powder fallout from the hair. Many women had followed the lead of men and powdered their hair white or grey in the mid-eighteenth century and later, for court wear, white, blue or black.

Some women plucked their eyebrows, or covered them with paste, and created new ones made of mouse skin, placing them where whim led. Pads of Spanish wool impregnated with vermillion added a blush to the cheeks of both sexes. If the cheeks had begun to age, "plumpers" were worn inside the mouth against the teeth.

Although Madame du Barry wore her own abundant blond hair, by mid-century women began to add false hair. Madame Hall in Illus. 10–31 has kept the front swept over a pad, Pompadour style, and added a false braid. The back of the hair at this time was fashioned into a chignon, hair dropped from the crown and turned under at the nape of the neck. Many women had followed the lead of men and powdered their hair white or grey by mid century. It took a revolution to collapse the towering heights these hair arrangements eventually achieved.

10–30 *Madame du Barry*, as painted by Francois-Hubert Drouais, c. 1770. National Gallery of Art, Washington. Timken Collection 1959. (See in color, plate four)

10-31 *Marie Adélaïde Hall*. Sculpture by Augustin Pajou. The Frick Collection, New York.

10-32 Detail from *"Le Rendez-vous pour Marly"* by J. M. Moureau, le Jeune, shows crisp rolls on the side of the head, with back hair braided and caught up with ribbon. The Metropolitan Museum of Art, Harris Brisbane Dick Fund, 1933.

10-33 J. M. Moreau le Jeune shows the side sausage curls and back chignon in detail from the engraving *"N'Ayez pas peur, ma bonne amie"*. The Metropolitan Museum of Art, Harris Brisbane Dick Fund, 1933.

10-34 EIGHTEENTH CENTURY WOMAN, MAKEUP CHART

Note: *Study color Plate *Four* for coloration
*Pale, fair skin, (called "dazzling white" by contemporary)
*Rouge placement: Rather low on cheeks, with faint touch on chin (dashed line)
*Clear, highlighted brow
*Rosebud lips
*Eyelids highlighted

1850's MEN;
ABRAHAM LINCOLN

From the 1830's, when beardlessness was encouraged, until the Civil War, most Americans remained clean-shaven. Then, it seems, hair began to creep down the side of the face, where it joined the moustache. This style, later popularized by General Burnside, Illus. 10–36, by reversal became known as "sideburns."

By the 1860's, the beard had become a badge of respectability. Abraham Lincoln had grown a beard by his inauguration in 1861. The wide variety of shapes and styles can be seen in the engravings of Grant and his generals, Illus. 10–37. Facial hair continued, unabated, for 30 years before younger men cleared their faces, leaving only a moustache.

10–36 Ambrose Burnside, whose distinctive and influential hair style became known as "sideburns". National Portrait Gallery, Smithsonian Institution, Washington, D. C. *Photograph by Mathew Brady, c 1861.*

10–35 Abraham Lincoln. National Archives, Washington, D.C.

10–37 Many variations in hair styles and facial hair are represented in Currier and Ives Print of *Grant and His Generals*, 1865. The Library of Congress, Washington D.C.

10–38 LINCOLN MAKEUP CHART

Note: *Deep set eyes
*Width of laugh lines
*Strong definition of mouth
*Width and angularity of cheekbones
*Study also 1–11, 1–12, 1–13

TURN OF THE CENTURY; THE GIBSON GIRL

At the beginning of the twentieth century, the "Gibson Girl," created by artist Charles Dana Gibson, was the ideal of men and women. See Illus. 10-40 and 10-41. Assured and at ease, her long hair was puffed into a soft pompadour (over false "rats") and her complexion suggested a natural, not artificial, glow. She exuded good health and enjoyed sports. Her spirit was embodied in the person of Alice Roosevelt Longworth, Illus. 10-39, the unpredictable daughter of President Theodore Roosevelt. At a time when the use of cosmetics was highly suspect, she came to represent the "liberated woman" who could not only go about unchaperoned and smoke cigarettes, but could dare to use rouge and powder. She was the most photographed young woman of her day, and her witty comments concerning society and politics continued to ricochet about Washington for the next 60 years.

At this time, cosmetic advertisements limited themselves to suggesting various creams, soaps, and lotions which would promote good health. It awaited the coming of the movies to launch makeup into popularity.

10-40 Gibson Girl Wall paper, "suitable for a bachelor apartment," shows an assortment of Gibson's girls, their long hair arranged with casual ease into knots at the nape of the neck or on top of the head.[14]

10-39 Alice Roosevelt Longworth, a contemporary counterpart to The Gibson Girl. *Courtesy Brown Brothers, Sterling, Pa.*

10-41 The Gibson Girl, created by Charles Dana Gibson in the 1880's.[13]

10–42 GIBSON GIRL MAKEUP CHART

Note: *Healthy, rounded contour of face
*straight, delicate nose
*full lips, sculptured
*accent on eyes as dominant feature

1920's WOMEN

By the 1920's, the pouf of the pompadour began to give way to the head-hugging waves of the Marcel. Women shed hair and pounds in emulation of popular dancer Irene Castle, whose boyish figure and bobbed hair prepared the way for the flapper. In Paris, Josephine Baker, Illus. 10–47, captivated the French as an entertainer in La Revue Nègre. In Hollywood, Clara Bow was declared to have "It," and "It" included, in addition to sex appeal, a pale face, large, dark-rimmed bedroom eyes peering out from under a tousled fringe of bands and curls, and a pair of pouting red lips, Illus. 10–43. Such movie stars became instant models to women around the world, supplanting the rich and queenly as image makers. Their influence is seen in the hair styles worn by women of the Miss America Pageant, 1931, Illus. 10–48.

The smoldering black smudged eyes of such screen sirens as Theda Bara and Pola Negri gave way to the incandescent beauty of Greta Garbo, Illus. 10–45,

10–43 Clara Bow, the "It" girl of the silver screen.   *United Press International Photo.*

10–44 CLARA BOW MAKEUP CHART

Note: *child-like features
      *short nose
      *rose-bud lips
      *brows far apart
      *full cheeks
      *strongly accented eyes

10-45 Greta Garbo, the glamorous star whose mysterious beauty dominated the first decade of the movies.   *United Press International Photo.*

10–46 GRETA GARBO MAKEUP CHART

Note: *high, thin eyebrows
　　　*Eyeliner extending outward at corners
　　　*Highlight on orbital bone under brow, and high on cheekbones
　　　*clear, high forehead
　　　*wide mouth, thinner upper lip

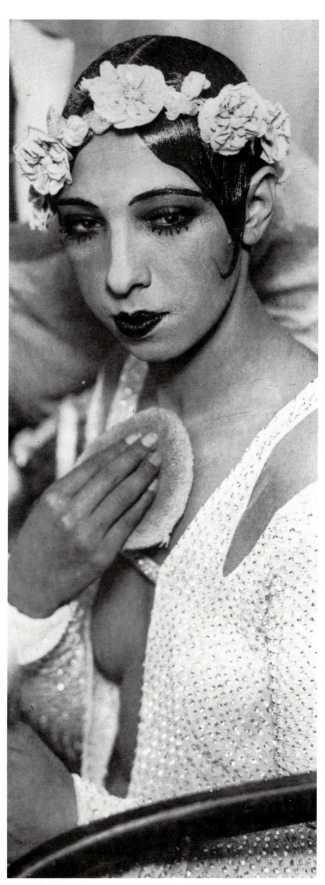

10-47 Josephine Baker, popular Black entertainer, created her own unique hair style with slicked down spit curls.

whose aura of mystery fascinated both men and women. Although she wore little makeup, her natural beauty was enhanced by eye liner which extended a line outward at the corners. Her incredibly long lashes were real, and were soon imitated with false ones by even her peer actresses. Such was her appeal, that revivals of the "Garbo look" recur regularly.

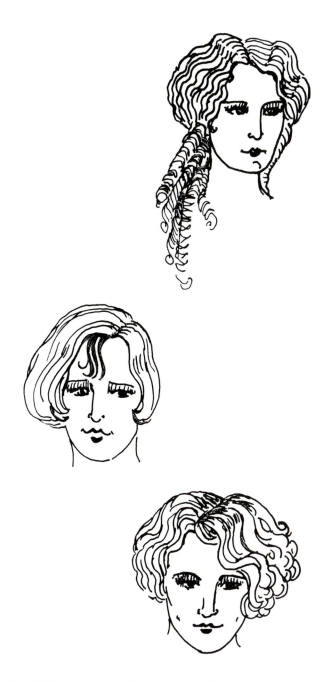

10-48 Divergent hair styles worn in the first Miss America Pageant, held in 1921, featured everything from the short bobs to the dangling long curls inspired by Mary Pickford.

1920's MEN

In 1905, J. C. Leyendecker, a noted illustrator, created the "Arrow Shirt Man" for an advertising campaign, thus launching the symbol for fashionable manhood for the next 25 years, Illus. 10–50. This fictitious, clear-eyed man, with chiseled features and an urbane manner provoked as many as 17,000 fan letters in a month—more than his film star counterpart, Rudolph Valentino.[16] By this time, the men had shorn off all facial hair, except perhaps for a small moustache, and slicked their hair back like Valentino into the sideburned "patent leather" look, Illus. 10–49. The use of hair pomades continued until the revolution invoked by the mop tops of the Beatles in the 1960's.

10-49a The Arrow Shirt Man created by J. D. Leyendecker.
Courtesy of Cluett, Peabody and Col, Inc. 15

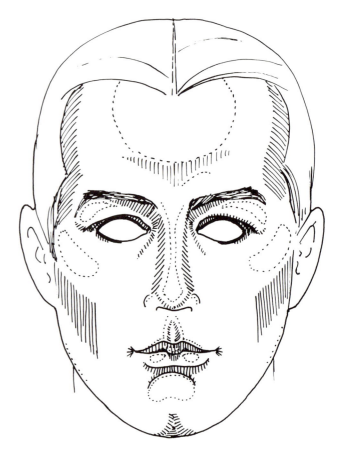

10-49b ARROW SHIRT MAN MAKEUP CHART

Note: *sharply chiseled features
*strong accenting highlights
*contoured mouth
*research variations in Michael Schau's book *J.C. Leyendecker.*
(Excellent reference for Noel Coward's characters)

10–50a Rudolph Valentino, romantic, sophisticated movie idol of the 1920's, with "patent leather" hair style. National Portrait Gallery, Smithsonian Institution, Washington, D.C. *(photographer) Russell Ball.*

10–51 Charles Chaplin, famous for his role of the little tramp. International Museum of Photography at George Eastman House.

10–50 Charles Lindbergh, tousle-headed all-American hero, first solo Trans-Atlantic pilot. National Portrait Gallery, Smithsonian Institution, Washington, D.C.

1930's WOMEN

"Glamour" was the elusive image sought by rich and poor in the 1930's. It was personified by the movies' Joan Crawford and society's wealthy Brenda Frazier. Cafe Society's glamour girls were led by Frazier, while deprived women in a depressed nation looked to her as an idealized woman. They were fascinated by pictures of her pale mask-like face, with its black penciled brows and scarlet lips photographed in the company of the world's most famous people in the most exclusive places, Illus. 10–53.

But it was Joan Crawford's look with her heavier brows, and fuller lips, exaggerated by dark red lipstick, which was widely imitated by the masses. Those who were entranced by the sparkling platinum blond hair of Jean Harlow made a rush for the peroxide bottle. Her brows were shaved, and she continued the use of the thin penciled line started in the twenties, Illus. 10–52.

Movie stars had benefited from innovations made by Max Factor in the previous decade in makeup application and the creation of new products. By the 1930's, cosmetics had become cheap and available to all. The at-home attempts to achieve "glamour" usually lacked subtlety and ended up a blatant slash of bright red lipstick, a spot of orangish rouge and a brow aided by an eyebrow pencil.

10–53 Joan Crawford in *tête-à-tête* with Brenda Frazier at the Stork Club in New York, 1939. *United Press International Photo*

10–54 1. Bangs created for Claudette Colbert by Perc Westmore.
2. Straight hair turning under all the way around in a soft roll, called a "Page Boy".
3. Remnants of the Marcel wave on the crown, ending in a tumble of curls.
4. Tight, close to the head style, with no lift on the top.

10–52 Jean Harlow, popular platinum blond star of the early 1930's. *United Press International Photo.*

10–55 JOAN CRAWFORD MAKEUP CHART

Note: *High forehead
     *Large space between eye and brow
     *Strong cheek bones
     *Large, squarish lips

1930's MEN

The movie stars continued to be the dominant influence in hair styles in the 1930's. The center, parted, "patent leather" look was out. However, although somewhat longer and fuller, the hair continued to be oiled and combed to the back. A slight wave began to be encouraged, as seen worn by Robert Taylor, who also retained a slim moustache, Illus. 10–56. The more rugged features of Clark Gable were topped by a stray forelock which endeared him to his fans. The styles continued with little change until the shorter cuts brought about by the war-time forties.

10–56 Clark Gable was considered the sexiest male star of the decade. His strong masculine characteristics constituted his appeal.   *United Press International Photo.*

10–57 Robert Taylor was among the top ten movie stars of 1936 and 1938. He typifies the slick good looks seen also in Tyrone Power, Cary Grant and Errol Flynn.   *United Press International Photo.*

10–58 ROBERT TAYLOR MAKEUP CHART

Note: *High angular cheek bones
*cleft in chin
*the angle of the brow, which leaves a wide space above the eye
*Widow's peak hair line

1940's WOMEN

The winners of the hair style show in Detroit, Michigan, in 1941, Illus. 10–59, show the elaboration and continuation of some of the preceding tight styles. The G. I.'s seemed to prefer the flowing curls of red-haired Rita Hayworth, whose hair was made to appear even more abundant by the first use of large rollers. Her hair, worn in a loose wave at the top, and cascading into curls, was a prevalent style of the day, Illus. 10–62 and 10–63.

Hair took a plunge downward to eight inches below the shoulders later in 1941, when Veronica Lake appeared with her blond hair hanging over one eye, Illus. 10–60b. Female factory workers who rushed to copy her, soon found it safer to fasten their hair up in a net snood, Illus. 10–60a. For dress occasions, long hair was brushed to the top of the head, secured, and the ends shaped into tight curls, Illus. 10–60d.

Marlene Dietrich's, Illus. 10–61, fine bone structure responded to the directional lights of the photographers, and they loved to accent her prominent cheekbones.[17] Soon, hollow cheeks were in, as others rushed to imitate. Her false lashes were applied on the outer half of the upper lid, and no confining line was added beneath the lower lashes.

In America, everyday makeup began to resemble that formerly displayed by women who depended upon sexuality for a living. The use of cake makeup as a base created a flawless makeup mask, which was accented by a liberal amount of rouge and brilliant lipstick.

10–60a G. I favorite style.

10–60b Veronica Lake.

10–60c Factory worker.

10–59 Hair styles, early 1940's.

10–60d Dress style.

10–61 Marlene Dietrich, a star whose unique mystique has spanned forty years.   *United Press International Phoro*

10–62 Rita Hayworth, called the Love Goddess of the 20th Century, was a favorite pin-up of American G. I.'s. *United Press International Photo.*

10-63 RITA HAYWORTH MAKEUP CHART

Note: *square face, accent on jaw line
*full lips, larger upper lip
*extreme, false lashes
*low hairline

1940's MEN

The military requirements which accompanied World War II were the cause of the major changes in hair styles of the forties. The close-cropped G. I.'s hair was not allowed to be over one and one-half inches long. The crew cut even emerged on the college campus. These two styles later grew into the geometric flat top, Illus. 10–66. If hair did not stand up in brush-like bristles, it was encouraged with wax. The crew cut became a venerable style which persisted for over twenty years, although later the hair was allowed to be a little longer and fuller, and was brushed toward the back on the sides.

On the civilian front, a skinny, youthful Frank Sinatra crooned, and adoring adolescents squealed, Illus. 10–65. He became the idol of a newly recognized group in our society—the teen-agers. For the first time, young people became a force with their own taste in dress and appearance. In subsequent years, they not only fell out of the pattern of being "little adults", but instigated changes in the appearance of their elders.

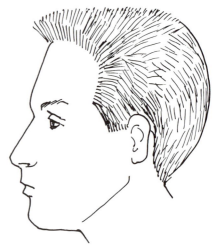

10–66 The flat top was similar to the crew cut, short all over, but standing straight up on top in a flat brush-like bristle.

10–64 British sailor and an American Merchant Marine typify the influence of the military in hair styles during the 1940's. *United Press International Photo.*

204

10-65 Frank Sinatra, 1942, wears his hair long and wavy on top, and combed back on the sides.   *United Press International Photo.*

1950's WOMEN

Teen-age girls in the early 1950's pulled their long hair back into pony tails, Illus. 10–68b. Soon long hair was swept away by the poodle cut, featuring all-over short curls, Illus. 10–68a, or the Italian boy, which was somewhat longer, with spit curls on the forehead and cheeks. Youthful Audrey Hepburn typified the little boy look, Illus. 10–69.

When short hair styles began to grow out, they were transformed into the bubble: a round, fluffed out-shape achieved by setting hair three inches long on large rollers.

Child-like vulnerability, combined with an open sensuality, established Marilyn Monroe as the reigning star of the decade. Her hair, in Illus. 10–67, represents a generally popular style.

In London, Mary Quant began to create styles and makeup aimed at the young. She introduced highlighters, lip glossers, and face shapers in cosmetics. Makeup was now merchandized with sexual innuendoes. "Bare face" makeup was in, which meant heavily accented eyes, and paler than pale lips. Throughout the 1950's, the eyes had a strong upper eye line extending outward and slightly upward at the corners. The Cleopatra eye, completely outlined in a bold black line with a straight line extended at the outer corner, was popularized by Elizabeth Taylor and Vivian Leigh. Compare with the original Egyptian makeup, Illus. 10–3 and 10–4. The earthy European stars, like Sophia Loren, added their influence, stressing dark-rimmed eyes and pale lips. All of these trends carried over into the sixties.

10-67 Marilyn Monroe, dominant star and sex symbol of the 1950's.   *United Press International Photo.*

10-69 Audrey Hepburn, gamin like actress, represented the youth and innocence desired by many women. Note her thicker brows, and use of strong eyeline which lifts up at the corner of the upper lid.   *United Press International Photo*

10-68 Hair styles of the 1950's: a. Poodle cut b. Pony tail.

10-70 MARILYN MONROE MAKEUP CHART

Note: *characteristics similar to child's face, (illus. 8-36)
    *widely spaced eyebrows, with their distinctive shape
    *beauty mark

1950's MEN

In the placid years of peace following the end of World War II, forty percent of the barber shop customers demanded flattops. Even the women followed suit, demanding "butch" cuts. But undercurrents of rebellion began to appear. James Dean, in the movie *Rebel Without a Cause*, created a cult following which represented a quiet revolt. His hair remained a modified crew cut, Illus. 10–71. It was Elvis Presley whose explosive music helped establish a new lifestyle for the generation, Illus. 10–72. There followed in his gyrating wake an eruption of sideburns and longer hair which was combed to the back where it was preened into a ducktail.

A raging controversy over hair arose. Conservative school boards viewed the growing hair in alarm and suspicion. In characterizing long hair as radical, they gave youth the outward symbol they needed for their declaration of independence from adult models.

10–72 Elvis Presley popularized Rock and Roll music, and along with it sideburns and longer hair. *United Press International Photo.*

10–71 James Dean, movie star and cult hero, represented the teenager's vision of himself. *United Press International Photo.*

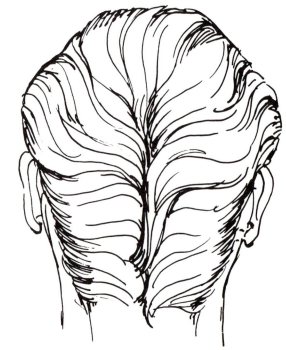

10–73 Back view of the duck tail.

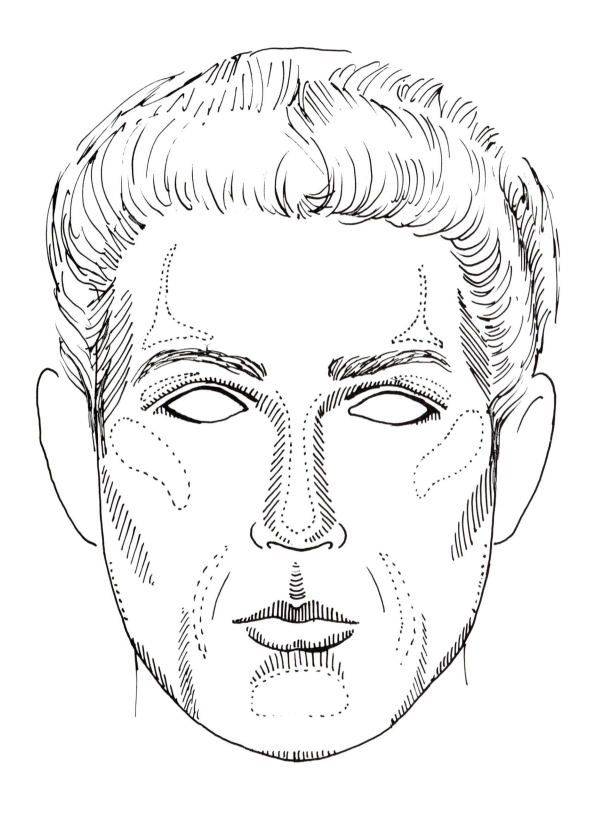

10-74 JAMES DEAN MAKEUP CHART

Note: *Placement of laugh lines, which are wide and do not originate at the nostril
*full lower lip
*strong accent on jaw bone

1960's WOMEN

Jacqueline, wife of the enormously popular President John F. Kennedy, exerted a potent influence on the women of the early 1960's, with her youth and simple elegance. The bouffant hair style she wore, Illus. 10–75, was imitated and then enlarged into swirling beehives. To achieve these silhouettes, the hair was back-combed into a tangled pile, the outer layer smoothed over, and then lacquered firmly in place.

Running concurrently with this style was the Twiggy influence from London. Her beanpole figure and boyish Sassoon cut suggested an eternal unisex-

ual youth. Her exaggerated eyes, with the lower lashes carefully painted in place, and her use of almost white lipstick fascinated the young, Illus. 10–76. It was the decade of eye shadow. Bold lines accented the upper lid. Multi-colors of eye shadow were available, and many were iridescent. Deeper shadows were drawn in the crease above the eyelid. A strong black line defined the upper lashes, which were heavily coated with mascara. The underlying structure of the face began to be emphasized with the use of blushers for the hollows, and highlighters for the cheekbones.

10–75 Jacqueline Bouvier Kennedy, dressed for a state dinner at the White House, 1963.   *United Press International Photo.*

10–76 Twiggy. Introduced Britain's "Mod" style to the U.S.
United Press International Photo.

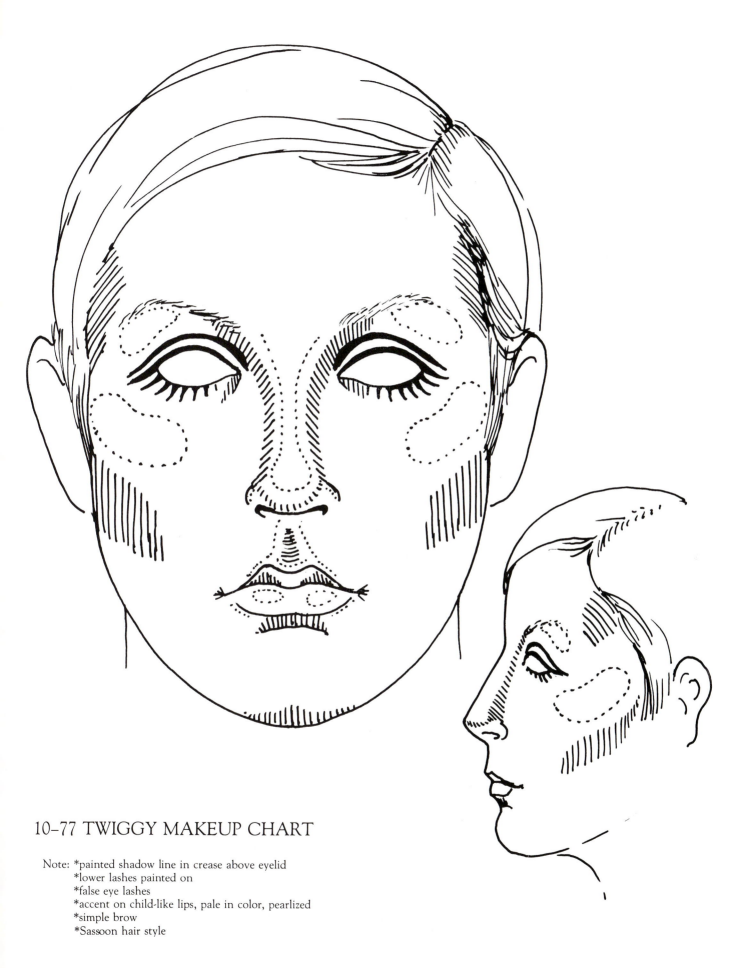

10-77 TWIGGY MAKEUP CHART

Note: *painted shadow line in crease above eyelid
    *lower lashes painted on
    *false eye lashes
    *accent on child-like lips, pale in color, pearlized
    *simple brow
    *Sassoon hair style

10-78 Cecily Tyson, wearing her hair braided in "corn rows." *United Press International Photo.*

Blacks began to claim their pride in race and color, and created their own version of bouffant — a round halo of curly hair known as the Afro, Illus. 10-80. Actress Cecily Tyson wore her hair plaited in corn rows, Illus. 10-78. Naomi Sims, top black model, appeared on the 1969 *Life* cover, her makeup a subtle blend of highlights and shadows, with red-brown lipstick. Cosmetics were finally available for black skins.

10-79 Hair style variations: a. Beehive, 1961,
  b. The fall, designed by Kenneth, 1968. Matching lengths of hair were attached to the top of the head.
  c. The flip, 1961, worn for casual occasions.
  d. Sasoon geometric cut.

10-80 Angela Davis wearing Afro hair style.   *United Press International.*

1960's MEN

1960 was the decade of extremes in hair styles for men, ranging from the abundant hair of President Kennedy, Illus. 10–81, to shaved heads. At the beginning of the sixties, business men still wore their hair trimmed short above the ears. The influence of youthful rebellion gained momentum, Beatlemania flourished, and furor continued in the schools. The ultimate witness to the death of the crew cut was the outcropping among the establishment of sideburns, moustaches, and hair which touched the ears and extended to the shirt collar. Hair represented a new channel to the fountain of youth. Hair "styling" for men was born, with all the attendant pampering usually associated with beauty parlors for women.

The transitions during this period can be clearly seen in the slicked-back hair of Ed Sullivan, which contrasted with the mops of the Beatles, when the popular rock stars first appeared on his TV show, Illus. 10–83; in the look-alike long hair of the guys and the gals, Illus. 10–84; and finally, in the invasion of long hair into the redneck territory of the hard hats, Illus. 10–85. Meanwhile, the bare pates of those influenced by the "Skin Heads" in London, as well as the Hari Krishna, began to polka dot this flowing sea of hair.

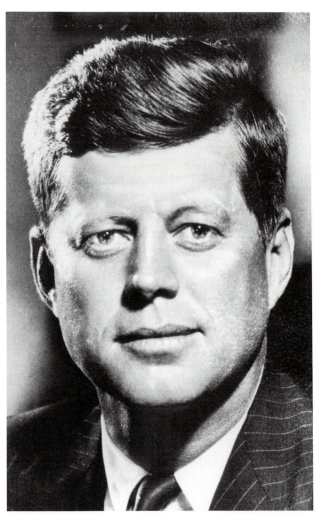

10–81 President John F. Kennedy. The official photograph distributed March, 1961.   *United Press International Photo.*

10–82 Shaved heads appeared in the 1960's. In London, they were a reactionary group called skin heads; in the U. S. they were usually associated with the Hara Krishna, a religious group.   *(photographer) Bruce Wilson*

214

10-83 The Beetles as they appeared on the Ed Sullvan show in 1964. *United Press International Photo.*

10-84 Long hair worn by both sexes. *United Press International Photo.*

10-85 Long hair invades the conservative strong hold of the hard-hat workers. *United Press International Photo.*

1970's WOMEN

Makeup in the 1970's could be typified by the look of Farrah Faucett, a star of television, Illus. 10–86. Contouring was used to stress the cheekbones, the lips were applied carefully with a lip liner, and a gloss added over the lipstick. The hard eye line of the sixties was now smudged on the edges and blended into the eye shadow. The orbital bone above the eye was highlighted, and the brows were natural, but controlled by plucking. Fawcett's long tousled hair style was popularized by the hair stylist, Jose Eber, who instructed his clients to bend over and "Shake Your Head Darling."[18] Others preferred long hair crinkled into a tight permanent wave, which could be washed and drip-dried without the use of rollers, Illus. 10–89c. The layered cut of Olympic skating star Dorothy Hamil, Illus. 10–89a, sent women in search of similar cuts which could move freely, and yet retain their shape. Those who could not make up their minds whether to have their hair long or short, opted for the "shag," a short-all-over cut, except for a fringe of longer hair at the nape of the neck, Illus. 10–89b. Black hair fashions included long, dangling braids, sometimes interspersed with beads. Compare Illus. 10–88 with the Egyptian wig, in Illus. 10–2.

10–86 Farrah Fawcett gained fame in *Charlie's Angels*, a television series.   *United Press International Photo.*

10–87 SEVENTIES MAKEUP CHART, FARRAH FAWCETT

Note: *Dotted lines indicate highlight; dashed lines indicate rouge placement
  *Cheek and eye contouring are stressed
  *Smudged shadow around eye, next to lashes

10–88 Tribal style made up of tiny braids, reflects Egyptian influence.   *(photographer) Bruce Wilson.*

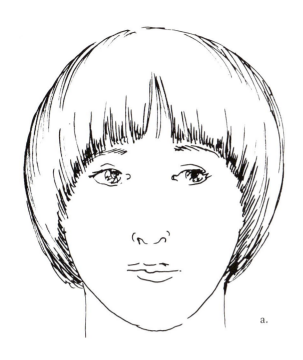

a.

10–89 Hair style variations, 1970's:
  a. Dorothy Hamil cut
  b. The Shag
  c. "Wet Dog" look of drip-dry style

b.

c.

1970's MEN

In the early seventies, school boards generally conceded that style of hair was an individual decision. Even the most conservative preacher, TV newsman, or politician, now wore longer hair. Grayed gentlemen with short cuts were known to say to their barber, "My wife says you should give me some sideburns." Hair dryers became standard equipment for men to chase their "blow dry" cuts into place, Illus. 10–92.

Those men without flourishing heads of hair bought wigs. In a surge of reverse wigging, young men stuffed their long hair under short wigs by day to meet the requirements of their jobs.

White versions of the Afro appeared on Caucasians like Art Garfunkel, Illus. 10–90. Afro wigs became abundant even in pastel colors. However, by the mid-seventies, the pendulum of change was weighted with so much hair that it began to swing back. Young men, particularly in the gay community, started to return to a shorter, cleaner cut, in order to disassociate from the establishment.

10–90 Art Garfunkel, wearing a "white" Afro.   *United Press International Photo.*

10–91 Trends begin a return to the more conservative "business man" look.   *(photographer) Bruce Wilson*

10–92a Blow dry Cut.

10–92b Typical hair and beard style worn by artists and professors in the 1970's.   *(photographer) Suzanne Dietz*

1980's WOMEN

If there was a dominant influence in the eighties, it was not a person, it was the media. Many styles co-existed and trends moved off center stage as rapidly as they entered. The *Time* magazine cover, August 30, 1982, featured the new body-conscious woman. Equal rights for women brought with it a desire for body fitness to complement a new sense of self-confidence. Participation in sports demanded simpler hair care. In collaboration and competition with men, the eighties woman no longer needed to win her place by feminine artifice. This did not mean an end to the use of cosmetics, merely a change in the basic motivation for its use. Its use varied according to the occasion.

Americans watched the courtship and marriage of Prince Charles with fascination, and there was an instant eruption of Princess Diana hair cuts, Illus.

10–93. Long hair was sometimes done up in variations of French braids, Illus. 10–95a. Looking backward to the fifties, women chose the mannish cut, complete with angled sideburns, Illus. 10–95b. Occasionally, the short mannish cut was slicked back a la Valentino. There were reflections of the iconoclastic images of the New Wave music groups. Entertainer Grace Jones took the flattop to its extreme, by creating a geometric silhouette, with the sides of the head shaved, and the hair extended on top, ending in a flat cut. Singer Cindy Lauper led her followers in multicolored hair. Makeup became more "natural," with the elimination of contouring. Extreme variations included the use of a black line totally surrounding the eye, off-beat colors of brownish purple to magenta for lipstick, and Geisha-inspired porcelain skin.

10–93 Princess Diana hairstyle.

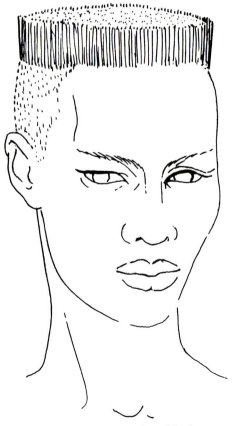

10–94 Grace Jones, entertainer and model, abstracts the flat-top into the geometric look.

10–95 Hair style variations, 1980:
   a. French braids
   b. Mannish cut, reflects crew cut of 1940's.

a.

b.

1980's MEN

The decade is one of wide diversity and multiple choice. The general look of the early 1980's was shorter hair which touched the ears but cleared the collar, reflecting a deliberate return to the 1950's, particularly on the part of the young. Men, weary of the blow dryer, returned to an easier wash and dry routine. The sideburns began to creep upward, until for some they were defined with a straight cut even with the top of the ear. Many men retained a queue at the nape of the neck, a vestigial remainder of formerly long hair, while others sprouted an unshaven stubble, influenced by Don Johnson in the popular TV show, *Miami Vice*.

Meanwhile, iconoclasts arose from the New Wave music influence, where the image breakers affected anything to shock, such as heads shaved except for a

10-96 Hair and makeup in the manner of Boy George and the Culture Club.

10-97 Steve Simpson, Wrestler, 1987, sports long curly hair.
(photographer) Doug Milner

224

10-98 Styles go their separate ways and the sexes are no longer differenciated by their hair. *(photographer) Doug Milner*

band of hair on top, hair glued into upright points, geisha makeup, and eyebrows extended back and over the ears, Illus. 10-96. Discord was in, harmony out. The makeup worn by Boy George, Michael Jackson, and Prince did not start an avalanche of makeup for men, despite their popularity and wide visibility.

The pervasive influence of the media is reflected in the look of the athletes. Formerly conservative in their personal style, their public exposure led to the development of distinct personae. Men such as runner Carl Lewis adapted the geometric flattop introduced by Grace Jones, while wrestlers like Steve Simpson, Illus. 10-97, affected a flowing cascade of long hair. As the decade came to a close, hair styles had become interchangeable between the sexes.

APPLYING FACIAL HAIR

Supplies

Alcohol or acetone: Solvent used to remove spirit gum; purchase at drug store.

Brush, cheap: Used to apply latex to the skin, this brush may have to be sacrificed, because the latex may dry in the bristles as you are working. Chinese water color brush, or utility brush.

Chamois skin or silk scarf: Used to press and hold beard in place while spirit gum is drying.

Combs, wide-tooth and rat-tail: The wide teeth are needed to rake through and straighten the crepe hair, without removing too many fibers. The rat-tail is useful for shaping and lifting the hair.

Crepe hair: Wool fibers braided together with strings. Available in natural hair colors; sold by the yard.

Eyebrow pencil: Used to mark outline of beard and mustache on skin.

Hair brush, wide-bristled: Used to shape and dress hair and beard.

Hair spray: Used to hold final shape of beard or wig.

Liquid latex: Used to form beards and attach the hairs for permanent hair pieces. Water soluble until dry. Order in flesh or tan. Ben Nye Liquid Latex is less apt to stick to itself when dry.

Mustache wax: Wax which is used to shape the ends of mustache, available at drug store or beauty supply. Can also use Derma Wax from theatrical supply.

Scissors: Used to prepare and trim the beard, they should be the narrow-bladed barber's scissors—sharp.

Spirit gum, matte: Adhesive for attaching facial hair. It comes in a bottle with its own brush.

Toupee plaster: Used to attach beards or wigs. The most useful form of this double-faced tape is that packaged in individual strips, like Band-Aids, with peel-off paper strips, allowing easy transfer to the face. It also comes in rolls with paper backing.

Wig lace, or tulle: Wig lace may be ordered from a makeup supply house, or tulle from a local fabric store. Do not confuse this with nylon net—the tulle is softer and has a finer mesh. Try to get as near a flesh tone as possible, since the beard is shaped on the fabric.

Wig and Beard Supplies and Sources

For made-to-order wigs and beards: Bob Kelly Wig Creation, 151 West 46th St., New York, NY, 10036, (212) 819-0030.

For further sources on supplies, wigs, and beards, see page 302.

Rather than ordering ready dressed wigs, you may have a local fashion wig shop where a selection can be made. Choose a full wig with the hair attached in close rows, which allows restyling. Also, some hairdressers will respond to the challenge of creating a period hair style if you provide adequate drawings or pictures of what you need.

Preparation of Crepe Hair

Crepe hair comes in ropes, braided with string. Unless you want a very kinky beard, the hair will need to be straightened. Move a ways from the end of the braid and snip the string. Pull it out. Wet the hair in warm water, squeezing out the excess moisture between towels. Stretch it by wrapping it around the back of a straight chair, and leave it to dry overnight. The tension applied in stretching determines the amount of wave left in the hair. You may prefer to place it between towels, and lightly stretch it as you iron it dry.

Selecting Colors

Study the hair or wig of the person for whom the beard is to be made. You will see that there are many variations of colors among the hairs. Choose at least two, or even three shades of crepe hair from which to construct the facial hair. A greying beard may be constructed to show streaks of uneven greying, by using a mixture of medium grey, dark grey, and white.

Making the Beard with Latex

The following instructions are for making a beard on a net and latex base that may be used repeatedly. A similar technique can be used to construct the beard against the skin, using spirit gum to adhere it and acetone to release it; the inside of the beard can then be coated with more spirit gum, or with latex, to make it stronger.

10-99

1. Lay the hair on a flat surface. Gently comb the end of the rope of hair, raking against the flat surface. Discard the tufts which come out (or save them as stubble). The end should lose its "cut" look, and have a natural feathered appearance.

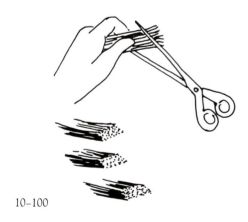

10-100

2. Cut off desired length with scissors, making sure it is long enough to allow for final trimming. Hold the cut-off feathered length in your hand and bevel-cut the opposite end. Lay it *carefully* aside, and continue cutting lengths. You may prepare the colors separately and mix them as you assemble the beard, or lay one color on top of the other, and comb through both to blend.

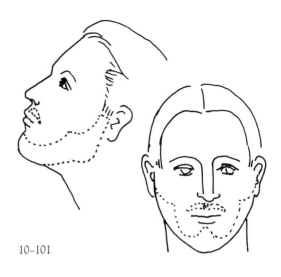

10-101

3. Refer to the beard design established by your research, and outline the shape of the facial hair on the actor's face, using an eyebrow pencil or brush. Indicate not only the top shape of the beard, but also how far it extends under the chin and along the jaw line. It could be useful to observe the natural beard line of the actor, unless the character designed requires a different shape.

4. Net is used as a reinforcing base on which to build the beard. Apply toupee tape at sideburn area, and on top of chin.

10-102

Stretch net around chin and up along jaw line, letting tape hold it in place. Cover marked areas. Slit and overlap at chin, or where necessary to make it fit. Trim away excess, leaving one-half inch outside lines.

227

5. Paint a line of latex one-fourth inch wide, starting under the chin, along the edge, next to the neck. Make it a thick, gooey coat, as it must catch and hold the ends of the hairs. Do not paint a very long area at a time, or the latex will dry too soon.

Keep water nearby to rinse brush after each application; stroke brush over a bar of soap and blot out excess water.

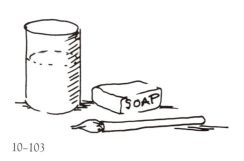

10-103

10-104

6. Study your beard design. (You do have one, don't you?) Place hair in direction it would naturally grow. It should seem to go downward in a vertical direction. Note arrows in chart, Illus. 10-107. Beveled cuts, particularly for the sides of the face, will make the hair attach in a natural manner.

10-105

7. Pick up a length of hair, and trim again to insure a neat, beveled edge against the latex. Press with the handle of a brush. Keep it clean with water (or acetone, if using spirit gum). Keep in mind at all times that you want to attach the ends of the hairs, not the sides; that is the reason for the bevel cut.

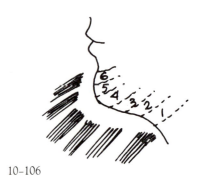

10-106

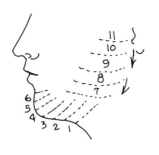

10-107

8. Continue painting small areas of latex and apply hair all along the lower line; then start another row above it. Continue until rows 1, 2, and 3 are covered. Reverse angle of bevel cut, rows 4, 5, and 6, Illus. 10-107. As you begin to layer the sides of the face, let the beveled edges help create the natural fall of the hair. Note that the beard is usually less full on the sides. Be careful to apply the hair evenly along the final line, and make every effort to embed the ends into the latex, so that the latex shows as little as possible. A hair dryer can be used to speed the drying of the latex.

9. After the latex is dry, use the hair brush and *gently* and *carefully* brush the beard downward. Some hairs not caught by the latex may come out. Fear not. Use rat-tail comb to lift and straighten.

10-108

NOTE: When removing beard freshly made with latex, peel it off carefully, and lightly dust talcum powder on the inside surface to keep it from sticking to itself.

Mustache

1. Outline mustache area on actor's face.
2. Cut net, and attach to face with tape.
3. Paint mustache area with latex on one side.
4. Choose a small wedge of hair, bevel cut the ends carefully, and apply in the direction you want the mustache to grow, starting at the outside edge. Repeat with another layer next to it and continue until you reach the center.

10-109

5. Begin again on the opposite side, reversing the direction of the hair. The net will serve to hold the two pieces of the mustache together.
6. Carefully brush the mustache, or comb it.

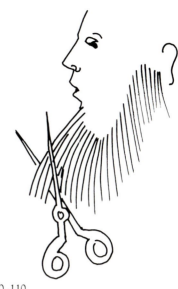

10-110

7. Both beard and mustache are now ready to trim according to the desired style. Hold the scissors vertically and trim small snippets at a time. Curls can be made with curling iron, or on hot rollers. Spray to set.

Building Beard with Spirit Gum

1–3. Follow steps 1,2, and 3 under *Making a Beard with Latex*.
4. Mark out the rows of hair with eyebrow pencil (Illus. 10-107) so that the placement of each tuft of hair is more exact.
5. Paint spirit gum over entire area for beard. Wait until it is tacky—test by tapping with finger.
6 and 7. Follow steps 6 and 7 under *Making a Beard with Latex*, only substitute spirit gum for latex.
8. Hold a chamois or silk scarf, folded on a diagonal, against the chin and pull back against the beard to secure it while it dries.
9. Smooth beard with wide-toothed comb, moving in the natural growth direction. Trim.
10. Spray to set.

Eyebrows

The same method used for making mustache would be used to construct bushy eyebrows. Block out real brows with soap and greasepaint, powdered, before attaching new brows with spirit gum.

229

Removing Hairpieces after Construction

Latex base: Carefully peel away the hair pieces. Lightly powder latex side with baby powder to keep it from sticking to itself.

Spirit gum: With acetone on cotton pad, apply along edges, and gently peel the beard away. Add more acetone as it peels back.

Attaching Beard and Mustache

The facial hair pieces can be attached with spirit gum directly to the clean skin, or on top of completed, powdered makeup. The latter method is less abrasive to the skin. Latex is not a satisfactory adhesive for securing a beard—it will sweat off.

1. To reattach beard pieces, hold them against the face to mark the line of attachment, so you will know where to apply the spirit gum.

2. Coat beard and mustache area of the skin, and the inside of the beard pieces with spirit gum. Let dry till tacky.

3. When both pieces are very tacky to touch, place them against the glued areas, and press firmly. The silk scarf or chamois skin can be used to exert pressure during the final drying. Keep acetone handy for cleaning fingers and brush.

4. Blend edge next to net with makeup, stroking in color to cover any latex which might show. The beard made with latex may have an edge which looks unnatural for intimate theatre. If desired, each night, paint a line of spirit gum along the latex edge where it joins the skin, and press a few fresh crepe hairs into it.

5. Reshape beard with hairbrush and rat-tail comb. Spray with hair spray.

Quick Change Method of Applying Hair Pieces

Apply strips of toupee tape along beard and mustache line, and press hair pieces in place.

After Performance

Peel beard and mustache away from the skin carefully, and immediately pin them to the wig stand. Remove spirit gum from the face with alcohol on a cotton ball. After many uses, the excess buildup of spirit gum on the hairpieces can also be removed with alcohol.

How to Measure for Wigs and Beards

Lee Baygan gives clear pictorial information in his book *Makeup for Theatre, Film and Television* on how to order ready-made beards. In general, he suggests that you secure Saran Wrap over the chin and mustache area (or over the hair area for wig) by holding it tightly in place with overlapping layers of Scotch tape. When a tape shell is built, outline the desired shape of the mustache, beard or hair with eyebrow pencil or Magic Marker. Remove, and reinforce as necessary. Allow four to five weeks for delivery, and indicate period, color and style.[19] Wig sources are listed in Appendix.

Care of Wigs

Wigs can be cleaned in acetone, or special wig cleaner ordered from theatrical supply houses. Shampooing a wig as if it were human hair will result in matting and tangling, and is not recommended.

Reference Books for Further Information on Hair

If you should want to learn to ventilate your own hair pieces, and learn more advanced techniques concerning this subject, consult the references at the end of the chapter.

10-111 Bust of Herodotus, Roman sculpture. Wig and beard study. The Metropolitan Museum of art., gift of George F. Baker.

Storage of Wigs and Beards during Production

Store wigs and beards on styrofoam wig forms available at beauty supply houses. To make a simple base, drill a 3/4" hole in the center of an 8" board, insert a 12" × 3/4" dowel and fasten with white glue. If the wig forms are unavailable, place a plastic gallon jug upside down over the dowel, put the wig on the jug, and pin the beard on with a corsage or T-pin.

BIBLIOGRAPHY

Batterberry, Michael and Ariane. *Fashion, the Mirror of History.* (New York: Greenwich House, 1982).

Bernard, Barbara. *Fashion in the 60's.* (London: Academy Editions; New York: St. Martin's Press, 1978).

Bernier, Oliver. *The Eighteenth-Century Woman.* (Garden City, N.Y.: Doubleday and Co., Inc. Published in association with The Metropolitan Museum of Art, New York. 1981).

Blum, Stella, Ed. *Eighteenth-Century French Fashion Plates in Full Color.* 64 Engravings from the "Galerie des Modes," 1779–1787. (New York: Dover Publications, Inc., 1982).

Cunnington, C. Willet and Phillis. *Handbook of English Costume in the Eighteenth Century.* (London: Faber and Faber Ltd., 1957).

Dorner, Jane. *Fashion in the Forties and Fifties.* (New Rochelle, N.Y.: Arlington House Publisher, 1975).

Galico, Paul. *The Revealing Eye.* Personalities of the 1920's. Photos: Nicholas Muray. (New York: Antteneum, 1967).

Hope, Thomas, *Costumes of the Greeks and Romans.* (formerly titled: *Costume of the Ancients*). Two Vols. bound as one. (New York: Dover Publications, Inc. 1962).

Keeman, Brigid. *The Women We Wanted to Look Like.* (New York: St. Martin's Press, 1977).

Kobal, John, Ed. *Movie-Star Portraits of the Forties.* 163 Glamor Photos. (New York: Dover Publications, Inc., 1977).

Newton, Stella Mary. *Renaissance Theatre Costume and the Sense of the Historic Past.* (London: Rapp and Whiting Limited. 1975). An in-depth study of the emotional attitudes of the period and their influence on the style.

Ridgeway, Brunilde Sismondo. *The Severe Style in Greek Sculpture.* (Princeton, N.J.: Princeton University Press, 1970). Excellent studies of front and back views of Greek hair styles.

Scott, Nora. *The Daily Life of the Ancient Egyptians.* Metropolitan Museum Booklet.

Teichmann, Howard, *The Life and Times of Alice Roosevelt Longworth.* (Englewood Cliffs, N.J.: Prentice-Hall, Inc., 1979).

_____. *Egyptian Wall Paintings: The Metropolitan Museum's Collection of Facsimiles.* Reprinted from The Metropolitan Museum of Art Bulletin, Spring 1979, by the Metropolitan Museum of Art.

_____. *This Fabulous Century. Sixty Years of American Life.* Editors of *Time-Life Books.* (New York: Time-Life Books, 1969).

Zamoyska, Betka. *Queen Elizabeth I.* (New York: McGraw-Hill Book Company, 1981).

NOTES

[9] Bill Severn. *The Long and the Short of It.* 5000 Years of Fun and Fury Over Hair. (New York: David McKay, Inc. 1971).

[10] Maggie Angeloglou. *A History of Make-up.* (London: Studio Vista, 1965).

[11] Severn. *The Long and the Short of It.*

[12] Angeloglou. *A History of Makeup.*

[13] Edmund Vincent Gillon, Jr. *The Gibson Girl and Her America.* The Best Drawings of Charles Dana Gibson. (New York: Dover Publications, Inc., 1969), p 95.

[14] Gillon. *The Gibson Girl and Her America.* p. 114.

[15] Michael Schau. *J. C. Leyendecker.* (New York: Watson-Guptill Pub. 1974). p. 110.

[16] Schau. *J. C. Leyendecker.* p. 30.

[17] Larry Carr. *Four Fabulour Faces.* The Evolution of Garbo, Swanson, Crawford and Dietrich. (New York: Arlington House, 1970).

[18] Jose Eber. *Shake Your Head Darling!* (New York: Warner Books, 1983).

[19] Lee Baygan. *Makeup for Theatre, Film and Television.* A Step by Step Photographic Guide. New York: Drama Book Publishers, 1982.

[20] _____ *Danjuro Ichikawa.* Wood block prints of roles played by Kabuki actor. (Tokyo: Hatsujiro Fukuda, 1896).

11

Patterning: Styling Human Features into Patterns

Most dramatic productions require realistic makeup. However, when the directorial concept calls for stylization—makeup becomes more theatrical, demanding a selection and simplification of facial forms. When this happens, the subtlety of realistically blended edges of shadows and highlights gives way to the formation of definite patterns of light and dark. Carried to its extreme, the effect is similar to the highly styled Kumadori makeup of the Japanese Kabuki or the Chinese Opera.

11-1a Danjuro Ichikawa, Kabuki Actor.[20]

11-2 Makeup design for the Monkey King character in the Chinese Opera.

233

Such makeup is non-realistic but has its origin in the observation of reality. According to Chang Pe-Chin, in *Chinese Opera and the Painted Face*, reality is first studied thoroughly then variations are tried until the most effective facsimile is found.[21] The mental and emotional attitudes of the characters are expressed with highly styled lines and patterns. See Illus. 11–1 featuring a Kabuki actor, and Illus. 11–3, makeup mask design from the Chinese Opera.

EXERCISE FOURTEEN:

Natural Shading Translated into Patterns

Perhaps the best way to understand patterning is to develop a simplification of the planes, shadows, and highlights based on your own aging makeup. In this process, the shapes of these areas become distinct, eliminating the fused edges.

1. Before beginning, study carefully the examples of stylized makeup, Illus. 11–3 through 11–6.

2. Place a sheet of tracing paper over your personal makeup aging chart on which you have recorded and shaded and highlighted areas. Use a lead pencil to draw around the shapes of the shadows. Be aware of how the patterns flow over the contours of the face. Eliminate the subtle blending from shadow into base and find shapes of the shadows.

3. In the same way, select the shapes of the highlighted areas. Not everything will be highlight or shadow; leave a space for base.

4. Apply base to your face.

5. Mix highlight and shadow colors the same way you did for aging, only make them a little lighter and a little darker than usual. The sharper the contrast between the three values of base, highlight, and shadow, the stronger the stylization will appear. However, if a production concept calls for a subtle stylization, then decrease the contrast in value. For this exercise, stick to colors related to natural flesh tones. After further experience, they might evolve into more intense colors. Do not divide the face into all highlight and shadow; let the base play its part in the overall design.

6. Outline the shadow areas on your face and fill them in with the flat of the brush.

7. Outline and fill in the highlight areas.

8. Stand back eight or ten feet from the mirror and see if the patterns project over the distance. Adjust values and areas as necessary. You may want to introduce a secondary shadow tone. There may be sides of certain patterns where you feel a blended edge would work better. Experiment with a combination of hard edged patterns and blended edges.

9. Powder with baby powder. Brush. Remove final powder with a wet sponge.

10. Make a new chart, recording your final patterned makeup.

By now, you should begin to see that the essential individuality of a face depends on the interrelationship between features taken as a whole. We recognize each other more through the overall pattern of a face than through details.

The purpose of the exercises in this chapter is to show how stylized makeup can be evolved out of realism and serves to intensify either the structural or emotional qualities reflected by the face. It is possible to lift out and stress different aspects embedded in the same countenance. In the following examples, the features of an elderly gentleman are first developed into a chart stressing the melancholy qualities of his face. Then, choosing the aspect of strength indicated by his features, a series of makeup charts begin with a realistic conception of the facial planes and then moves through several stages of simplification into pure pattern. The result is very similar to Kumadori makeup. Such stylization can be based on the physical muscular structure of the face or on an interpretation of attitude.

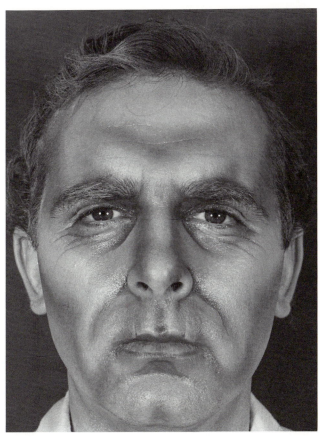

11-3 and 11-5 Age makeup using realistic shading of highlights and shadows.   (photographer) Bruce Wilson.

11-4 and 11-6 Stylized patterns of light and shadow developed from naturalistic shading.   (photographer) Bruce Wilson

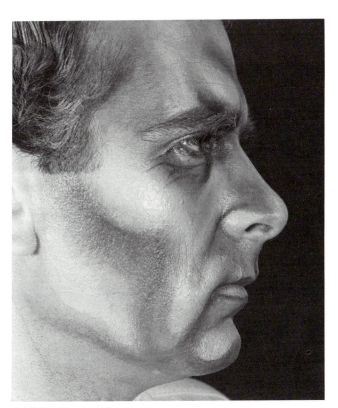

11-5 Profile of 11-3.   (photographer) Bruce Wilson

11-6 Profile of 11-4.   (photographer) Bruce Wilson

11–7 through 11–9 Sequence illustrating stylization evolved from a photograph.   *(photographer) Karl Stone.*

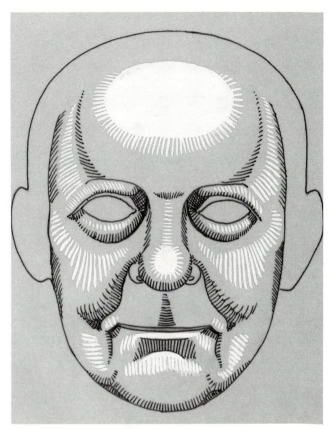

11-8

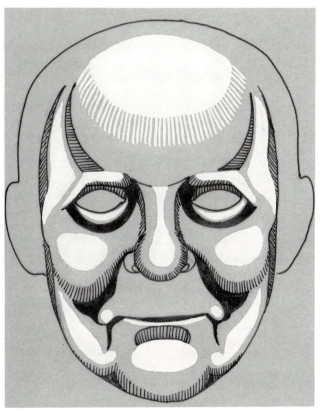

11-9

EXERCISE FIFTEEN:

Patterning from a Photograph

1. Select a full front, *large*, non-smiling photograph which portrays striking character, such as Illus. 11–14.

2. Explore the face by tracing features with lead pencil, as in Chapter 9, Steps 2 through 5 under *Comparing Photograph With Your Face*. Discover the basic planes and locate the highlights and shadows. Study the sequence from photograph to patterning in Illus. 11–7 through 11–13 and Illus. 11–14 through 11–21.

3. Transfer the contour information to your personal makeup chart blank, defining shadows with parallel lines and highlights with dots.

4. For further refining, lay another tracing paper on top of your last stylization and continue the selecting and refining of shapes until the features have been reduced to their essence. If you carry the process far enough, you may end up with a Kumadori stylization, as in the series developed in Illus. 11–14–11–21. In the final design, the colors of the areas would be chosen for psychological impact and would become more abstract. See Plates 7 and 8 in color section at the back of the book.

Stylization is a potent design tool for our theatre. When wedded with a strong directorial concept, it enlarges the actor's statement and adds greatly to the dramatic impact. Makeup can simplify an actor's task by telegraphing at one glance the distilled nature of the character, leaving the actor free to refine and elaborate upon it. Although it took centuries for the Oriental theatre to evolve its evocative makeup traditions, we need not wait. Using their example, we can select specific character studies for a given play and develop them into distilled personalities which rise out of, and integrate with, the script.

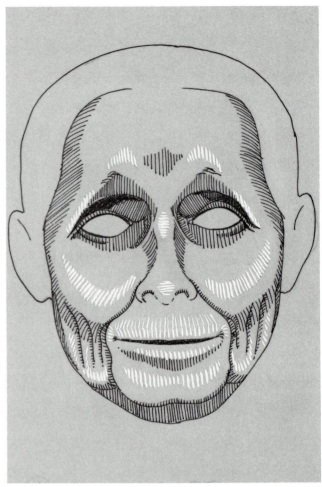

11-11

11-10 through 11-13 Sequence illustrating stylization
evolved from a photograph of a 100 year old woman.

11-10   *(photographer) Beth Odle*

238

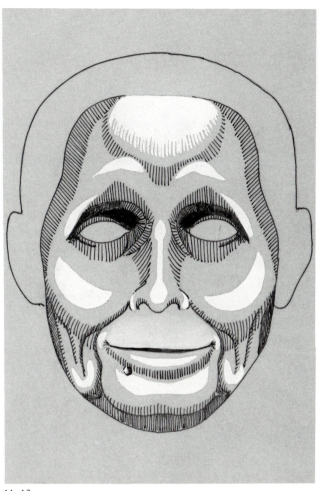

11–12

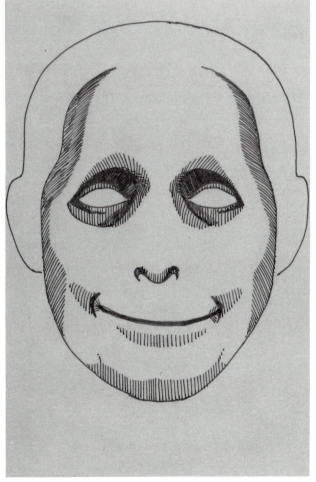

11–13

11-14   *(photographer) Karl Stone*

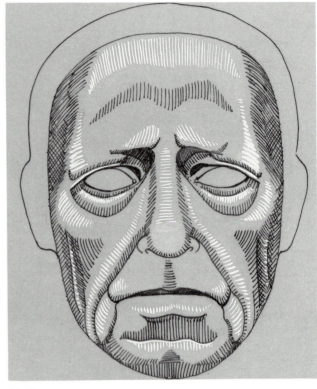

11-15

11-14 In studying the face in photograph 11-14, one can discover the emotional quality of suffering, as well as the evidence of great strength. Charts 11-15 through 11-19 accent the aspect of suffering.

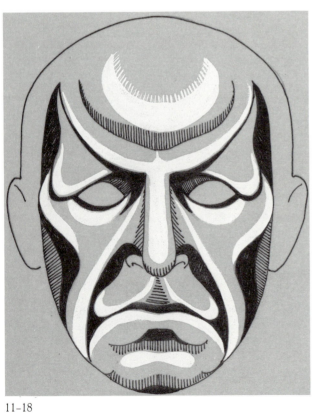

11-18

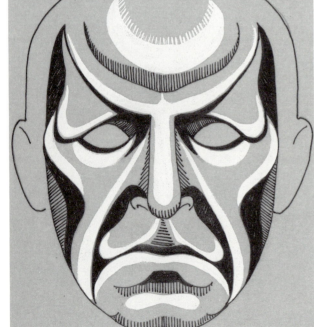

11-19

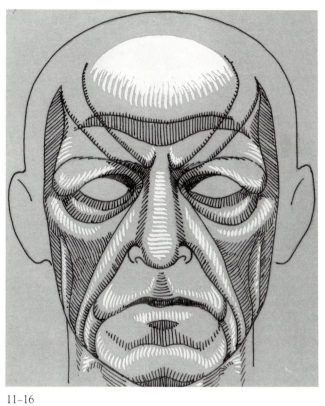

11–16

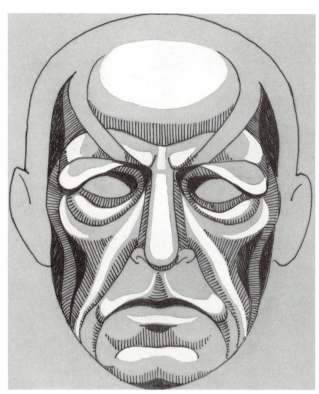

11–17

The quality of strength is selected and refined in charts 11–16 through 11–21.

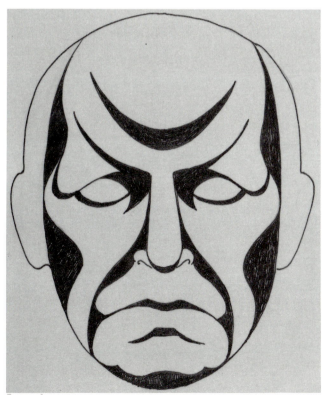

11–20

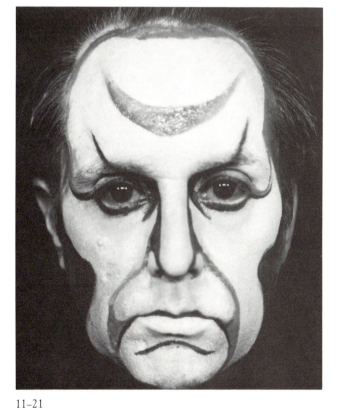

11–21

INTEGRATING STYLIZED DESIGN INTO TOTAL PRODUCTION

Only an occasional production will call for the extreme stylization of Kumadori makeup. However, the process is valuable for reaching beyond traditional realism in order to make a more dynamic statement. The stylization should be integrated into the makeup designs for the entire cast. A strong directorial hand and eye would be presupposed.

Stylized makeup for a specific play is exemplified by an Everyman Player production of Shakespeare's *The Tempest*.[22] The directorial concept was to place Prospero on a sunken Atlantis island, where everything "did suffer a sea change," and where the elements of sea life permeated all designs.

Prospero is interpreted as a visionary. Design elements are chosen to reflect the mystique of this magic powers. The design concept synthesizes the inner iridescence of a jelly fish, the watchful eye of an octopus, and the intricate weavings of a brain coral. A nylon tricot beard is softened by the floating strands of a feather boa. His magnetic eyes dominate the features which have been intensified by stylization. See Illus. 11–22 through 11–24.

When Prospero exerts his power and causes the storm which wrecks the ship, the characters from the mainland also reflect sea motifs. Their garb becomes a combination of land fashion and sea fantasy. In garments which reflect the qualities of water—transparent, shining, floating—they arrive in slow motion into the underwater world controlled by Prospero.

Old Gonzolo, a gentle friend, is cloaked in a moss green cape transparent except for a web of veins which seems to be an extension of his care-worn features.

Wearing a cape patterned after the spines of a sea urchin, King Alonso reflects his sorrow over the believed death of his son. Calaban blends with the coral encrusted scenery, mottled in the manner of a Sargassum fish. Trinculo reflects the bright yellows of the Long-nose Butterfly fish, and Stephano takes on the clownish colors of the Harlequin fish.

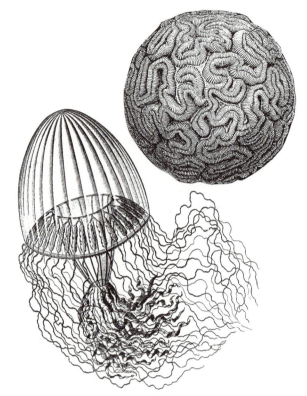

11–22 Brain coral and jelly fish, prototypes for design of Prospero headdress.[23]

11–23 Design for Prospero's makeup and headdress in *The Tempest*, by Shakespeare.

11-24 Actor Hal Proske as Prospero. The inner lights of his magic dome were operated by remote control.

11-26 Design for Alonso, in *The Tempest*.

11-25 Makeup design for Old Gonzolo in *The Tempest*.

11-27 Actor David Cooper as Gonzolo in *The Tempest*.

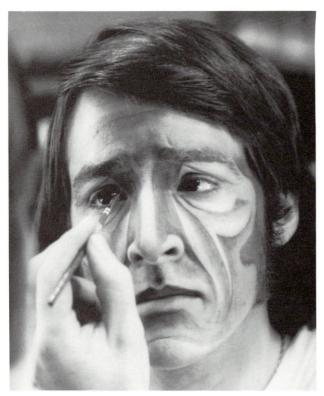

11-28 Ronlin Foreman in makeup as Alonso, King of Naples.

11-29a Design for Ariel in *The Tempest*, with motifs derived from sea anemone and flying fish.

The design for Ariel is based on a combination of elements of the flying fish and sea anemone. His face bears the marks of wood graining impressed there during his imprisonment in a tree. These patterns flow into the floating streamers of the anemone. At the end, when he is freed by Prospero, the fins symbolize his flight to freedom.

The research for these designs was based on a study of photographs of underwater creatures. In looking through the books, the images were first noted because of their color or form. Later, specific characters were aligned with their visual counterpart. Thus sea images permeated all design decisions, unified the selection of color, texture and line, and extended from settings, properties and costumes—to makeup.

NOTES

[21]Chang Pe-Chin, Ph.D., *Chinese Opera and the Painted Face*. (Taipei, Taiwan: Mei Ya Publishers, Inc. Rev. Ed., 1978).

[22]The Everyman Players, a professional ensemble company founded in 1957, directed by Orlin Corey, with productions designed by Irene Corey. Toured widely in the U. S. and abroad from 1958 to 1978.

[23]Ernst Haeckel. *Art Forms in Nature*. (New York: Dover Pub. Inc., 1974), p. 9, p. 36.

[24]Irene Corey, ". . . *First You Find the Animal!*" *Dramatics*, 47, No. 3 (Jan/Feb. 1976). pp. 10–15.

[25]Corey. *Dramatics*, 47, No. 3, (Jan/Feb. 1976).

[26]Arthur Fauquez. *Reynard the Fox*. (New Orleans, La. P.O. Box 8067:Anchorage Press, 1962).

12

Styling from Nature

Nature is a never-ending source of designs for makeup. Whether you are seeking the external reality or the internal spirit, the variations in shapes, colors, and intensities will be inexhaustible. Descending into the microscopic world, the design structure continues with ever more startling rhythms and formations. The forms, patterns, and shapes which nature offers the makeup artist in an array of fishes, birds, insects, flowers, and animals forever eliminates the excuse for mundane designs.

12-1 Lion, courtesy the Dallas Zoo, Dallas Tx.

12-2 Noble, the Lion, played by Allen Shaffer in *Reynard the Fox.*   *(photographer) Jerry Mitchell.*

Selection

Since we are using the face as a canvas without any mask extensions, certain long-nosed creatures will be impossible to create. This excludes those animals which require a longer canvas than our faces provide, such as the toucan, unicorn, anteater, and deer. However, we are still left with multitudes of animals as fair game.

Styling Animals

Plays are usually peopled with humans, but occasionally a playwright will ask an animal to answer the call. The lion is a frequent visitor to the boards as Androcles' debtor or as a frightened coward keeping company with a tin man and a scarecrow. The Greeks were not timid about calling for frogs, birds, or even wasps. The horses of *Equus* have shared the footlights with *Peanuts'* Snoopy and the ever popular stuffed companions of Christopher Robin.

Where does the theatre artist begin to meet the challenge of designing a foxy Reynard, an arrogant toad, or man's ubiquitous friend, the dog? Frequently the animal itself, the most obvious source of all, is overlooked in favor of an accepted stereotype. Ears bounce atop a loose fitting hood worn with an ample pair of footed pajamas, followed by an abject tail. Makeup, an echo of a pale memory of a dog listening to a phonograph, consists of a black spot around one eye, a black nose, and a set of glued-on broomstraw whiskers.

The process of creating animal makeup is always the same; *first you find the animal!*[24] The following instructions for the dog and squirrel illustrate the procedure for creating animal makeup. Plan to execute at least one of these exercises in order to experience the process. The experience will prepare you for the less detailed examples included in the book, as well as for the creation of your own stylization.

STYLING ANIMALS

Creating Dog Makeup

If you are designing makeup for a special dog in a particular script, such as Toto in *The Wizard of Oz*, choose the breed of dog best suited for the character. Once the breed is chosen, find the facial expression which best captures the personality depicted by the author. Any dog lover knows that no two dogs are alike. A well-written play depicting animals will contain as much character delineation for them as for a person.

EXERCISE SIXTEEN:

Making a Chart for a Dog[24]

1. *Photograph*: Choose a photograph which is large enough to show planes and contours of the head. Preferably, it should be a frontal view with the mouth closed. Information on the skull is also very helpful in understanding the structure which lies beneath the fur.

2. *Trace the photograph*: Outline the dominant features: eyes, nose, mouth, chops, cheekbone, chin furrows, and bags. Use extremely thin tracing paper or draw directly on the photograph, using lead pencil.

12-3 Basic lines and planes of a dog's face traced from a photograph.

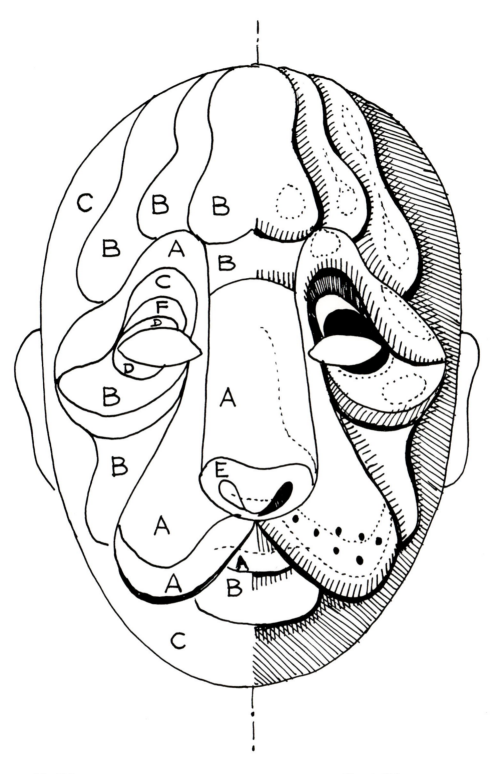

Areas	Mix Colors	Generic Colors
A	Highlight: light cream color	Muted yellow
B	Medium tone: light yellow-brown	Muted yellow plus red-brown
C	Shadow: dark brown	Red-brown
D	Black: Pupil, nostril, whisker dots, thick lines indicating mouth and chops, eye bag, and fold crevices	
E	Light pink	White with touch of moist rouge
F	White: Eye	

12–4 DOG MAKEUP CHART

3. *Ask yourself questions*: What is the angle or axis of the eye? Is there more space between the dog's eyes than the human eyes? Is the nose longer? Wider? Is the chin shorter? What is the slant of the forehead? Can you determine the cheekbone?

4. *Transfer the dog's features to your face chart*: Some portion of the dog's eyes and mouth must correspond to the actor's; the rest of the face can be relocated. For example, notice the following things on this chart for dog makeup:

   a. The dog's eyes do not start at the inner corner of the actor's eyes, but further to the side, away from the nose. This will give the illusion of more space between the eyes. For animal makeup, *always start with the eyes.*

12–5

   b. The pupil of the dog's eye is drawn around the outside corner of the actor's eye and encompasses much of the upper lid.

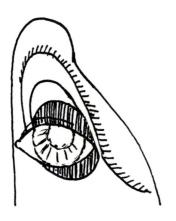

12–6

   c. Ignore the natural eyebrow and draw the dog's eyelid above the false pupil.

   d. Establish the "sad" eye line. The angle of this pouch is important.

   e. Start the side of the dog's nose next to the tear duct and extend it downward. The tip-end of

12–7

the dog's nose will start at the lower *edge* of the actor's nose and extend onto the face. The dog's nostrils will encompass the actor's nostrils and extend onto the face.

   f. Note that the dog's mouth starts at the center of the upper lip and droops down off the actor's mouth, not necessarily extending all the way to the corner.

   g. The dog's chin is about half-way down the actor's chin.

5. *Choose colors for chart*: Select warm colors and light values for the dog's features which need to appear to project forward; the nose, muzzle, and eyelids (Areas A).

The cheekbone, forehead, and chin (Areas B) must be a shade or two darker in order to appear farther back.

For portions of the human face you wish to "erase" or ignore, use an even darker tone (Areas C). Correlate this color with costume. It may be necessary to adjust the actual colors of your chosen animal in order to allow these principles to work. For example, it would be impossible to create the effect of a whole nose jutting forward if the nose were black. It would have to be altered to a lighter shade of grey. However, a black nostril is okay.

Indicate the colors on your chart with colored pencils. Look at the chart from across the room; does the form carry? Make dotted areas to indicate additional highlight and slanted lines to show additional shadow.

Applying Makeup for a Dog

1. Prepare face for makeup.

2. Pre-mix all colors. The planes of the animal's face should appear separate from each other in *value*, as well as color. In the mixing of the colors, paint touching rows of the colors side by side on your wrist or hand. Hold this test patch in front of the mirror and squint at it to check value contrast.

3. Block out your eyebrows with soap.

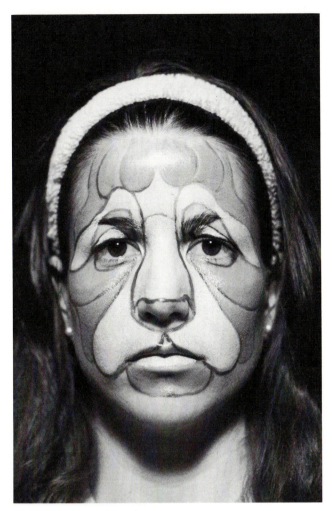

12–9 Fill in areas with colors.

12–8 Establish basic areas with medium toned lines. *(photographer) Nick Dalley*

4. Choose a medium shade and draw in the outlines of features and planes as established on the chart. Start with the eyes, and then draw the mouth and nose in relation to them. Follow the chart carefully. Review the steps outlined under *Transfer the dog's features.*

5. Fill in the light cream color first, all Areas A in solid color. Some blending between areas may be done later by the patting technique.

6. Continue painting, filling in light yellow-brown in all *B* areas and then darker shadow in *C* areas, until the original layout lines have been obliterated.

249

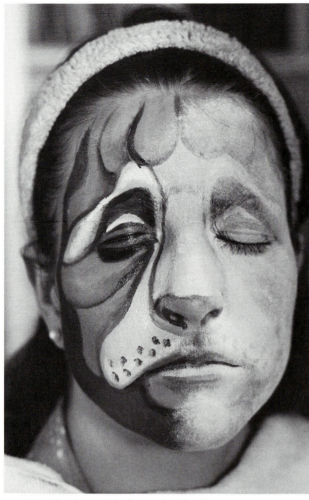

12-10 Powder thoroughly; let set; brush off excess. *(photographer)*
Nick Dalley

10. Black is used to fill in the dog's pupil, which incorporates the top of actor's eye-lid, and to accent lines under Area B, eye pouch, mouth, and chin. Black outlines outer contours of dog's features and is blended by feathering into Areas C.

11. Powder thoroughly. Wipe with damp sponge.

12. Retouch black with brush, holding only a small amount of pigment or use liquid black over for sharper contrast.

7. Highlight where dotted areas appear on the chart by stroking white into the base color already applied. Pat to blend.

8. Create shadow accents by using a dark brown to reset lines in the light yellow-brown areas. This includes the brow furrows, eye pouch and bags, and outline of muzzle. Paint in all shadow lines shown on the chart and then feather them.

9. Fill in dog's nose and the triangle on the upper lip with pink.

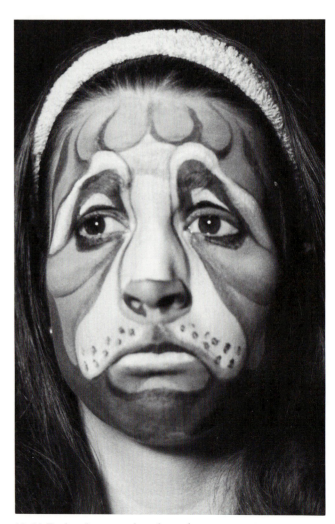

12-11 Dark colors complete the makeup.

BASIC PROCEDURE FOR ADAPTING ANIMAL CHARACTERISTICS TO A HUMAN FACE

1. Find a full front, *large* photograph of the animal or sketch him first hand.

2. Trace the major planes and features to familiarize yourself with the structure.

3. Ask yourself questions, comparing your face with the animal. Most creatures, ourselves included, have two eyes, a nose, and a mouth, but we do not all look alike. The subtle shifting of a feature distinguishes a rabbit from a hare, a mouse from a marmot.

4. Transfer the animal planes to your face chart. The eyes and mouth become points of departure from which animal features can be made larger, smaller, wider, or rounder. The rest of the human features are disregarded, and animal parts are distributed over them.

5. Choose a color scheme based on the principle that light values and warm colors show advancing planes and dark values and cool colors indicate receding planes. Fill in the areas on the chart with colored pencils. Overlay shades of color to create the effect you want. You may need to exercise "artistic license" to make the parts of the face lighter and warmer than nature, in order to make them appear to project forward.

6. Prepare your face for makeup. Wet a bar of soap and rub it backwards into your eyebrows. Spread the hairs to flatten them against the skin. Continue smoothing and pressing with the bar of soap until the brow is "glued" down. Allow to dry before applying greasepaint. If you have particularly heavy brows, you may want to use derma wax.

7. Mix the necessary colors for your animal, based on your chart. Most animals will need two shades of a light warm value and two shades of a darker color. To test for value contrast, paint adjoining strokes of each color and squint at them to see that there are distinct steps between them. Colors on the outer part of the face should blend with the headdress of costume.

8. Choose a medium color (never black!) and draw with your brush the "map" which indicates the areas. *Start with the position of the eyes,* then establish the mouth in relation to the eyes. All these lines will be painted out as you fill in the areas.

9. Fill in the lightest colors first, then the darker ones. Leave black until last.

10. Powder liberally with white baby powder (see Illus. 12–10.) Press powder into all crevices, until all makeup disappears under a white coat of powder. Wait two or three minutes and brush off excess with a soft complexion brush. Finally, wipe with a damp sponge or piece of wet cotton.

11. Black can be reintensified by going over it with a brush containing a little black greasepaint.

12–12 Chimpanzee, Courtesy the Dallas Zoo, Dallas, Texas.
(photographer) Rosa Finsley

251

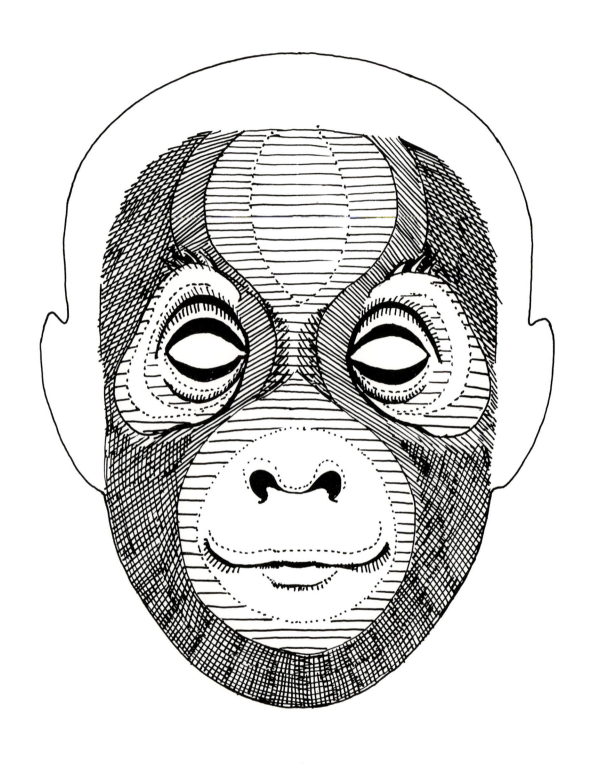

12–13 CHIMPANZEE MAKEUP CHART

I would like to encourage further experimentation with other design possibilities based on animals. I first created animal makeup charts to accompany the play scripts, *Reynard The Fox*[25] and *The Great Cross Country Race*[26] in 1962. These plays were widely toured both in the U.S. and abroad by the Everyman Players. Since that time, stylized animal makeup has become a traditional part of the theatre. The makeup-mask provides mobility of expression for the actor, enlarges his expression, and unlike hard masks does not inhibit vocal projection. The stylized makeup-mask avoids a certain monotony which grows out of watching a completely masked face. Such makeup is equally effective whether the animal's features are being projected across a large distance or when being viewed through the eyes of a camera. Please study examples of this process in Illus. 12–12 through 12–18.

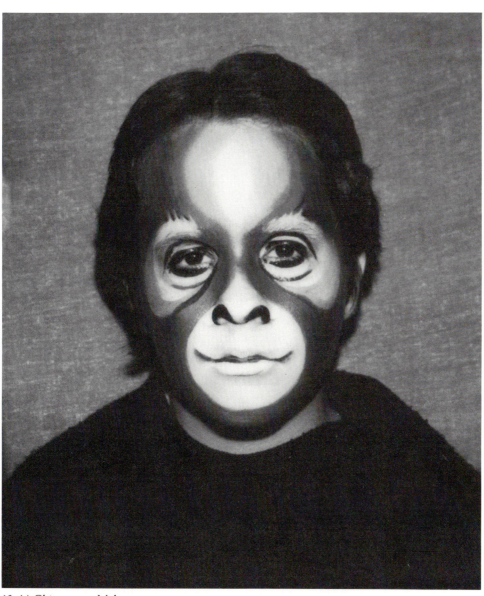

12-14 Chimpanzee Makeup.

12–15 ARMADILLO MAKEUP CHART

12–16 Armadillo Makeup.

12–17 Galapagos Tortoise, courtesy the Dallas Zoo, Dallas, Texas.   *(photograph) Rosa Finsley*

12–18 Mr. Sloe, as played by Ken Holamon, in *The Great Cross Country Race*. An Everyman Player Production.

THE ANIMAL IN MAN

It is not unusual for us to assume similarities between the features of animals and the countenance of man. Charles Le Brun does so in this seventeenth century drawing, in which he not only integrates the physical characteristics of the lion with the man, but also suggests a strong and forceful personality.

Since the time of Aesop, writers have taken delight in exploring the foibles of man while presenting the antics of animals. One of the more brilliant examples is a play written by Ben Jonson in 1606, called *Volpone*, or *The Foxe*. Larry Gelbart updated the story in 1977, calling it *Sly Fox*.

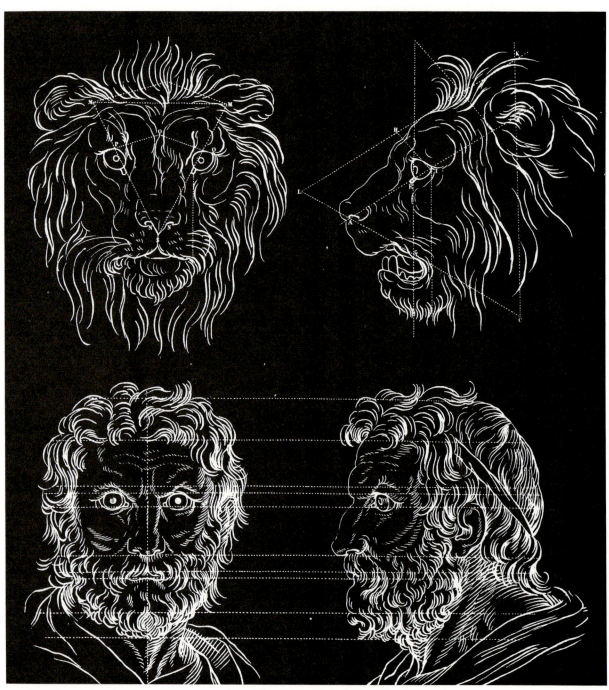

12–19 Seventeenth century artist Charles Le Brun drew parallels between men and animals.

12–20 Design for Foxwell J. Sly in *Sly Fox*.

12–21 Randy Moore as Foxwell J. Sly.

Illustrations 12–20, 22, 25, 28 and 29 are designs which were created for a production of *Sly Fox* at the Dallas Theatre Center, Dallas, Texas. Animal counterparts were assigned to all characters, resulting in vulture-like friends, mice-like servants, and monkey-like judges and constables.

12-23 Allen Hibbard as Chief of Police.

12-22 Design for Chief of Police.

12-24 Lynn Mathis as Captain Crouch in *Sly Fox*.

12–25 Mouse-like characteristics given to the design for a servant.

12–26 Actress Maria Figueroa as the mousy servant.

After consultation with the director concerning characterization, the cast members made a trip to the zoo to observe their counterparts in action. As a result, animal movements, such as the circling of vultures around their prey, was incorporated into the actions of Sly's avaricious "friends," as they hovered around his sickbed. My designs suggested an anthropomorphic combination of human and animal qualities, which were then expanded by the actors.

12-27 Vultures used for prototype for Sly's "friends".[28]

12-29 Design for Lawyer Craven.

12-28 Design for Jethro Crouch in *Sly Fox*.

12-30 Campbell Thomas, left, as Jethro Crouch, and John Henson as Lawyer Craven, right, in *Sly Fox*.

MAKEUP DERIVED
FROM INSECTS

Sometimes, it may take an act of courage to research your subject, but there is no substitute for the variations to be discovered in studying photographs of the actual species. To further substantiate the infinite design possibilities offered by nature, look at the photography done with the scanning electron microscope by David Scharf in his book *Magnifications*.[28] He presents us with the comic visage of a feathery midge, and the helmeted Mediterranean fruit fly, looking as if it is armored for attack.

Two makeups are developed from the photograph of the Jumping Wolf Spider, Illus. 12–31. (Did you know that he has *four* eyes?) The first chart, Illus. 12–32, is a realistic translation, however, Illus. 12–33 indicates a far stronger statement—an abstraction of the spider's visage.

12-31 Jumping wolf spider.   *(photographer) E. S. Ross*

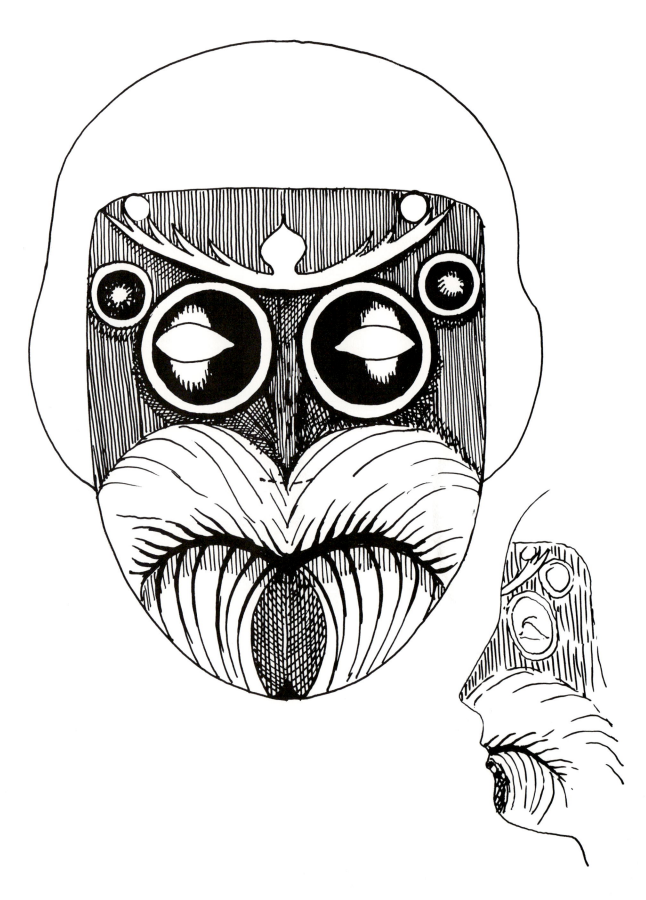

12–32 SPIDER MAKEUP CHART, realistic approach

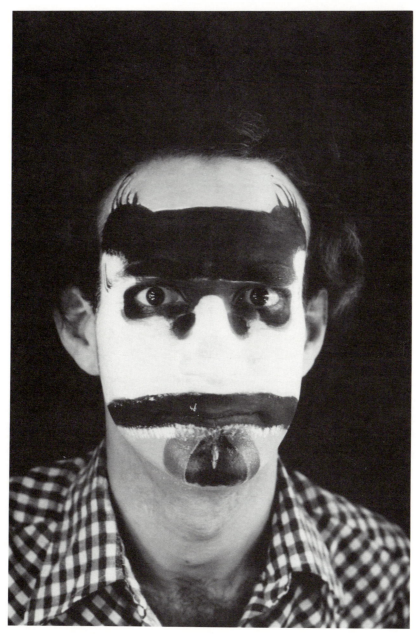

12–33 Stylized makeup for a spider, designed and worn by Andrew Gaup.

MAKEUP DERIVED
FROM FLOWERS

Extend your inspiration for makeup to the world of flowers and leaves. If you must design Peasblossom for *Midsummer Night's Dream*, go look up the flower! Whether you wrap a face in rose petals, detail with the exotic throat of an orchid, or define the simple countenance of a pansy, you will be the richer for the patterns and colors observed there. For developments on these themes, see Illus. 12–34 through 12–37; also Plates 9 and 10 in Color Section.

12-34 Pansy prototype.

12–35 MAKEUP DESIGN BASED ON A PANSY

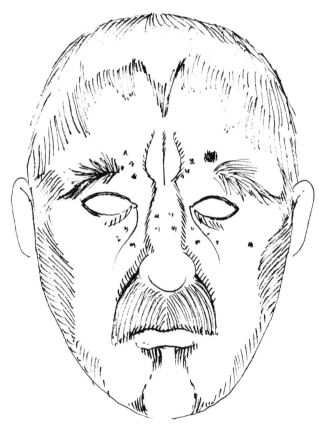

12-36 Throat of a Dendrobium orchid.

MAKEUP DERIVED FROM BIRDS

At first glance, it may seem that birds can only be portrayed by a mask which projects the beak. In the crow makeup designed for the playscript of *Reynard The Fox*,[29] the illusion of the beak was created by painting the beak yellow, which caused it to advance against the black surround. The actress' teeth were blacked out with toothwax to heighten the effect. Although Aristophanes' *The Birds* is an obvious vehicle for birds, I once modeled all of the characters for *A Midsummer Night's Dream*, except the court, after various birds. Thus Puck adopted the harlequinesque mask of the Masked Tanager, Titania, the exotic feathers of Birds of Paradise, Oberon, the Ruffled Grouse, and Snout, the Tinker, the bald pate of the Vulturine Guinea fowl.[30]

The preceding exploration of the world of nature should reassure you that, should your inspiration falter, nature is ready to assist. If your character needs crisp, clean definition, study crystals; if the need is for grace and gentleness, observe the flow of underwater sea life. All is there waiting to be observed. Leonardo

12-37 Chart for realistic makeup based on the throat of a Dendrobium orchid. See variation in Color Plate Ten.

12-38 Owl. Courtesy Dallas Museum of Natural History.

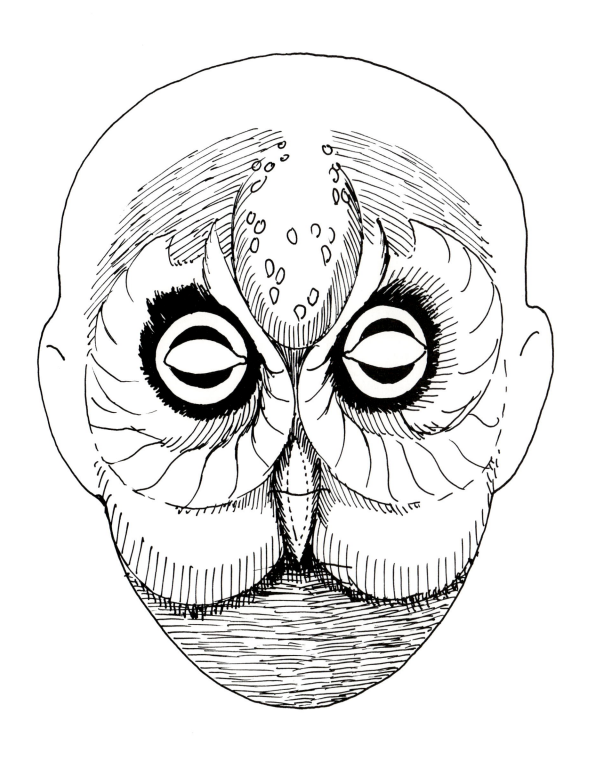

12–39 OWL MAKEUP CHART

da Vinci has advised that you stop sometimes and look into the stains of walls, or ashes of a fire, or clouds or mud, or like places so that you might find really marvelous ideas. Try it.

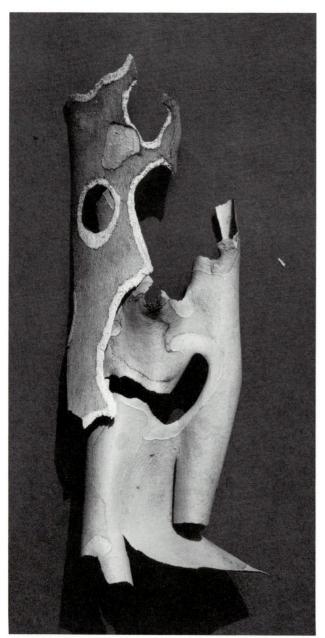

12–40 Tree bark.

BIBLIOGRAPHY

Sorel, Edward. *Resemblences*. Amazing faces by Charles Le Brun. (New York: A Harlequin Quist Book. 1980).

Periodicals:

Ranger Rick. Washington D.C.: National Wildlife Federation. 8925 Leesburg Pike, Vienna, Va. 22180.

The best close up views of animal heads available.

Zoobooks. San Diego, Calif: Wildlife Education, Ltd. 830 West Washington St., 92103.

Excellent series of animal booklets showing many views and perspectives, including skeletons.

NOTES

[27]Alan Broadhurst. *The Great Cross Country Race*. (New Orleans, La. P.O. Box 8067, Anchorage Press, 1965).

[28]Jim Harter. *Animals*. 1419 Copyright free Illustrations of Mammals, Birds, Fish, Insects, etc. (N. Y.: Dover Publications, Inc., 1979), p. 238.

[29]David Scharf. *Magnifications*: Photography with the Scanning Electron Microscope. (New York: Schocken Books, 1977).

[30]Arthur Fauquez. *Reynard the Fox*. (New Orleans, La. P.O. Box 8067, Anchorage Press, 1962).

[31]Irene Corey. *The Mask of Reality: An Approach to Design for Theatre*. (New Orleans, La. P.O. Box 8067, The Anchorage Press, 1968).

13

Styling from
Art Forms

Speaking of the creative process, Llewelyn Powys says, "True style has nothing to do with imparting matter lucidly . . . It is the scent of the herb, the mist over the blackberry hedge, the soul of the man. It is begotten of the senses, it is the quintessential thought, of those fleet immediate messengers finding unity at last in the person of the being they serve."[31] An artist is a seer who shares his vision. He is aware of the nuances of the day and mixes these with the mysterious flood of images of the night where the known merges with the unknown, creating new insights. He perceives with sensitivity, synthesizes his response, and then gives shape to his experience. He thus focuses our attention on an object or idea and enhances our perception of the world. The works of artists, present and past, offer us thousands of such visualizations. Each time we truly *see* and experience them, we recreate their original energy. The life force in these paintings and sculptures is regenerated through our participation. Why not carry this a step further, bring these concepts into three dimensional form, and then harness them with the dynamics of the stage?

The purpose of this book is to explore the craft of makeup and to expose the designer to possible sources of inspiration. When seeking to use forceful art forms, it is essential to take the motivating concept from the play. The creative process can be generated from any aspect of a project, but as a rule, one does not start with an idea for makeup and impose it on a script. Rather, the imagery of the script may demand a visualization of some abstract principle, something beyond realism. It is then that the makeup artist should be armed with an awareness of the multitudes of forceful visual concepts already expressed by artists, past and present.

Following, are two examples of the integration of art form and play concept which I have designed and experienced. The productions of *The Book of Job* and

13-1 *Miserere: Who Does Not Paint Himself a Face?* by Georges Rouault. Collection, The Museum of Modern Art, New York, Gift of the artist.

Romans by St. Paul, as performed by The Everyman Players[32] are given as examples of how an art form comes to be melded with a script. Since I was the designer for all physical aspects of these productions, perhaps it was easier to achieve unity of style.[33] It is unfortunate that in many situations, design unity is sometimes jeopardized by the difficult necessity of correlating the ideas (and the egos) of many people— the director and the designers of settings, costumes, and lights. Makeup seldom has its own spokesman and can fall to the varied whims of individual actors, all of whom come from different experiences and backgrounds. If makeup is to reach its potential in contributing to the artistic strength of a production and integrate into the other visual elements, it must have full support of the director and producer.

USING THE ART FORM OF THE MOSAIC

The decision to use mosaics as a theme for *The Book of Job*, adapted and directed by Orlin Corey, arose out of several concepts. It had to be suitable for sanctuary presentation; it needed to stress the beauty of the faith of Job, rather than the ugliness of his misfortunes; and it required a sense of universality commensurate with the archetypal importance of the figure of Job. In voicing the recurring questions of mankind, Job is not just one man, but a representation of all men. Clothing him, his friends, and his chorus in a mosaic motif submerged the individuals into a greater whole; they became larger than life.

When harnessing such potent art forms, be prepared for the dynamic power which is released. When the actors in *The Book of Job* first stepped forth, fully made up and costumed, they ceased to be George, Joe, and Pat, and became an awesome presence. When the original concepts were wedded to a strong visual form and an equally strong ritualistic choral production voicing the poetic King James language, the cohesion resulted in a dramatic presentation which lasted twenty years on the national and international scene.

13-2 Head of a court dignitary. Sketch taken from a mosaic at San Vitale, Ravenna.

13-3 George Bryan as Eliphaz in *The Book of Job*.

(photograph) Jerry Mitchell.

271

The features, as designed in the *Job* makeup, are typical of the way the features are depicted in Romanesque paintings and Medieval manuscripts. Thus boldly outlined, they project a solemn universality and strength.

When designing makeup for the theatre, it has been my custom to consider it an extension of the same character interpretation expressed by the costume. Once the mosaic theme was chosen, it implied a consistency for the whole figure. Satin mosaics were fixed to gloved hands and to costumes. In this context it would have been a violation of the design style to surround such a mosaic face with real hair and a real beard. Instead, wigs and beards were made of folded spears of organdy, accented with squares of laminated satin. To have used the mosaic costume without the mosaic makeup would also have weakened the impact. Once the art form is embraced, it must permeate the entire production.

USING SCULPTURE AS A DESIGN STYLE

In the early years of the Christian church, art forms, such as stained glass and sculpture, were used as reinforcement for verbal teaching in an age that did not read. In searching for a concept for a production of *Romans by St. Paul*, arranged and directed by Orlin Corey, it seemed that the straightforward teaching attitude of Paul correlated with the stoic intensity found in the figures sculpted in the great cathedrals of France. It was decided to treat the players as if they were saints who stepped out of their niches to amplify the rhetorical questions of Paul.

Execution of the sculptural style then required that the figures be elongated by means of raised shoes, lengthened fingers, and raised foreheads. Color was monochromatic throughout the costume and extended into the makeup. Weighted hems established the verticality of the figures, and when accented by strong side lighting, the overall effect was that of living sculpture.

13-4 Head of St. Thomas, a sculptural figure on the South-Central portal of Chartres Cathedral.　*(photograph) Orlin Corey*

The Sumerian sculpture in Illus. 13–6 could be effective as a makeup-mask, especially if completed with stylized hair and beard.

272

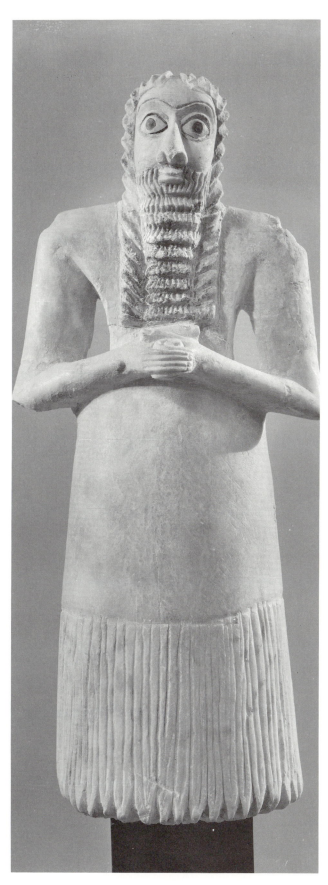

13-5 Hal Proske as Saint Paul in *Romans by Saint Paul*. An Everyman Player production. *(photographer) Jerry Mitchell.*

13-6 Sumerian Sculpture, ca. 3000 B.C. The Metropolitan Museum of Art, Fletcher Fund, 1940.

13-7 SUMERIAN MAKEUP CHART

MASKS AS AN ART FORM FOR THEATRE

It is largely through our faces that we identify each other. When features are stylized, the statement of the underlying personality becomes even stronger.

Masks call forth a stereotypical response, and have a similarity with myth, in that both are abstractions of human experience. Writers frequently relate figures to mythical stories, thus infusing their characters with a related power and strength. The actor-artist can do the same by being aware of the larger universal associations which mask imagery suggests.

The fascinating power of the facial image is enlarged by mask. As such, the mask has been put to many uses, including the curing of disease, establishing protection in afterlife, and confirming leadership. For the primitive tribal priest, it served to conceal his common mortality and enhanced him with a super-human personality.

In some cases, masks are effective because they deviate from the pattern we expect them to have. The growing popularity of Halloween masquerade substantiates the fascination of creating mystery through the unexpected.

Whether used as a whole or partial face covering, or stylized into the makeup-mask, this facial extension should not be ignored by the designer. It should be noted, also, that glasses are a minor form of mask, reflecting not only period, but character.

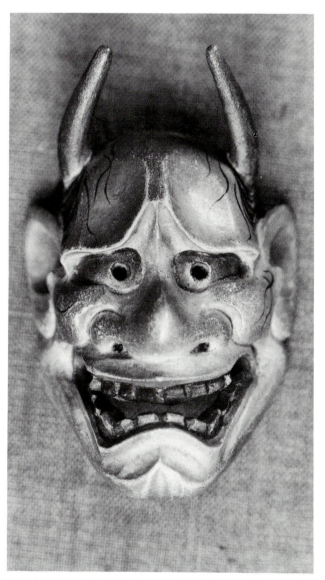

13-8 Mask Netsuke, 14th Century Noh character Hannya, the demon of a once beautiful woman. From the Hobson Collection.

275

PAINTINGS
AS INSPIRATION
FOR MAKEUP

Many works of art can be translated into makeup studies and can become possible points of departure for makeup design. Since I believe that design concepts should grow out of the signal within the script, I will not presume to attach play suggestions to the categories; that could be limiting and misleading. It is true that certain plays, hungry for strong styling, leap into mind—*Sweeny Todd*, *The Balcony*, *Three Penny Opera*, *Lear*, *The Orestian*, and *The Mad Woman of Chaillot*, but I leave the challenge of correlation up to you. I suggest that you immerse yourself in the script, and then, with the aura of the play's visions about you, turn through the art forms until you hear a "click."

13-10 Makeup created by Merlin Fahey, based on a woodcut by Sidney Chafetz. *(photograph) Bruce Wilson*

13-9 *I Myself Am Good Fortune*, woodcut by Sidney Chafetz. With permission of the artist.

In the *Portrait of a Woman*, Color Plate 2, notice Rembrandt's use of rich colors in the skin tones—including green. Some of the most original coloration can be found in a study of the Postimpressionists and the Expressionists. To realize the impact of the images these painters can have, I suggest you translate several of them onto your face with makeup. Be as brave as the artist! Paint *exactly* what you see in the painting, as illustrated in the black and white makeup done in the manner of the woodcut by Sidney Chafetz, Illus. 13–9 and 13–10, using dark lines against a light base.

Discover the joy of color through recreating Paul Klee's *The Actor's Mask*, Illus. 13–11. If you look up this painting in color, you will find horizontal lines in red-orange across a lime green base, with yellow filled in between the lines of the brow, eyes and mouth; pink interspersed with lime on the neck.

13-11 *Actor's Mask.* (1924) Paul Klee. The Sidney and Harriet Janis Collection, the Museum of Modern Art, New York.

While you are researching artists' use of color, study Rouault's luminous stained glass colors, and try his *Miserere: Who Does Not Paint Himself a Face?*, Illus. 13-1. Or, translate into makeup the brilliant colors in *Head* by Jawlensky, Color Plate Six, and *Woman in a Large Hat* by Van Dongen, Color Plate Five. By learning from the painters, you will be on your way to discovering more inventive ways of using line and color in theatrical makeup.

I close this book with an example of the remarkable makeup created by a South-East Nuban man from the Sudan. There, remote from civilization, these men have elevated face and body painting to a sophisticated art form. Attuned to colors and nature, they create constant variations in patterns, sometimes changing their designs twice a day. The purpose seems to be purely for enhancement of appearance. We are indebted to the courageous photography of Leni Riefenstahl for recording this artistry in her book, *The People of Kau*.[35] I can think of no better place for you to continue your search for inspiration.

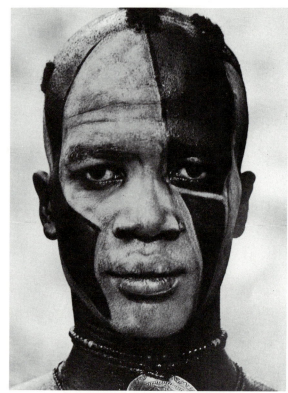

13–12 Original abstract makeup created by a man from South East Nuba in the Sudan. Photograph from *The People of Kau.*© by Leni Riefenstahl©, Reprinted by permission of Harper and Row, Publishers, Inc.

BIBLIOGRAPHY

Ghiselin, Brewster, ed. *The Creative Process*, A Symposium. (New York: A Mentor book from New American Library, 1952).

Huet, Michel. *The Dance, Art and Ritual of Africa*. (New York: Pantheon Books, 1978).

Kirk, Malcolm. *Man as Art, New Guinea*. (New York: A Studio Book, The Viking Press, 1981).

Sorell, Walter. *The Other Face: The Mask in the Arts*. (New York: The Bobbs-Merrill Co. Inc., 1973).

An investigation of the magic and the mystery of the mask, and its universal significance.

Virel, Andre. *Decorated Man*. The Human Body as Art. (New York: Harry N. Abrams, Inc. 1979).

A study of the psychological significance of adornment, and a study of the mask as a means of camouflage and transformation.

Riefenstahl, Leni. *The People of Kau*. Photographs, text, and layout by Leni Riefenstahl. Trans. from German by J. Maxwell Brownjohn. (New York: Harper and Row, Pub. 1976).

Corey, Orlin. *An Odyssey of Masquers: The Everyman Players*. (New Orleans, La: Rivendell House, Pub. 1990).

NOTES

[32]Llewelyn Powys, *Types and Times in the Essay*, Ed. Warnor Taylor, (Harper and Brothers, 1932).

[33]Corey. *The Mask of Reality*

[34]Leni Riefenstahl. *The People of Kau*. Photographs, Text and Layout by Leni Riefenstahl. Trans. from German by J. Maxwell Brownjohn. (New York: Harper and Row, Pub. 1976).

Plate One: *Madonna and Child*, (detail). Domenico Ghirlandaio.
The National Gallery of Art, Washington, D.C. Samuel H. Kress Collection.

Plate Two: *Portrait of a Woman*. H. van Rijn Rembrandt.
The Metropolitan Museum of Art, N.Y.

Plate Three: *A Young Man with His Tutor*, (detail). Nicolas de Largillière.
National Gallery of Art, Washington D.C., Samuel H. Kress Collection.

Plate Four: *Madame du Barry*. Francois-Hubert Drouais.
National Gallery of Art, Washington D.C. Timken Collection.

Plate Five: *Woman in a Large Hat*, (detail) 1908. van Dongen.
The Museum of Modern Art, New York. Private collection.

Plate Six: *Head.* (detail) A. Jawlensky, 1965.
The Museum of Modern Art, N. Y.

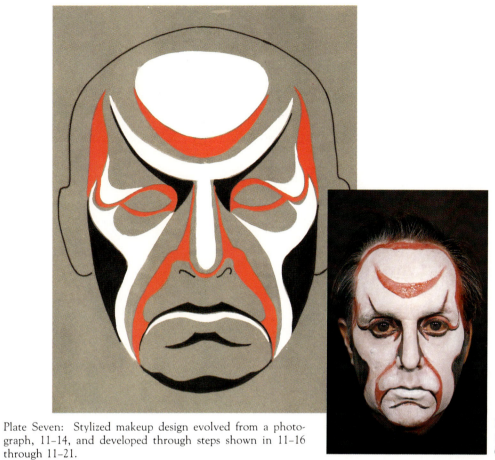

Plate Seven: Stylized makeup design evolved from a photograph, 11–14, and developed through steps shown in 11–16 through 11–21.

Plate Eight: Kabuki style makeup interpreted by Allen Shaffer. (photograph by Irene Corey)

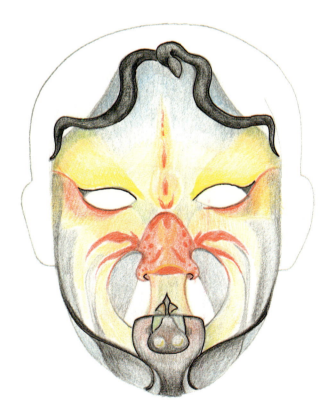

Plate Nine: Makeup design based on the throat of an orchid.

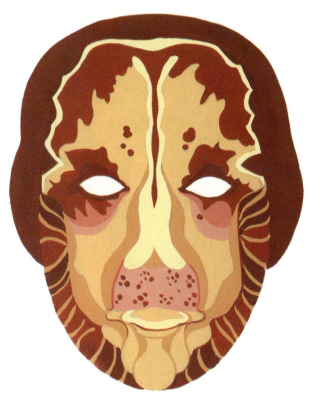

Plate Ten: Makeup design based on a Dendrobium Orchid. (See photograph 12–45 for prototype).

Plate Eleven: Makeup and costume design evolved from sea life images for the role of Prospero in Shakespeare's *The Tempest*, enacted by actor Hal Proske; an Everyman Player production.

HAVE FUN!

PICTURE IDENTIFICATION
The Face Is a Canvas
Irene Corey

MS Number	Identification: Title, or Subject, Sitter	Artist or Photographer	Permissions Credit
1-1	Mountain woman and grandchild sitting on the porch of their home up Frozen Creek, Breathitt County, Ky.	Marion Post Wolcott	F.S.A. Collection, Library of Congress, Washington, D.C.
1-2	Thomas Taylor, San Augustine, Tx.	Doug Milner	
1-3	Migrant Field Worker, Tulare Migrant Camp, Visalia, Calif., 1940	Arthur Rothstein	F. S. A. Collection, Library of Congress, Washington, D. C.
1-4	Elizabeth Throckmorton	Nicolas de Largillière, 1656–1746	Alisha Mellon Bruce Fund, 1964, National Gallery of Art, Washington, D. C.
1-5	Wife and children of sharecropper, in Washington County, Ark., 1935	Arthur Rothstein	F.S.A. Collection, Library of Congress, Washington, D. C.
1-6	A resettlement administration client, Boone County, Ark., Oct. 1935	Ben Shahn	F.S.A. Collection, Library of Congress, Washington, D. C.
1-7	Rehabilitation client's wife, Jackson Co., Oh., 1936	Theodor Jung	F.S.A. Collection, Library of Congress, Washington, D. C.
1-8	Farmer in cut-over area, Chippewa County, Wis., 1939	John Vachon	F.S.A. Collection, Library of Congress, Washington, D. C.
1-9	Neighbor comforts a grandmother as she watches the flames of a tenement where her two-year-old grandson has perished, Providence, R. I., 1978.		United Press International Photo
1-10	Sir Alec Guinness in various roles played in the movie *Kind Hearts and Coronets*		Courtesy Weintraub Entertainment
1-11	Abraham Lincoln, Springfield, Ill., 1846	N. H. Shepherd, Daguerreotype	Library of Congress, Washington, D. C.
1-12	Abraham Lincoln, Chicago, Ill. Oct. 4, 1859.	Samuel M. Fassett	Library of Congress, Washington, D. C.
1-13	Abraham Lincoln. Last Portrait, April 10, 1865	Alexander Gardner	Library of Congress, Washington, D.C.
2-1	Joanne Grant	Suzanne Dietz	
2-2	Joanne Grant	Suzanne Dietz	
2-18	Felix Frankfurter, caricature	Oscar Berger	National Portrait Gallery, Smithsonian Institution, Washington, D. C.
2-19	Santa Claus	Thomas Nast	
2-20	Luba painted wooden and china-clay mask, Congo-Kinshasa		*African Designs From Traditional Sources.* Geoffrey Williams. New York: Dover Publications, Inc. 1971. Public domain
2-21	Portrait Head of the Emperor Caracalla Roman sculpture, III c. A.D.		The Metropolitan Museum of Art, Samuel D. Lee Fund, 1940
2-22a	12 year old son of a cotton sharecropper, near Cleveland, Miss., June 1937	Dorothea Lange	Library of Congress, Washington, D. C. F.S.A. Collection

MS Number	Identification: Title, or Subject, Sitter	Artist or Photographer	Permissions Credit
2-22b	Keith Tompkins, San Augustine, Tx.	Doug Milner	
2-22c	Farmer, Park County, In., 1940	Arthur Rothstein	F.S.A. Collection, Library of Congress, Washington, D.C.
2-22d	Robert A. Wood, engineer and surveyor, San Augustine, Tx.	Doug Milner	
2-23	Ruby Fitzgerald, Martha Garrett, Mandy Garret, San Augustine, Tx.	Doug Milner	
2-24a	John H. Oglesbee, Sr., San Augustine, Tx.	Doug Milner	
2-24b	John H. Oglesbee, Sr., San Augustine, Tx.	Doug Milner	
2-24c	John H. Oglesbee, Jr., San Augustine, Tx.	Doug Milner	
2-24d	John H. Oglesbee, Jr. San Augustine, Tx.	Doug Milner	
2-24e	John H. Oglesbee III, San Augustine, Tx.	Doug Milner	
2-24f	John H. Oglesbee III, San Augustine, Tx.	Doug Milner	
2-25	Starving child in Karamoja, Uganda aided by UNICEF, 1981		United Press International Photo
2-26	Anti-war demonstration, Madison, Wis., 1967	Dennis Conner	United Press International Photo
2-27a	Hands of retired farmer, San Augustine, Tx.	Doug Milner	
2-27b	Hands of old couple and their granddaughter	John Vachon	F.S.A. Collection, The Library of Congress, Washington, D.C.
2-28b	Walt Whitman, September, 1887	George C. Cox	National Portrait Gallery, Smithsonian Institution, Washington. D.C. Gift of Mr. and Mrs. Charles Feinberg
2-29	Anna Eleanor Roosevelt, 1885-1975	Clara Sipprell	National Portrait Gallery, Smithsonian Institution, Washington, D. C.
2-30	Martin Luther King, 1965		United Press International Photo
2-31	Marquis de Lafayette, c. 1834	Nicholas Eustache Maurin, lithograph	National Portrait Gallery, Smithsonian Institution, Washington, D.C.
2-32	Frederick Douglass, 1817-1895		National Portrait Gallery, Smithsonian Institution, Washington, D. C.
2-33	James P. Teel, Handyman, San Augustine, Tx.	Doug Milner	
2-34	Conway Massey, Athletic Director, San Augustine, Tx.	Doug Milner	
2-35	Nathan Tindall, Sheriff, San Augustine County, Tx.	Doug Milner	
2-36a	J. P. Matthews, Proprieter, Dry Goods Store, San Augustine, Tx.	Doug Milner	
2-36b	J. P. Matthews	Doug Milner	

MS Number	Identification: Title, or Subject, Sitter	Artist or Photographer	Permissions Credit
2-37a	Mrs. Rose Carrendeno, Italian-American, New York City, 1943	Gordon Parks	Office of War Information Photo, Library of Congress, Smithsonian Institution, Washington, D. C.
2-37b	Armenian woman, farmer, West Andover, Mass., 1941	Delano	F.S.A. Collection, Library of Congress, Washington, D. C.
2-37c	Portugese fisherman, West Andover, Mass., 1940	Edwin Rosskam	F.S.A. Collection, Library of Congress, Washington, D. C.
2-37d	Stephanie Cortner Smith, Monteagle, Tenn., American, 1983.	Irene Corey	
2-38	Chinese woman, Chinatown, New York City, 1942	Marjory Collins	Office of War Information, Library of Congress, Washington, D. C.
2-39a	Ardis Mosky, San Augustine, Tx.	Doug Milner	
2-39b	Ardis Mosky	Doug Milner	
2-40	Mandrill Monkey	Rosa Finsley	Courtesy the Dallas Zoo, Dallas, Tx.
2-41	Dendrobium orchid	Irene Corey	Courtesy Earl Jones, Florist
2-42	Slipper orchid	Irene Corey	
2-43a	Weathered Wood	Irene Corey	
2-43b	Odessa Harrison, San Augustine, Tx.	Doug Milner	
2-43c	Odessa Harrison, front view	Doug Milner	
2-44	Death's Head Hawk-Moth		*Animals; 1419 Copyright-Free Illustrations of Mammals, Birds, Fish, Insects, etc.* Jim Harter. 1979
2-45	Emmett Kelly, 1981	Donald Lee Rust	National Portrait Gallery, Smithsonian Institution, Washington, D. C.
3-3	Orlin Corey in makeup as hound dog in *The Great Cross Country Race.*	Irene Corey	An Everyman Player Production
3-30b	Jill Dalley in hound dog makeup	Irene Corey	
4-1a		Irene Corey	
4-1b	Nick Dalley	Irene Corey	
4-2a		Irene Corey	
4-2b	Nick Dalley	Irene Corey	
4-3a		Irene Corey	
4-3b	Nick Dalley	Irene Corey	
4-4a		Irene Corey	
4-4b	Nick Dalley	Irene Corey	
4-5	Study of an Angel	Annibale Carracci	The Metropolitan Museum of Art, Gustavus A. Pfeiffer Fund, 1962.
6-1a	Joanne Grant,	Suzanne Dietz	
6-1b	Joanne Grant, contoured.	Suzanne Dietz	
6-2a	Merlin Fahey	Bruce Wilson	
6-2b	Merlin Fahey	Bruce Wilson	
6-2c	Merlin Fahey	Bruce Wilson	

MS Number	Identification: Title, or Subject, Sitter	Artist or Photographer	Permissions Credit
6-2d	Merlin Fahey	Bruce Wilson	
6-2e	Merlin Fahey	Bruce Wilson	
6-4a	Millicent Flowers	Irene Corey	
6-4b	Millicent Flowers	Irene Corey	
6-4c	Millicent Flowers	Irene Corey	
6-4d	Millicent Flowers	Irene Corey	
6-5a	Jesus L. Ramirez	Irene Corey	
6-5b	Jesus L. Ramirez	Irene Corey	
7-5	Woman from Brown County, In., 1935	Theodor Jung	F.S.A. Collection, Library of Congress, Washington, D. C.
7-7a	Joanne Grant	Suzanne Dietz	
7-7b	Joanne Grant	Suzanne Dietz	
7-9	Frank Mathews, San Augustine, Tx.	Doug Milner	
7-10	Detail, Mrs. Carrie Ward	Delano	F.S.A. Collection, Library of Congress, Washington, D.C.
7-11	Detail, Wayne Garrett, San Augustine, Tx.	Doug Milner	
7-12	Tontey Roberts, age 95, San Augustine, Tx. Detail, forehead	Doug Milner	
7-16a, 16b	Makeup chart for Aging	Irene Corey	
7-16	Hands	Doug Milner	
7-19	Migratory worker's wife, Robstown, Tx., 1942	Arthur Rothstein	F.S.A. Collection, Library of Congress, Washington, D. C.
7-20a	Cynthia E. Partin, San Augustine, Tx.	Doug Milner	
7-20b	Cynthia E. Partin, San Augustine, Tx.	Doug Milner	
7-21	Robert A. Wood, San Augustine, Tx.	Doug Milner	
7-22a	Alice Roosevelt Longworth and daughter Paulina, c. 1932		United Press International Photo
7-22b	Alice Roosevelt Longworth, later years		United Press International Photo
7-23a	John C. Calhoun, c. 1834	James Barton Longacre	National Portrait Gallery, Smithsonian Institution, Washington, D. C.
7-23b	John C. Calhoun, 1850	D'Avignon after Brady	National Portrait Gallery, Smithsonian Institution. Washington, D.C.
7-24	Daughter of migrant worker, 1942, Bridgeton, N.J.	John Collier	F.S.A. Collection, Library of Congress Washington, D. C.
7-25	Cora Jean Davis, San Augustine, Tx.	Doug Milner	
7-26	Louella Walker, San Augustine, Tx.	Doug Milner	
7-27	Ex-slave on farm near Greensboro, Ala., photographed May, 1941	Jack Delano	F. S. A. Collection, Library of Congress, Washington, D. C.
7-28	Mosa, young Indian child	Edward S. Curtis	Library of Congress, Washington, D. C.
7-29	Indian Brave	Edward S. Curtis	Library of Congress, Washington, D. C.

MS Number	Identification: Title, or Subject, Sitter	Artist or Photographer	Permissions Credit
7–30	Wife of On High	Edward S. Curtis	Library of Congress, Washington, D. C.
7–31	Big Head	Edward S. Curtis	Library of Congress, Washington, D. C.
7–32	Mattie Garret Odle, age 24	Courtesy Odle family	
7–33	Sketch, Makeup, age 24	Irene Corey	
7–34	Mattie Garret Odle, age 40	Beth Odle	
7–35	Makeup chart, age 40	Irene Corey	
7–36	Mattie Garret Odle, age 74	Courtesy Odle family	
7–37	Makeup chart, age 74	Irene Corey	
7–38	Mattie Garret Odle, age 101	Beth Odle	
7–39	Makeup chart, age 101	Irene Corey	
7–40	Young Hispanic	unknown	*The San Antonio Light* collection, University of Texas, Institute of Texan Cultures at San Antonio
7–41	Older Hispanic	unknown	The University of Texas Institute of Texan Cultures at San Antonio
7–42	Older Hispanic	unknown	The University of Texas Institute of Texan Cultures at San Antonio
8–1a	Nick Dalley	Irene Corey	
8–1b	Nick Dalley	Irene Corey	
8–1c	Nick Dalley	Irene Corey	
8–2	Fat/Skinny Makeup chart	Irene Corey	
8–5	Jean Simboli, New York City	Bruce Wilson	
8–6	Helen Jean Lake, San Augustine, Tx.	Doug Milner	
8–7	Jean Simboli, New York City	Bruce Wilson	
8–8	Helen Jean Lake, San Augustine, Tx.	Doug Milner	
8–9	Alice Hollis, San Augustine, Tx.	Doug Milner	
8–10	F. K. Parker, San Augustine, Tx.	Doug Milner	
8–11	Alice Hollis, San Augustine, Tx.	Doug Milner	
8–12	F. K. Parker, San Augustine, Tx.	Doug Milner	
8–13	Nick Dalley	Irene Corey	
8–14	Makeup Chart for Fat Face	Irene Corey	
8–15	Joanne Grant	Suzanne Dietz	
8–35	Young girl living near Washington, D. C. 1942	Gordon Parks	F.S.A. Collection. Library of Congress, Washington, D. C.
8–36	Makeup chart for Youth	Irene Corey	
8–38	Sharp Nose, an Arapaho Indian	unknown	National Archives, Washington, D.C.
8–39	Makeup chart for Indian	unknown	
8–40	Tim Green	Irene Corey	
8–41	Herman Wheatley	Irene Corey	
8–42	Herman Wheatley	Irene Corey	

MS Number	Identification: Title, or Subject, Sitter	Artist or Photographer	Permissions Credit
8-43	Leroy Lane, San Augustine, Tx.	Doug Milner	
8-44	Hasako Yamamoto	Linda Blase, 1983©	
8-45	Chih Kai, Wu	Irene Corey	
8-46	Oriental makeup chart, male	Irene Corey	
8-47	Oriental makeup chart, female	Irene Corey	
8-48	Caucasian makeup for Oriental	Irene Corey	
9-1	Grace Dwyer	Karl Stone	
9-3	Head of a Heavenly King (Lokapala) A. D. 12th Century	Japan; late Heian Period	Dallas Museum of Fine Arts, The Eugene and Margaret McDermott Fund
9-5	Nat Jensen	Karl Stone	
9-10a	Merlin Fahey	Bruce Wilson	
9-10b	Merlin Fahey	Bruce Wilson	
9-10c	Merlin Fahey	Bruce Wilson	
9-12a	Unknown	Doris Ulmann	Used with special permission from Berea College and the Doris Ulmann Foundation
9-12b	Unknown	Doris Ulmann	Used with special permission from Berea College and the Doris Ulmann Foundation
9-12c	Mrs. Bird Patten	Doris Ulmann	Used with special permission from Berea College and the Doris Ulmann Foundation
9-12d	Mr. Ritchie	Doris Ulmann	Used with special permission from Berea College and the Doris Ulmann Foundation
9-12e	Orlenia Ritchie	Doris Ulmann	Used with special permission from Berea College and the Doris Ulmann Foundation
9-12f	Mrs. Stewart	Doris Ulmann	Used with special permission from Berea College and the Doris Ulmann Foundation
9-12g	James Duff	Doris Ulmann	Used with special permission from Berea College and the Doris Ulmann Foundation
10-1	The Chess Players, detail of Italian painting.	Girolamo da Cremona, c. 1467–1473	The Metropolitan Museum of Art, Bequest of Maitland F. Griggs, 1943 Maitland F. Griggs Collection
	Angela Davis, "Afro"		United Press International Photo
10-2	Wig of Princess Nany, Dynasty XXI		The Metropolitan Museum of Art, Museum Excavations, 1928–29
10-3	Head of a Canopic Jar representing Princess Mert-Aten Egyptian Dynasty XVIII		The Metropolitan Museum of Art, The Theodore M. Davis Collection, Bequest of Theodore M. Davis, 1915
10-4	Makeup chart for Egyptian Woman	Irene Corey	

MS Number	Identification: Title, or Subject, Sitter	Artist or Photographer	Permissions Credit
10–5	Head from a fragmentary statue of The Diadoumenos, Roman copy of a bronze statue by Polikleitos, of about 430 B. C.		The Metropolitan Museum of Art, Fletcher Fund, 1925
10–6	Sketch of Male Deity, Zeus or Dionysos Roman copy of a Greek work, V Century B. C.		The Metropolitan Museum of Art, Rogers Fund, 1913
10–7	Sketch, after Apollo West Pediment of Temple of Zeus at Olympia, 460 B.C.		
10–8	Sketch, Kritian Boy		
10–9	Sketch, Omphalos Apollo		
10–10	Makeup chart for Greek Man	Irene Corey	
10–11	Madonna and Child	Domenico Ghirlandaio	The National Gallery of Art, Washington, D. C. Samuel H. Kress Collection
10–12	Sketch after Sandro Botticelli's *Young Woman*	Sandro Botticelli	Gemäldegalerie, Berlin
10–13	Sketch after *Madonna* by Pietro Perugino	Pietro Perugino	National Gallery of Art, Washington, D.C. Samuel H. Kress Collection.
10–14	Sketch after *Ginevra Bentivoglio*	Ercolel Roberti	The National Gallery of Art, Washington, D. C. Samuel H. Kress Collection
10–15	Renaissance woman, 15th century	Irene Corey	
10–16	Henry VIII, England	artist unknown	National Portrait Gallery, London
10–17	Philip Melanchton	Albrecht Durer	National Gallery of Art, Washington, D.C. Rosenwald Collection
10–18	Frederick The Wise, Elector of Saxony	Albrecht Durer	National Gallery of Art, Washington, D. C. Rosenwalk Collection
10–19	*Portrait of a Man with a Gold Embroidered Cap.*	Cranach, Lucas The Elder	The Metropolitan Museum of Art Bequest of Gula V. Hirschland, 1980
10–20	Makeup chart for Henry VIII	Irene Corey	
10–21	Elizabeth I	M. Gheeraerdts	National Portrait Gallery, London
10–22	Sketch after tomb figure in Pershore Abbey, Worcester, England		
10–23	Sketch, hair style variation. French.		
10–24	Sketch after Margaret, wife of Sir Peter Legh, Tomb in Church of All Saints, Fulham, England		
10–25	Makeup chart for Elizabeth I	Irene Corey	
10–26	*A Young Man with his Tutor*, Detail	Nicolas de Largillière	National Gallery of Art, Washington, D.C.
10–27	*Game of Billiards*	Antoine Trouvain	The Metropolitan Museum of Art. The Elisha Whittelsey Collection, The Elisha Whittelsey Fund, 1949
10–28	Sketch of sculpture of Louis XIV	French school, after Bernini	National Gallery of Art, Washington, D.C. Samuel H. Kress Collection

MS Number	Identification: Title, or Subject, Sitter	Artist or Photographer	Permissions Credit
10–29	Makeup chart for Restoration man	Irene Corey	
10–30	*Madame du Barry*	François-Hubert Drouais	National Gallery of Art, Washington, D. C. Timken Collection
10–31	Marie-Adélaïde Hall	Augustin Pajou	The Frick Collection, New York
10–32	*Le Rendez-vous pour Marly*	J. M. Moreau, le Jeune	The Metropolitan Museum of Art, Harris Brisbane Dick Fund, 1933
10–33	*N'Ayez pas peur, ma bonne amie*	J. M. Moreau le Jeune	The Metropolitan Museum of Art, Harris Brisbane Dick Fund, 1933
10–34	Makeup chart for Eighteenth Century Woman	Irene Corey	
10–35	Abraham Lincoln		National Archives, Washington, D.C.
10–36	Ambrose Burnside	Mathew Brady	National Portrait Gallery, Smithsonian Institution, Washington, D.C.
10–37	*Grant and His Generals*	Currier and Ives, 1865	Library of Congress, Washington, D.C.
10–38	Makeup chart for Lincoln	Irene Corey	
10–39	Alice Roosevelt Longworth		Brown Brothers, Sterling, Pa.
10–40	Gibson Girl wall paper	Charles Dana Gibson	*The Gibson Girl and Her America. The Best Drawings of Charles Dana Gibson* Dover Publications, Inc. N. Y. 1969
10–41	Gibson Girl	Charles Dana Gibson	*The Gibson Girl and Her America. The Best Drawings of Charles Dana Gibson* Dover Publications, Inc. N. Y. 1969
10–42	Makeup chart for Gibson Girl	Irene Corey	
10–43	Clara Bow		United Press International Photo
10–44	Makeup chart for Clara Bow	Irene Corey	United Press International Photo
10–45	Greta Garbo		United Press International Photo
10–46	Makeup chart for Greta Garbo	Irene Corey	
10–47	Josephine Baker, entertainer 1920's		The Bettmann Archives, Inc.
10–48	Miss America Pageant, 1921	Irene Corey	
10–49a	Arrow Shirt Man	J. C. Leyendecker	Courtesy of Cluett, Peabody and Co, Inc.
10–49b	Makeup chart for Arrow Shirt Man	Irene Corey	
10–50	Charles Lindbergh		National Portrait Gallery, Smithsonian Institution, Washington, D.C.
10–50a	Rudolph Valentino	Russell Ball	National Portrait Gallery, Smithsonian Institution, Washington, D. C.
10–51	Charles Chaplin		International Museum of Photography at George Eastman House
10–52	Jean Harlow		United Press International Photo
10–53	Joan Crawford and Brenda Frazier		United Press International Photo
10–54	Hair styles	Irene Corey	

MS Number	Identification: Title, or Subject, Sitter	Artist or Photographer	Permissions Credit
10–55	Makeup chart for Joan Crawford	Irene Corey	
10–56	Clark Gable		United Press International Photo
10–57	Robert Taylor		United Press International Photo
10–58	Makeup chart for Robert Taylor		Irene Corey
10–59	Hair styles	Irene Corey	
10–60	Hair styles	Irene Corey	
10–61	Marlene Dietrich		United Press International Photo
10–62	Rita Hayworth		United Press International Photo
10–63	Makeup chart for Rita Hayworth	Irene Corey	
10–64	British Sailor and American Merchant Marine		United Press International Photo
10–65	Frank Sinatra, 1942		United Press International Photo
10–66	Crew cut	Irene Corey	
10–67	Marilyn Monroe		United Press International Photo
10–68	Hair styles	Irene Corey	
10–69	Audrey Hepburn		United Press International Photo
10–70	Makeup chart for Marilyn Monroe	Irene Corey	
10–71	James Dean		United Press International Photo
10–72	Elvis Presley		United Press International Photo
10–73	Sketch of ducktail	Irene Corey	
10–74	Makeup chart for James Dean	Irene Corey	
10–75	Jacqueline Kennedy, 1963		United Press International Photo
10–76	Twiggy		United Press International Photo
10–77	Makeup chart for Twiggy	Irene Corey	
10–78	Cecily Tyson		United Press International Photo
10–79	Hair styles	Irene Corey	
10–80	Angela Davis		United Press International Photo
10–81	President John F. Kennedy		United Press International Photo
10–82	Matthew Nash	Bruce Wilson	
10–83	Beatles and Ed Sullivan		United Press International Photo
10–84	Guys and gals, long hair styles-Suzanne Gregory and Jay Craven		United Press International Photo
10–85	Hard hat workers		United Press International Photo
10–86	Farrah Fawcett		United Press International Photo
10–87	Makeup chart for 1970's Woman	Irene Corey	
10–88	Valerie Drafts	Bruce Wilson	
10–89	Hair styles	Irene Corey	
10–90	Art Garfunkel		United Press International Photo
10–91	Merlin Fahey	Bruce Wilson	

MS Number	Identification: Title, or Subject, Sitter	Artist or Photographer	Permissions Credit
10–92a	Hair style	Irene Corey	
10–92b	John H. Barr III	Suzanne Dietz	
10–93	Lady Diana	Irene Corey	
10–94	Grace Jones		
10–95	a. Braids b. Butch cut	Irene Corey	
10–96	Makeup in manner of Boy George	author	
10–97	Steve Simpson, wrestler, 1987	Doug Milner	Courtesy The Dallas Times Herald
10–98	Jill & Nick Dalley, 1987	Doug Milner	
10–111	Bust of Herodotus, Roman Sculpture		The Metropolitan Museum of Art, Gift of George F. Baker, 1891.
11–1a	Danjuro Ichikawa, Kabuki Actor		*Danjuro Ichikawa.* Wood block prints of Kabuki Actor. Publisher: Hatsujiro Fukuda, Tokyo, 1896
11–2	Monkey King, Chinese Opera Mask	Irene Corey	
11–3	Merlin Fahey, Age makeup	Bruce Wilson	
11–4	Merlin Fahey, Age makeup, profile	Bruce Wilson	
11–5	Merlin Fahey, Stylized makeup	Bruce Wilson	
11–6	Merlin Fahey, Stylized makeup, profile	Bruce Wilson	
11–7	O. D. Montgomery	Karl Stone	
11–8	Stylized makeup chart, Montgomery, Phase 1	Irene Corey	
11–9	Stylized makeup chart, Montgomery, Phase 2		
11–10	Mattie Garret Odle	Beth Odle	
11–11	Stylized makeup chart, Odle, Phase 1	Irene Corey	
11–12	Stylized makeup chart, Odle, Phase 2	Irene Corey	
11–13	Stylized makeup chart, Odle, Phase 3	Irene Corey	
11–14	W. C. Hogue	Karl Stone	
11–15	Stylized makeup chart, Hogue, Stressing suffering	Irene Corey	
11–16	Stylized makeup chart, Hogue, Stressing strength, Phase 1	Irene Corey	
11–17	Stylized makeup chart, Hogue, Phase 2	Irene Corey	
11–18	Stylized makeup chart, Hogue, Phase 3	Irene Corey	
11–19	Stylized makeup chart, Hogue, Phase 4	Irene Corey	
11–20	Stylized makeup chart, Hogue, Phase 5	Irene Corey	
11–21	Allen Shaffer, makeup, Phase 5	Irene Corey	
11–22	Brain coral and jelly fish		*Art Forms In Nature.* Ernst Haeckel. Dover Publications, Inc., N. Y. 1974
11–23	Design for Prospero's makeup and Magic garb	Irene Corey	An Everyman Player Production

MS Number	Identification: Title, or Subject, Sitter	Artist or Photographer	Permissions Credit
11–24	Hal Proske as Prospero in *The Tempest*	Irene Corey	An Everyman Player Production
11–25	Design for Gonzolo, *The Tempest*	Irene Corey	An Everyman Player Production
11–26	David Cooper applying makeup as Gonzolo	Irene Corey	An Everyman Player Production
11–27	Design for Alonso, *The Tempest*	Irene Corey	An Everyman Player Production
11–28	Ronlin Foreman in makeup as Alonso, King of Naples, in *The Tempest*.	Irene Corey	An Everyman Player Production
11–29	Design for Ariel, *The Tempest*	Irene Corey	An Everyman Player Production
12–1	Lion		Courtesy of the Dallas Zoo, Dallas, Tx.
12–2	Allen Shaffer, as Noble in *Reynard the Fox*	Jerry Mitchell	An Everyman Player Production
12–4	Makeup chart for Dog	Irene Corey	
12–8	Jill A. Dalley being made up as dog	Irene Corey	
12–9	Jill A. Dalley, areas painted in for dog makeup	Irene Corey	
12–10	Jill A. Dalley, powdering stage	Irene Corey	
12–11	Jill A. Dalley, completed dog makeup	Irene Corey	
12–12	Chimpanzee monkey	Rosa Finsley	Courtesy of the Dallas Zoo, Dallas, Tx.
12–13	Makeup chart for Monkey	Irene Corey	
12–14	Randall T. Lockridge in makeup as a monkey	Irene Corey	
12–15	Makeup chart for Armadillo	Irene Corey	
12–16	Andy Haynes, in makeup of armadillo	Irene Corey	
12–17	Galapagos tortoise	Rosa Fensley	Courtesy of the Dallas Zoo, Dallas, Tx.
12–18	Ken Holamon, as Mr. Sloe, in *The Great Cross Country Race*	Irene Corey	An Everyman Player production
12–19	The lion, animal and man	Charles Le Brun, 17th c.	Public domain
12–20	Design for Foxwell J. Sly, in *Sly Fox*	Irene Corey	
12–21	Randy Moore as Foxwell J. Sly in *Sly Fox*	Irene Corey	Dallas Theatre Center, Dallas ,Tx.
12–22	Design for the Chief of Police in *Sly Fox*	Irene Corey	
12–23	Allen Hibbard as the Chief of Police in *Sly Fox*	Irene Corey	Dallas Theatre Center, Dallas, Tx.
12–24	Lynn Mathis as Captain Crouch in *Sly Fox*	Irene Corey	Dallas Theatre Center, Dallas, Tx.
12–25	Design for the mousy servant in *Sly Fox*	Irene Corey	
12–26	Maria Figueroa as mousy servant in *Sly Fox*	Irene Corey	Dallas Theatre Center, Dallas, Tx.
12–27	Vultures	Irene Corey	Public domain
12–28	Design for Jethro Crouch in *Sly Fox*	Irene Corey	Dallas Theatre Center, Dallas, Tx.

MS Number	Identification: Title, or Subject, Sitter	Artist or Photographer	Permissions Credit
12–29	Design for Lawyer Craven in *Sly Fox*		Dallas Theatre Center, Dallas, Tx.
12–30	Campbell Thomas, left, as Jethro Crouch, and John Henson as Lawyer Craven, right, in *Sly Fox*	Irene Corey	Dallas Theatre Center, Dallas, Tx.
12–31	Jumping Wolf Spider	E.S. Ross	
12–32	Makeup chart for realistic spider	Irene Corey	
12–33	Andrew Gaup, makeup for a stylized spider	Irene Corey, photograph Andrew Gaup, makeup design	
12–34	Pansy	Irene Corey	
12–35	Pansy makeup design chart	Irene Corey	
12–36	Dendrobium Orchid	Irene Corey	
12–37	Makeup chart based on Dendrobium orchid	Irene Corey	
12–38	Owl	Irene Corey	Courtesy Dallas Museum of Natural History
12–39	Makeup chart based on the owl	Irene Corey	
12–40	Tree bark	Irene Corey	
31–1	*Miserere: Who Does Not Paint Himself a Face?* Etching, aquatint and roulette over heliogravure. Plate 22 $^5/_{16}''$ × $^{15}/_{16}''$	Georges Rouault	Collection, The Museum of Modern Art, New York, Gift of the Artist
13–2	Head of a Court Dignitary sketched after a mosaic at San Vitale, Ravenna	Irene Corey	
13–3	George Bryan as Eliphaz in *The Book of Job*	Jerry Mitchell	
13–4	Sculptural figure of St. Thomas from the South-Central Portal of Chartres Cathedral	Orlin Corey	
13–5	Hal Proske as Saint Paul in *Romans by St. Paul.*, Arranged by Orlin Corey	Jerry Mitchell	An Everyman Player Production
13–6	Sumerian sculpture, c. 3000 B.C.		The Metropolitan Museum of Art, Fletcher Fund, 1940
13–7	Makeup chart based on Sumerian Sculpture	Irene Corey	
13–8	Mask Netsuke, 14th Century Noh character Hannya, the demon of a once beautiful woman	Irene Corey	From the Hobson Collection, Shreveport, La.
13–9	*I Myself Am Good Fortune*, woodcut	Sidney Chafetz	*The Ohio Journal.* Winter 1978. Vol 4, No. 2, page 32
13–10	Merlin Fahey in makeup after Chafetz' woodcut	Bruce Wilson	
13–11	*The Actor's Mask.* 1924. Oil on canvas mounted on board, 14$^1/_2''$ × 13$^1/_2''$	Paul Klee	The Sidney and Harriet Janis Collection, Gift to The Museum of Modern Art, New York

MS Number	Identification: Title, or Subject, Sitter	Artist or Photographer	Permissions Credit
13–12	Nubian man with his own makeup design; From South East Nuba in the Sudan	Leni Riefenstahl	*The People of Kau.* Photographs, Text and Layout by Leni Riefenstahl. Trans. from the German by J. Maxwell Brownjohn. N. Y.: Harper and Row, Pub. 1976

COLOR PLATES, IDENTIFICATION

One	*Madonna and Child.* Transferred from wood to Masonite, 28 7/8″ × 20″	Domenico Ghirlandaio	The National Gallery of Art, Washington, D.C.
Two	*Portrait of a Woman*	H. van Rijn Rembrandt	The Metropolitan Museum of Art, New York
Three	*A Young Man with His Tutor*, Detail, Canvas, 57½″ × 45 1/8″	Nicolas de Largillière	National Gallery of Art, Samuel H. Kress Collection. Washington, D.C.
Four	*Madame du Barry*, Canvas, oval, 28 × 23 3/8″	François-Hubert Drouais	The National Gallery of Art, Washington, D.C. Timken Collection, 1959
Five	*Woman In a Large Hat*, 1908	van Dongen	The Museum of Modern Art, New York. Private Collection
Six	*Head (detail)*	A. Jawlensky, 1965	The Museum of Modern Art, New York.
Seven	Stylized makeup design evolved from a photograph, 11–5, and developed through steps shown in 11–16 through 11–21	Irene Corey	
Eight	Actor Allen Shaffer in stylized makeup	Irene Corey	An Everyman Player Production
Nine	Makeup design based on throat of an orchid	Irene Corey	
Ten	Makeup design based on a Dendrobium orchid	Irene Corey	
Eleven	Makeup and costume design for Prospero in Shakespeare's *The Tempest*, with imagery based on sea life. See front cover of this book for actor Hal Proske's interpretation of this makeup	Irene Corey	
Cover 1	Actor Hal Proske in makeup as Prospero in Shakespeare's *The Tempest*	Design by Irene Corey	

SOURCES

If you do not have an immediate source for makeup, write one of the makeup companies for a catalog:

Bob Kelly Cosmetics and Bob Kelly Wig Creation
151 West 46th Street, New York, N. Y. 10036
Phone: (212) 819-0030
FAX: (212) 869-0396

Ben Nye, Inc.
5935 Bowcraft St., Los Angeles, California 90016
Phone: (213) 839-1984
FAX: (213) 839-2640
   *Ben Nye offers an Irene Corey Basic Makeup Kit.

Mehron, Inc.
45E Route 303, Valley Cottage, New York, 10989
Phone: (914) 268-4106
FAX: (914) 268-0439

Stein Cosmetics/Zauder Bros, Inc.
10 Henry Street
Freeport, N. Y., 11520
Phone: (516) 379-2660
FAX: (516) 223-3397

Kryolan
132 Ninth Street
San Francisco, CA 94103
Phone: (415) 863-9684
FAX: (415) 863-9059
   *Kryolan offers an Irene Corey palette, colors only.
   Note: Although each manufacturer provides a variety of *types* of makeup, if you are interested in a particular kind, the following information might be useful.

Liquid Makeup, in wide range of skin tones: Mehron, Kryolan

Liquid Makeup, in Primary colors: Mehron, Kryolan, Stein

Dry Pressed Powder Colors, wide range of colors: Nye

Cake Makeup, water based in wide range of colors: Mehron, Stein

Moist Cake Makeup, in wide range of colors: Kryolan
   *Note: These cakes can be used in the same way as dry pressed powder, *if they are never wet with water.*

The following regional companies offer the major brands of makeup:

Alcone Co.
5-49 49th Ave.
Long Island City, NY 11101
Phone: (718) 351-8373
FAX: (718) 729-8296

Olesen Co.*
1535 Ivar
Hollywood, CA 90028
Phone: (213) 461-4631
FAX: (213) 464-0444
   *Their catalog has helpful makeup chart (in color) indicating correlation between brands of most popular colors.

Norcostco, Northwestern Costume
3203 N. Highway 100
Minneapolis, MN 55422
Phone: (612) 533-2791
FAX: (612) 533-3718

Norcostco, Atlanta Costume
2089 Monroe Dr. N. E., Atlanta, GA 30324
Phone: (404) 874-7511
FAX: (404) 873-3524

A general source book helpful in makeup and other related theatrical areas:

New York Theatrical Source Book
Broadway Press
120 Duane St.
New York, N.Y. 10007
Phone: (212) 693-0570

INDEX

(photographer) Walt Strickland

Irene Corey's designs have influenced the theatre world for a generation. The look of more than one long-running Broadway and touring production has been derived from her book *The Mask of Reality: An Approach to Design for Theatre*—the designers may or may not have known her pioneering animal makeup directly; her style has made its way into the public domain. Her blended costume-makeup design for *The Book of Job*, inspired by Byzantine mosaics, has been featured in many major publications in the Western world that publish color photography. *Job* ran for two decades as an outdoor production in addition to tours in this country and parts of Europe; it was seen on the BBC and as a Spanish-language film in South America. *Romans by Saint Paul*, with her giant "carved" saints, appeared on CBS in addition to church and theatre performances in the U.S. and a cathedral tour of England. Her splendid animals romped through the race of *The Tortoise and the Hare*

at the Venice Biennale as well as in England, South Africa, and the U.S. Overall, her designs have been featured in national tours of the Everyman Players, international tours, seasons in New York City, and two World's Fairs. Examples of her work appear in more than twenty textbooks on theatre.

In addition to her partnership in the specialty costume company Irene Corey Design Associates, based in Dallas, TX, she continues to give lectures and workshops to theatre groups across the nation, occasionally serving as guest designer.

Spare time finds her in her English-style flower garden, where she carves out space for yet one more irresistible lily or iris. "If time lasts," she says, "I would love to concentrate on painting and sketching, try a new recipe everyday, invite courageous friends, cook a little, entertain a lot, squeeze out some clay pots, build a studio in Taos . . ., write another book?"